THE PSYCHOLOGY
OF
IMAGINATION

JEAN-PAUL SARTRE

THE PSYCHOLOGY OF IMAGINATION

A Citadel Press Book
Published by Carol Publishing Group

The Intentional Structure of the Image

This Book aims to describe the great function of consciousness to create a world of unrealities, or "imagination" and its noetic correlative, the imaginary.

The author has permitted himself to use the word "consciousness" in a sense somewhat different from the which it usually receives. The expression "state of consciousness" implies a sort of inertia, or passivity of the mental structures, which seems to the author to be incompatible with the known facts of reflection. The term "consciousness" will be used in this work to designate not only the unity and the totality of its psychical structures, but to indicate each of these structures in its concrete particular nature. We shall, therefore, speak of the consciousness of the image, of the perceptual consciousness, etc., using the term in one of the senses of the German word *Bewusstsein*.

TRANSLATED FROM THE FRENCH

First Carol Publishing Group Edition 1991

A Citadel Press Book
Published by Carol Publishing Group

Editorial Offices
600 Madison Avenue
New York, NY 10022

Sales & Distribution Offices
120 Enterprise Avenue
Secaucus, NJ 07094

In Canada: Musson Book Company
A division of General Publishing Co. Limited
Don Mills, Ontario

Citadel Press a registered trademark of
Carol Communications, Inc.

Manufactured in the United States of America

ISBN 0-8065-0305-X

Carol Publishing Group books are available at special discounts
for bulk purchases, for sales promotions, fund raising, or
educational purposes. Special editions can also be created to
specifications. For details contact: Special Sales Department,
Carol Publishing Group, 120 Enterprise Ave., Secaucus, NJ 07094

16 15 14 13 12 11 10 9 8

CONTENTS

The Intentional Structure of the Image

PART ONE
THE CERTAIN

Part I
THE CERTAIN

1

DESCRIPTION

1. The Method

DESPITE several preconceptions, to which we shall return shortly, it is certain that when I produce the image of Peter, it is Peter who is the object of my actual consciousness. As long as that consciousness remains unaltered, I could give a description of the object as it appears to me in the form of an image but not of the image as such. To determine the properties of the image as image I must turn to a new act of consciousness: I must *reflect*. Thus the image as image is describable only by an act of the second degree in which attention is turned away from the object and directed to the manner in which the object is given. It is this reflective act which permits the judgment "I have an image."

It is necessary to repeat at this point what has been known since Descartes: that a reflective consciousness gives us knowledge of absolute certainty; that he who becomes aware "of having an image" by an act of reflection cannot deceive himself. There have been psychologists, no doubt, who maintained that a vivid image could not be distinguished from a faint perception. Titchener even cites some experiments in support of this view. But we shall see further on that such claims rest on an error. In fact, the confusion is impossible; what has come to be known as an "image" occurs immediately as such to reflection. But it is not a metaphysical and ineffable revelation that concerns us here. If this consciousness is immediately distinguishable from all others, it is because it presents itself to

3

reflection with certain traits, certain characteristics, which at once determine the judgment "I have an image." The act of reflection thus has a content of immediate certainty which we shall call the *essence* of the image. This essence is the same for everyone; and the first task of psychology is to explain this essence, to describe it, to fix it.

Why, then, should there be so many different theories concerning this immediate knowledge on which all psychologists should certainly be of one mind? Our answer is that the majority of psychologists ignore this primary knowledge and prefer to build explanatory hypotheses concerning the nature of the image.[1] These like all other scientific hypotheses, never possess more than a certain probability: the data of reflection are certain.

All new studies of the image should therefore begin with a basic distinction: that it is one thing to *describe* the image and quite another to draw *conclusions* regarding its nature. In going from one to the other we pass from certainty to probability. The first duty of the psychologist is obviously to formulate into concepts the knowledge that is immediate and certain.

So we shall ignore theories. We want to know nothing about the image but what reflection can teach us. Later on we shall attempt, as do other psychologists, to classify the consciousness of the image among the other types of consciousness, to find a "family" for it, and we shall form hypotheses concerning its inherent nature. For the present we only wish to attempt a "phenomenology" of the image. The method is simple: we shall produce images, reflect upon them, describe them; that is, attempt to determine and to classify their distinctive characteristics.

2. First Characteristic: The Image Is a Consciousness

The very first reflective glimpse shows us that up to now we have been guilty of a double error. We believed, without

[1] Cf. our critical study *L'Imagination*, Alcan, 1936.

giving the matter any thought, that the image was *in* consciousness and that the object of the image was *in* the image. We pictured consciousness as a place peopled with small likenesses and these likenesses were the images. No doubt but that this misconception arises from our habit of thinking in space and in terms of space. This we shall call: *the illusion of immanence.* The clearest expression of this illusion is found in Hume, where he draws a distinction between impressions and ideas:

Those perceptions, which enter with most force and violence, we may name *impressions.* . . . By *ideas* I mean the faint images of these in thinking and reasoning. . . .[1]

These ideas are none other than what we called *images.* Now Hume adds several pages further on:

But to form the idea of an object, and to form an idea simply is the same thing; the reference of the idea to an object being an extraneous denomination, of which in itself it bears no mark or character. Now as 'tis impossible to form an idea of an object, that is possest of quantity and quality, and yet is possest of no precise degree of either; it follows, that there is an equal impossibility of forming an idea, that is not limited and confined in both these particulars.[2]

According to this view my actual idea of chair has but an extraneous relation to an existing chair. It is not the chair of the external world, the chair I just perceived; it is not the chair of straw and wood by which I am able to distinguish my idea from the idea of a table or an inkwell. But, my actual idea is nevertheless an idea *of* chair. What can this mean but that, for Hume, the idea of chair and the chair as an idea are one and the same thing. To have an idea of chair is to have a chair in consciousness. That this is so is shown by the fact that what is true of the object is also true of the idea. If the object must have a determined quantity and quality, so must the idea.

[1] A Treatise of Human Nature. Oxford, 1941, p. 1.
[2] *Ibid*, p. 20.

Psychologists and philosophers have in the main adopted this point of view. It is also the point of view of common sense. When I say that "I have an image" of Peter, it is believed that I now have a certain picture of Peter in my consciousness. The object of my actual consciousness is just this picture, while Peter, the man of flesh and bone, is reached but very indirectly, in an "extrinsic" manner, because of the fact that it is he whom the picture represents. Likewise, in an exhibition, I can look at a portrait for its own sake for a long time without noticing the inscription at the bottom of the picture "Portrait of Peter Z. . . ." In other words, an image is inherently like the material object it represents.

What is surprising is that the radical incongruity between consciousness and this conception of the image has never been felt. It is doubtless due to the fact that the illusion of immanence has always been taken for granted. Otherwise it would have been noticed that it was impossible to slip these material portraits into a conscious synthetic structure without destroying the structure, without breaking the contacts, arresting the flow, breaking the continuity. Consciousness would cease being transparent to itself; its unity would be broken in every direction by unassimilable, opaque screens. The works of men like Spaier, Buhler and Flach, in which the image is shown to be supple by being full of life, suffused with feeling and knowledge are useless; for by turning the image into an organism they did not make it any the less unassimilable by consciousness. It is for this reason that certain logical minds, like F. Moutier,[1] have felt that the existence of mental images must be denied if the integrity of the mental synthesis is to be saved. Such a radical solution is contradicted by the data of introspection. I can, at will, think of an image of a horse, tree or house. But if we accept the illusion of immanence, we are necessarily led to construct the world of the mind out of

[1] F. Moutier, *L'aphasie de Broca*. Thèse de Paris. Steinheil, 1908. Cf. p. 244: "We absolutely deny the existence of images."

objects entirely like those of the external world, but which simply obey different laws.

Let us ignore these theories and see what reflection teaches us, so that we may rid ourselves of the illusion of immanence.

When I perceive a chair it would be absurd to say that the chair is *in* my perception. According to the terminology we have adopted, my perception is a certain consciousness and the chair is the *object* of that consciousness. Now I shut my eyes and I produce an image of the chair I have just perceived. The chair, now occurring as an image, can no more enter *into* consciousness than it could do so as an object. An image of a chair is not, and cannot be a chair. In fact, whether I perceive or imagine that chair of straw on which I am seated, it always remains outside of consciousness. In both cases it is there, *in* space, in that room, in front of the desk. Now—and this is what reflection teaches us above all—whether I see or imagine that chair, the object of my perception and that of my image are identical: it is that chair of straw on which I am seated. Only consciousness is *related* in two different ways to the same chair. The chair is envisioned in both cases in its concrete individuality, its corporeality. Only, in one of the cases, the chair is "encountered" by consciousness; in the other, it is not. But the chair is not in consciousness; not even as an image. What we find here is not a semblance of the chair which suddenly worked its way into consciousness and which has but an "extrinsic" relation to the existing chair, but a certain type of consciousness, a synthetic organization, which has a direct relation to the existing chair and whose very essence consists precisely of being related in this or that manner of the existing chair.

And what exactly is the image? Evidently it is not the chair: in general, the object of the image is not itself an image. Shall we say then that the image is the total synthetic organization, consciousness? But this consciousness is an actual and concrete nature, which exists in and for itself and which can always occur to reflection without any intermediary. The word image can therefore only indicate the relation of consciousness to the object; in other words, it means a certain manner in which the object makes its appearance to consciousness, or, if one prefers, a certain way in which consciousness presents an object to itself. The fact of the matter is that the expression "mental image" is confusing. It would be better to say "the consciousness of Peter as an image" or "the imaginative consciousness of Peter." But since the word image is of long standing we cannot reject it completely. However, in order to avoid all ambiguity, we must repeat at this point that an image is nothing else than a relationship. The imaginative consciousness I have of Peter is not a consciousness of the image of Peter: Peter is directly reached, my attention is not directed on an image, but on an object.[1]

Thus, in the woof of the synthetic acts of Consciousness there appear at times certain structures which we shall call imaginative consciousness. They are born, develop and disappear in accordance with laws proper to them and which we shall try to ascertain. And it would be a grave error to confuse this life of the imaginative consciousness, which lasts, becomes organized, and disintegrates, with the object of this consciousness which in the meantime can well remain immutable.

3. Second Characteristic: The Phenomenon of Quasi Observation

When we began this study we thought our concern was with *images*, that is, with some elements of consciousness. Now we see that we are dealing with complete consciousnesses, that is, with complex structures which "intend" certain objects. Let us now see whether reflection can teach us more about

[1] Cases may be cited in which I produce an image of an object which has no real existence outside of myself. But the chimera does not exist "as an image." It exists neither as such nor otherwise.

these consciousnesses. The simplest procedure will be to examine the image in its relationship to the concept and the percept. To perceive, conceive, imagine: these are the three types of consciousnesses by which the same object can be given to us.

In perception I *observe* objects. By this we must understand that although the object enters into my perception in its completeness, I nevertheless see it only from one side at a time. Consider the example of the cube: I know it is a cube provided I have seen its six sides; but of these I can see only three at a time, never more. I must therefore apprehend them successively. And when I pass, for example, from sides ABC to sides BCD, there always remains a possibility that side A has disappeared during my change of position. The existence of the cube therefore remains doubtful. But let us note that when I see three sides of the cube at the same time, these three sides never present themselves to me as squares: their lines become flat, their angles become obtuse, and I must reconstruct their squareness at the very beginning of my perception. All this has been said hundreds of times: the characteristic of a perception is that the object appears only in a series of profiles, of projections. The cube is certainly present to me, I can touch it, see it; but I always see it only in a certain fashion which includes and excludes at one and the same time an infinity of other points of view. We must *learn* objects, that is to say, multiply upon them the possible points of view. The object itself is the synthesis of all these appearances. The perception of an object is thus a phenomenon of an infinity of aspects. What does this mean for us? It means that we must *make a tour* of objects, wait until the "sugar melts," as Bergson said.

When, on the other hand, I *think* of a cube as a concrete concept,[1] I think of its six sides and its eight angles all at once;

---

[1] The existence of such concepts has at times been denied. Nevertheless a perception and an image presuppose a concrete knowledge without image and without words.

I think that its angles are right angles, its sides squared. I am at the center of my idea, I seize it in its entirety at one glance. This does not mean, of course, that my idea does not need to complete itself by an infinite progression. But I can think of the concrete essences in a single act of consciousness; I do not have to re-establish the appearance, I have no apprenticeship to serve. Such is, no doubt, the clearest difference between a thought and a perception. This is the reason why we can never perceive a thought nor think a perception. The two phenomena are radically distinct: the one is knowledge which is conscious of itself and which places itself at once at the center of the object; the other is a synthetic unity of a multiplicity of appearances, which slowly serves its apprenticeship.

What shall we say of the image? Is it apprenticeship or knowledge? Let us note first that it seems to belong to perception. In the one, as in the other, the object presents itself in profiles, in projections, in what the Germans designate by the apt term "*Abschattungen*." Only we no longer have to make a tour of it: the cube as an image is presented immediately for what it is. When I say: "the object I perceive is a cube," I make an hypothesis that I may have to reject at the close of my perceptions. When I say: "the object of which I have an image at this moment is a cube," my judgment is final: it is absolutely certain that the object of my image is a cube. What does this mean? In perception, a knowledge forms itself slowly; in the image the knowledge is immediate. We see now that the image is a synthetic act which unites a concrete, nonimagined, knowledge to elements which are more actually representative. The image teaches nothing: it is organized exactly like the objects which do produce knowledge, but it is complete at the very moment of its appearance. If I amuse myself by turning over in my mind the image of a cube, if I pretend that I see its different sides, I shall be no further ahead at the close of the process than I was at the beginning: I have learned nothing.

And this is not all. Let us consider this piece of paper on the table. The longer I look at it the more of its features are revealed to me.

Each new orientation of my attention, of my analysis, shows me a new detail: the upper edge of the sheet is slightly warped; the end of the third line is dotted . . . etc. No matter how long I may look at an image, I shall never find anything in it but what I put there. It is in this fact that we find the distinction between an image and a perception. In the world of perception every "thing" has an infinite number of relationships to other things. And what is more, it is this infinity of relationships—as well as the infinite number of relationships between the elements of the thing—which constitute the very essence of a thing. From this there arises something of the *overflowing* in the world of "things": there is always, at each and every moment, infinitely *more* than we see; to exhaust the wealth of my actual perception would require infinite time. Let us not deceive ourselves: this manner of "brimming over" is of the very nature of objects. When we say that no object can exist without having a definite individuality we mean "without maintaining an infinity of determined relationships with the infinity of other objects."

Now, the image, on the other hand, suffers from a sort of essential poverty. The different elements of an image have no relationship with the rest of the world, while among themselves they have but two or three relationships, those, for instance, that I have been able to ascertain; or those it is now essential for me to hold on to. We must not say that the other relationships exist in secret, that they wait for a bright searchlight to be directed upon them. No: they do not exist at all. Two colors, for instance, which in reality possess a certain discordant relationship can exist together in imagery without any sort of relationship between them. Objects exist only in so far as they are thought of. This is what all those who consider the image to be a reborn perception fail to understand. The difference is not that of vividness but rather that the objects of the world of images can in no way exist in the world of perception; they do not meet the necessary conditions.[1]

In a word, the object of the perception overflows consciousness constantly; the object of the image is never more than the consciousness one has; it is limited by that consciousness: nothing can be learned from an image that is not already known. It can, of course, happen that a memory image presents itself unexpectedly, and presents some new aspects. But even in such a case it presents itself in one piece to intuition, it reveals at a single stroke what it is. If I perceive a bit of turf, I must study it for a considerable period to determine where it comes from. In the case of an image I know it immediately; it is the grass of this meadow, in such a place. And this origin cannot be determined from the image: the very act that gives me the object as an image includes the knowledge of what it is. It is true that occasionally a memory-image does remain unidentified: all of a sudden I see again a dreary garden under a gray sky and I cannot recall when or where I saw that garden. But this is simply a determination that lacks an image, and no observation, no matter how prolonged, will yield the knowledge I lack. If I later discover the name of the garden it is by means of processes which have nothing to do with pure and simple observation: the image gave everything it possessed in a lump.[2]

Thus the object presents itself in the image as having to be apprehended in a multiplicity of synthetic acts. Due to this fact, and because its content retains a sensible opacity, like a phantom, because it does not involve either essences

[1] This is what Jaensch understood so well when, pushing the theory of revived perceptions to the limit, he made of the eidetic image an object which could be observed and learned.

[2] What can deceive us here is:

    (a) The use we make of images in mathematical thinking. Many believe that we perceive new relationships between figures by means of the image.

    (b) Cases in which the image comprises a sort of affective instruction. We shall consider these different cases later.

or generating laws but only an irrational quality, it gives the impression of being an object of observation: from this point of view the image appears to be more like a perception than a concept. But in other respects the image teaches nothing, never produces an impression of novelty, and never reveals any new aspect of the object. It delivers it in a lump. No risk, no anticipation: only a certainty. My perception can deceive me, but not my image. Our attitude towards the object of the image could be called "quasi-observation." Our attitude is, indeed, one of observation, but it is an observation which teaches nothing. If I produce an image of a page of a book, I am assuming the attitude of a reader, I *look* at the printed pages. But I am not *reading*. And, actually, I am not even looking, since I already *know* what is written there.

Without leaving the realm of pure description, we may attempt to explain this characteristic property of the image. In the image a certain consciousness does indeed present itself with a certain object. The object is therefore a correlative of a certain synthetic act, which includes among its structures a certain knowledge and a certain "*intention*." The intention is at the center of the consciousness: it is the intention that envisages the object, that is, which makes it what it is. The knowledge, which is inseparable from the intention, specifies that the object is this or that, adds some determinations synthetically. To construct a certain consciousness of a table as an image is at the same time to construct the table as the object of an imaginative consciousness. The object as an image is therefore contemporaneous with the consciousness I take of it, and it is determined exactly by that consciousness: it includes nothing in itself but what I am conscious of; but, inversely, everything that constitutes my consciousness has its counterpart in the object. My knowledge is none other than a knowledge *of* the object, a knowledge concerning the object. In the act of consciousness the representative element and the element of knowledge are united in a synthetic act.

The correlative object of that act becomes at one and the same time a concrete, sensible object, and an object of knowledge. This gives rise to the paradoxical result that the object is present to us externally and internally at the same time. Externally, because we observe it; internally, because it is *in the object* that we perceive what it is. This is the reason why extremely poor and curtailed images, images which are reduced to a few spatial determinations, can nevertheless have a rich and profound meaning. And that meaning is there, immediate, *in* these lines, it occurs without a need to decipher it. This is also the reason why the world of images is a world in which nothing *happens*. I can at will develop this or that object into an image, make a cube turn, make a plant grow, make a horse run, without producing the least shift between the object and consciousness. Not a moment of surprise: the object which is moving is not alive, *it never precedes the intention*. But neither is it inert, passive, "worked" from without, like a marionette: *consciousness never precedes the object*, the intention reveals itself to itself at the same time that it realizes itself, in and by its realization.[1]

4. Third Characteristic: The Imaginative Consciousness Posits Its Object as Nothingness

All consciousness is consciousness *of* something. Non-reflective consciousness envisions heterogeneous objects for consciousness: for example, the imaginative consciousness of tree envisions a tree, that is, a body which is by nature external to consciousness; consciousness rises out of itself, transcends itself.

If we wish to describe this consciousness, we must, as we

---

[1] There exist in the condition between wakefulness and sleep certain cases that are strange enough to pass as resistances of images. For instance, I happen to see some vague object turning on itself like the hands of a watch without being able to stop it or to make it reverse itself. We shall have a few words to say about these phenomena when we study hypnagogic images to which they belong.

have seen, produce a new consciousness called "reflection." For the first consciousness is entirely consciousness of tree. But we must be cautious: all consciousness is consciousness through and through. If the imaginative consciousness of tree, for instance, were conscious only by virtue of the object of reflection, then it would be unconscious of itself in the state of non-reflection, which is a contradiction. Since this consciousness has no other object than the tree as an image, and since it is itself but an object of reflection, it follows that it must possess a certain consciousness of itself. Let us say that it possesses an immanent and natural consciousness of itself. It is not our business to describe this natural consciousness. But it is evident that our description of the imaginative consciousness would be very incomplete were we to make no attempt to find out:

1. How the non-reflective consciousness posits its object.
2. How this consciousness appears to itself in the non-thetic consciousness which accompanies the position of the object.

The transcendental consciousness of tree as an image posits the tree. But it posits it *as an image*, that is, in a manner which is not that of the perceptual consciousness.

We have often proceeded as if the image were at first a perception and then something (a reducer, knowledge, etc.) came along to put it in its proper place as an image. The object as an image is supposed to be built up at first in the world of things only to be driven out of it *after the event*. But this thesis does not fit in with the facts of phenomenological description; moreover, we have seen in another work that if perception and imagery are not by nature distinct, if their objects do not occur in consciousness as *sui generis*, we have no means of drawing a distinction between these two ways of experiencing objects; in a word, we have demonstrated the inadequacy of external criteria for the image. But since we do speak of images, since the term does have a meaning for us, it must be that the image contains in its very nature an element of basic distinction. Reflective investigation will show us that this element lies in the positional act of the imaginative consciousness.

Every consciousness posits its object, but each does so in its own way. Perception, for instance, posits its object as existing. The image also includes an act of belief, or a positional act. This act can assume four forms and no more: it can posit the object as non-existent, or as absent, or as existing elsewhere; it can also "neutralize" itself, that is, not posit its object as existing.[1] Two of these acts are negations: the fourth corresponds to a suspension or neutralization of the proposition. The third, which is positive, assumes an implicit negation of the actual and present existence of the object. This positional act—and this is essential—is not superimposed on the image after it has been constituted. The positional act is constitutive of the consciousness of the image. Any other theory, besides running contrary to the facts of reflection, leads us into the illusion of immanence.

This position of absence or non-existence can occur only on the level of *quasi-observation*. On the one hand, in fact, perception posits the existence of its object: on the other hand, concepts and knowledge, posit the existence of *natures* (universal essences) composed of relationships and are indifferent to the "flesh and bone" existence of objects. To think the concept "man," for instance, is to posit nothing but an essence; for, as Spinoza said:

(1) the true definition of each thing involves nothing and expresses nothing but the nature of a definite thing. From which it follows (2) that clearly no definition involves any certain number of individuals nor expresses it. . . .[2]

To think of Peter by a concrete concept is to think of a collection of relationships. Among these relationships will be

---

[1] This suspension of belief remains a positional act.
[2] Ethics, I, Prop. VIII, Note 2, trans. A. Boyle.

found some determinations of place. (Peter is on a trip to Berlin—he is a lawyer in Rebat, etc.) But these determinations add a positive element to the concrete nature "Peter"; they never have that privative, negative character of the positional acts of the image. It is only in the realm of sensible intuition that the words "absent," "far from me" can have a meaning, it is only in this realm in which the idea of "not having taken place" can occur. For instance, if the image of a dead loved one appears to me suddenly, I have no need of a "reduction" to feel the ache in my heart: it is a part of the image, it is the direct consequence of the fact that the image presents its object as not existing.

No doubt there are some perceptual judgments which involve a neutralized positional act. This is what happens when I see a man coming towards me and I remark "this may be Peter." But this suspended belief refers only to the *man who is approaching*. My doubt is only whether it is Peter; not that it is a man. But to say "I have an image of Peter" is equivalent to saying not only "I do not see Peter," but also "I see nothing at all." The characteristic of the intentional object of the imaginative consciousness is that the object is not present and is posited as such, or that it does not exist and is posited as not existing, or that it is not posited at all.

To form an image of Peter is to make an intentional synthesis which gathers up a mass of past events, which proclaims the identity of Peter by means of these diverse appearances and which presents this selfsame object in a certain form (in profile, three fourths, full-length, half-length, etc.). This form is necessarily intuitive; what my actual intention grasps is the corporeal Peter, the Peter I can see, touch, hear, if I did see him, hear him or touch him. It is a body which is necessarily a certain distance from mine, which necessarily has a certain position in relation to me. But at this moment I know that the Peter whom I could touch is not being touched by me. It is of the very nature of my image of him not to touch him or see him, a way he has *of not being* at such a distance, in such a position. In the image, belief posits the intuition but not Peter. The characteristic of Peter is not to be non-intuitive, as we might be tempted to believe, but to be "intuitive-absent," given to intuition as absent. In this sense it can be said that the image involves a certain nothingness. Its object is not a simple portrait, it asserts itself: but in doing so it destroys itself. Alive, appealing, and strong as an image is, it presents its object as not being. This does not prevent us from reacting to the image as if its object were before us; we will see later that it is possible for us to attempt to react to an image as if it were a perception. But the false and ambiguous condition we reach thereby only serves to bring out in greater relief what we have just said: that we seek in vain to create in ourselves the belief that the object really exists by means of our *conduct* towards it: we can pretend for a second, but we cannot destroy the immediate awareness of its nothingness.

5. Fourth Characteristic: Spontaneity

The imaginative consciousness of the object, as we noted above, is not sure of itself. This consciousness, which might be called transversal, has no object. It posits nothing, refers to nothing, is not knowledge: it is a diffuse light which consciousness releases for itself, or, to drop analogies, it is an indefinable quality which attaches itself to every consciousness. A perceptual consciousness appears to itself as being passive. An imaginative consciousness, on the contrary, presents itself to itself as an imaginative consciousness, that is, as a spontaneity which produces and holds on to the object as an image. This is a sort of indefinable counterpart of the fact that the object occurs as a nothingness. The consciousness appears to itself as being creative, but without positing that what it has created is an object. It is due to this vague and fugitive quality that the image-consciousness is not at all like a piece of wood floating on the sea, but like a wave among waves. It feels itself to be a consciousness through and through and one with the other consciousnesses which have preceded it and with which it is synthetically united.

Conclusion

It would be possible for us to learn much more that is certain about images but to do so would require that we compare the mental image with other phenomena possessing a similar structure and attempt a comparative description. Simple reflection has yielded us, it seems, everything within its power. It has pointed out to us what may be called the static nature of the image, or the image considered as an isolated phenomenon.

It is impossible to disregard the importance of these characteristics. If we attempt to classify and order them, we see first that the image is not a condition, a solid and opaque residue, but a consciousness. Most psychologists believe that they find the image when they make a cross-section of the stream of consciousness. For them the image is one element in an instantaneous synthesis, and each consciousness includes or can include one or more images: so that an investigation of the role of the image in the thought process consists of trying to find the place of the image among the variety of objects which constitute a present consciousness; it is in this sense that they can speak of a thought which is *supported* by images. We now know that we must drop these spatial metaphors. The image is a consciousness which is *sui generis*, which can in no way form a part of a larger consciousness. There is no image *in* a consciousness which contains it, in addition to the thought, signs, feelings and sensations. The image-consciousness is a synthetic form which appears like a certain moment of a temporal synthesis and organizes itself with other forms of consciousness which precede and follow it, to make one continuous whole. It is as absurd to say that an object occurs at the same time as an image and as a concept as it would be to speak of a body which is both solid and gaseous.

This imaginative consciousness may be said to be representative in the sense that it goes out in search of its object in the realm of perception and that it envisions the sensible elements that constitute this realm. At the same time it orients itself in relation to this realm as does perception in relation to the object perceived. But, it is spontaneous and creative; it maintains and sustains the sensible qualities of its object by a continuous creation. In perception the actual representative element corresponds to a passivity of consciousness. In the image, this element, in what it has of the primary and incommunicable, is the product of a conscious activity, is shot through and through with a flow of creative will. It follows necessarily that the object as an image is never anything more than the consciousness one has of it. This is what we called the phenomenon of quasi-observation. To be vaguely conscious of an image is to be conscious of a vague image. We are far from Berkeley and Hume, who denied the possibility of general images, of non-specific images. But we are fully in agreement with the subjects of Watt and Messer:

"I saw," said subject I, "something that looked like a wing." Subject II saw a face without knowing whether it was that of a man or woman. Subject I had "an image that looked like a human face; a typical image, not individual." [1]

Berkeley's error lay in ascribing to the image conditions which apply only to perception. A hare vaguely perceived is nevertheless a specific hare. But a hare which is an object of a vague image is a vague hare.

The final outcome of the preceding is that the *flesh* of the object is not the same in an image and in a perception. By

[1] Messer, cited by Burloud: *La Pensée d'après les Recherches expérimentales de Watt, de Messer et de Bühler*, p. 69.

"flesh" I understand the intimate texture. The classical authors describe the image as a faint, vague perception but in all other respects like the perception in the "flesh." Now we know this to be an error. The object of perception is constituted of an infinite multiplicity of determinations and possible relations. The most definite image, on the other hand, possesses in itself only a finite number of determinations, namely, only those of which we are conscious. These determinations can remain unrelated to each other, unless we are aware that they do possess such relationships. Hence, the discontinuity at the very heart of the object of the image, something of a clash, qualities which dash towards existence and stop halfway, an essential poverty.

We still have much to learn. For instance, the relationship between the image and its object is still very obscure. We said that the image was a consciousness of an object. The object of the image of Peter, we said, is the Peter of flesh and bone, who is actually in Berlin. But, on the other hand, the image I now have of Peter shows him to be at his home, in his room in Paris, seated in a chair well known to me. Consequently the question can be raised whether the object of the image is the Peter who actually lives in Berlin or the Peter who lived last year in Paris. And if we persist in affirming that it is the Peter who lives in Berlin, we must explain the paradox: why and how the imaginative consciousness envisions the Peter of Berlin through the Peter who lived last year in Paris?

But as yet we know only the statics of the image; we cannot at once form a theory concerning the relationship of the image to its object: to do this we must first describe the image as a functional attitude.

2

THE IMAGE FAMILY

WE HAVE described certain forms of consciousness called images. But we know neither where the class of images begins nor ends. For instance, in the external world there exist objects which are also called images (portraits, reflections in a mirror, imitations, etc.). Is this but a matter of the same name, or is the attitude of our consciousness to these objects the same as it is to the phenomenon of the "mental image"? In the latter case the idea of the image would have to be considerably expanded to make it fit a number of types of consciousness which have as yet not been discussed.

1. Image, Portrait, Caricature

I wish to recall the face of my friend Peter. I make an effort and I produce a certain imaginary consciousness of him. But my objective is very imperfectly attained: certain details are lacking, others are suspect, the whole is very blurred. There is a certain feeling of sympathy and pleasantness that I want to restore to the face but which will not come. I do not give up, I rise and take a photograph from a drawer. It is an excellent portrait of Peter, it gives me all the details of his face, even some that had escaped me. But the photograph lacks life; it presents perfectly the external traits of Peter's face; it does not give his expression. Fortunately I possess a skillfully drawn caricature of him. This time the facial features are deliberately distorted, the nose is much too long, the cheeks too prominent, etc. Nevertheless, what is missing in the photograph, vitality, expression, is clearly present in the drawing: I "rediscover" Peter.

Mental representation, photograph, caricature; these three very different realities appear in our example as three stages of the same process, three moments of a unique act. From beginning to end the aim is the same: to recall the face of Peter which is not present. Nevertheless, it is only the subjective representation that psychology calls an image. Is this justified?

Let us examine our example more thoroughly. We have used three procedures to recall the face of Peter. In the three cases we found an "intention," and the intention envisions the same object in each of them. This object is neither the representation, nor the photo, nor the caricature: it is my friend Peter. Further, in the three cases I envision the object in the same manner: I want the face of Peter to appear as a perception. I want "to make him present" to me. And as I cannot bring him before me directly as a perception I have recourse to a certain material which acts as an *analogue*, as an equivalent, of the perception.

In the first two cases, at least, the material can be perceived for itself: it is not intended to function as the material of an image. This photo, taken by itself, is a *thing*: I can try to ascertain the duration of its exposure by its color, the product used to tone it and fix it, etc.; the caricature is a *thing*: I can take pleasure in studying its lines and colors without thinking that they were intended to represent something.

The material of the mental image is more difficult to determine. Can it exist outside the intention? This problem we shall consider later. But in any case it is evident that the mental image must also have a material, and a material which derives its meaning solely from the intention that animates it. To see this clearly all I need do is compare my initial empty intention to my mental image of Peter. At first I wanted to produce Peter out of the void, and then something loomed up which filled in my intention. The three cases are therefore strictly parallel. They are three situations with the same form, but in which the material varies. From these differences in material there flow naturally the internal differences which we must describe and which, no doubt, reach all the way to the structure of the intention. But our first concern is with intentions of the same class, of the same type and with materials which are functionally identical.

We may be charged with being unfair in choosing for our example of a mental image a representation which has been voluntarily produced. In most cases, no doubt, the image springs up with a deep spontaneity which is independent of the will. It seems that the involuntary image appears to consciousness as my friend Peter might appear to me from around the corner of a street.

But, here again we are the victims of the illusion of immanence. It is true that in what we incorrectly call an "involuntary evocation" the image is built up outside of consciousness and then appears for consciousness as a finished product. But involuntary and voluntary images represent two very similar types of consciousness, one of which is produced by a voluntary spontaneity and the other by an involuntary spontaneity. We must under no circumstances confuse intention, in our sense of the term, and will. To say that there can be an image without will implies in no way that there can be an image without intention. In our opinion, it is not only the mental image which needs an intention in order to be constructed: an external object functioning as an image cannot exercise that function without an intention which interprets it as such. If someone suddenly shows me a photo of Peter the case is functionally the same as when an image of him suddenly and involuntarily appears to my consciousness. As a perception, the photograph is but a paper rectangle of a special quality and color, with shadows and white spots distributed in a certain fashion. If that photograph appears to

me to be the "photo of a man standing on a pedestal," the
mental phenomenon is necessarily already of a different structure: another intention animates it. And if that photo seems
to me to be the photo "of Peter," if perchance I see Peter
behind it, it must be that the piece of cardboard is animated
by some help from me, giving it a meaning it had not as yet
had. If I see Peter by means of the photo *it is because I put
him there*. And how could I have put him there if not by a
particular intention? And if the intention is necessary what
does it matter whether the image is presented all of a sudden
or is deliberately sought? All that could happen, in the former
case, is a slight lag between the presentation of the photo
and its apprehension as an image. We can imagine three successive stages of apprehension: photo, photo of a man standing on a pedestal, photo of Peter. But it may also happen that
the three stages occur so close to each other as to make but
one; it can happen that the photo does not function as an object but presents itself immediately as an image.

We could repeat this demonstration with the mental image.
It can of course appear without being wanted: nonetheless
it needs a certain intention, the one that turns it into an image.
However, we must mention one important difference: a photo
serves at first as an object (at least theoretically). A mental
image occurs immediately as an image, because the existence
of a psychic phenomenon and the meaning it has for consciousness are identical.[1] Mental images, caricatures, photos
are so many species of the same genus, and from now on we
can attempt to ascertain what it is they have in common.

The purpose of all three is the same: to make an object
"appear." That object is not before us, and we know it is not.
We thus find, in the first place, an intention directed on an
absent object. But this intention is not empty, it is not directed
on any content whatsoever, but on one which is to present

---

[1] We are not forgetting that these remarks compel us to deny entirely the
existence of an unconscious. This is no place to discuss this point.

some analogue to the object in question. For instance, if I wish to bring before me the face of Peter, I must direct my intention upon some chosen objects, and not on my pen or on that piece of sugar. I apprehend these objects as images, that is they lose their own meaning in acquiring another meaning. Instead of existing for themselves, in a free state,[2] they become integrated into a new form. The intention serves only as a means for evoking its object, just as table-turning is used to call forth spirits. They serve as *representatives* of the absent object, without, however, in any way eliminating the characteristic of objects of an imaginary consciousness: namely, their absence.

In the preceding account we supposed that the object is absent and that we posit its absence. We can also posit its non-existence. Behind their physical representation in Durer's engraving, Death and the Knight are surely objects for me. But for these objects I posit non-existence and not absence. This new class of objects, which we will call fictions, includes classes like those we have just surveyed: engravings, caricatures, and mental images.

So our conclusion is that the image is an act which envisions an absent or non-existent object as a body, by means of a physical or mental content which is present only as an "analogical representative" of the object envisioned. The specifications are determined by the material, since the informing intention remains the same. We shall therefore distinguish between images whose material is borrowed from the world of things (images of illustrations, photos, caricatures, actors' imitations, etc.), and those whose material is borrowed from the mental world (consciousness of movements, feelings, etc.). There are intermediary types which present us with syntheses of external elements and psychical elements, as when we see a face in a flame, in the arabesques of a tapestry, or in the case

[2] We shall see later what "to exist in a free state" means for the material content of the mental image.

of hypnagogic images, which are constructed, as we shall see, on a foundation of entoptic lights.

The mental image cannot be studied by itself. There is not a world of images and a world of objects. Every object, whether it is present as an external perception or appears to intimate sense, can function as a present reality or as an image, depending on what center of reference has been chosen. The two worlds, real and imaginary, are composed of the same objects: only the grouping and interpretation of these objects varies. What defines the imaginary world and also the world of the real is an attitude of consciousness. We shall therefore study in turn the following consciousnesses: looking at a portrait of Peter, a schematic drawing, a music hall singer impersonating Maurice Chevalier, a face in the fire, "having" a hypnagogic image, "having" a mental image. By proceeding thus from the image which draws its material from perception to the one which finds it among objects of intimate sense, we shall be able to describe and determine, through their variations, one of the great functions of consciousness: the "image" function or imagination.

2. The Sign and the Portrait

I look at a portrait of Peter. Through the photo I envision Peter in his physical individuality. The photo is no longer the concrete object which gives me the perception; it serves as material for the image.

But here is a phenomenon which seems to be of the same nature: I approach some heavy black strokes printed on a placard nailed above the door of a railway station. These strokes suddenly lose their own dimensions, color, place: now they spell the words "Office of the Assistant Manager." I *read* the words by means of the placard and I now know that I must enter this place to put in my claim: it shows that I understood how "to interpret" the words. But this is not absolutely correct: it would be better to say that I created them out of these black strokes. These strokes are no longer of importance to me, I no longer perceive them: what I have really done is to assume a certain attitude of consciousness which envisions another object through them. That object is the office where I have business to attend to. The object is not in these words, but, thanks to the inscription, it does not escape me completely: I assign a place to it, I have knowledge of it. The material on which my intention was directed, becoming transformed by that intention, now forms an integral part of my actual attitude; it is the material of my act, it is a *sign*. In the case of the sign, as in that of the image, we have an intention which envisions an object, a material which it transforms, an envisioned object which is not present. At first glimpse it might seem as if we were dealing here with the same function. We should note, moreover, that classical psychologists often confuse sign and image. When Hume tells us that the relationship between the image and its object is external he turns the image into a sign.[1] But, conversely, when a word as it appears in internal speech is turned into a mental image, the function of the sign is assigned to the image. Later on we shall see that an inner word is not the mental image of a printed word, as a psychology based on hasty introspections believed, but that it is in itself and directly a sign. Just now our need is to investigate the relationships between the physical sign and the physical image. Do they belong to the same class?

1. The material of the sign is totally indifferent to the object it signifies. There is no relationship whatsoever between "Office," black strokes on white paper, and the "office" as a complex object which is not only physical but social. The source of the association is custom; and subsequently strength-

[1] M. I. Myerson, in his chapter "Les Images." Dumas, *Nouveau Traité*, t. II, constantly confuses (cf. particularly pp. 574 and 581) sign, image and symbol.

ened by habit. Without habit, which motivates a certain
mental attitude as soon as the word is perceived, the word
"office" would never evoke its object.

But the relationship between the material of the physical
image and its object is altogether different; the two *resemble*
each other. What are we to understand by this?

The material of our image, when we look at a portrait, is
not only that jumble of lines and colors, as we just called it
in the interest of simplicity. It is, in reality, a quasi-person,
with a quasi-face, etc. In the museum of Rouen, on suddenly entering an unfamiliar room, I happened to take the
figures in a large picture for men. The illusion was of very
short duration—perhaps a quarter of a second—and during
this extremely brief period my experience was not imaginary
but perceptual. No doubt the synthesis was poorly made and
the perception was false, but the false perception was nonetheless a perception. In the picture there is the form of a man.
If I come close, the illusion disappears, but its cause remains:
the picture, made like a human being, acts on me as if it were
a man, regardless of what the attitude I assumed towards
it may be otherwise; that knitting of the brows, on the canvas, moved me directly, because the synthesis "brows" clev-
erly prepared is carried out of its own accord, even before I
myself turn these brows into "image-brows" or real brows;
the repose of that figure moved me directly, whatever may
be the interpretation that I might give it. In short, these elements are themselves neutral; they can enter either into an
imaginary or perceptual synthesis. But although they are
neutral, they are *expressive*. If I decide to hold on to the
perception, if I look at the picture purely aesthetically, if I
observe the color relationships, the form, the touch, if I study
the purely technical processes of the painter, the expressive
value will nevertheless not vanish; the figure in the painting
begs me gently to look upon it as a man. Likewise, if I am
acquainted with the original of the portrait, there will be a

real force, a resemblance in the portrait, prior to all interpretation.

It would be a mistake to believe that it is this resemblance
which causes the mental image of Peter to arise in my mind.
Such a notion belongs to the objection raised by James against
the associationists. The resemblance between A and B, he said,
cannot act as a force which brings B into consciousness when
A is given. To perceive the resemblance between A and B,
both must be presented together.

The resemblance of which we speak is therefore not a force
which tends to evoke the mental image of Peter. But the portrait of Peter does have a tendency to stand for Peter in
person. The portrait acts upon us—almost—like Peter in person, and because of this fact the portrait invites us to make
the perceptual synthesis: Peter of flesh and bone.

My intention is here now; I say: "This is a portrait of
Peter" or, more briefly: "This is Peter." Then the picture is
no longer an object, but operates as material for an image.
The entreaty to perceive Peter has not disappeared, but it has
entered into the imagined synthesis. It is really the entreaty
that functions as *analogue* and it is because of it that my intention is directed to Peter. I say to myself: "Look, it's true,
Peter is like that, he has such brows, such a smile." Everything I perceive enters into a projective synthesis which aims
at the true Peter, a living being who is not present.

2. As meaning, a word is but a beacon: it presents itself,
awakens a meaning, and this meaning never returns to the word
but goes out to the thing and the word is dropped. In the
case of a physical image, however, the intentionality constantly
returns to the image-portrait. We face the portrait and we
observe it; [1] the imaginary consciousness of Peter is being
constantly enriched; new details are being constantly added
to the object: that wrinkle I had not noticed in Peter until I

---

[1] It is this observation which becomes the quasi-observation in the case
of the mental image.

saw it in his portrait becomes a regular part of his features from now on. Each detail is perceived, but not for itself, not as a spot of color on a canvas: it becomes a part of the object at once, that is a part of Peter.

3. These reflections prompt us to raise the question concerning the relation of image and sign to their objects. Concerning the sign, it is clear that the significant consciousness as such is not positional. When accompanied by an affirmation, this affirmation is reunited with it synthetically and we have a new consciousness: a judgment. But to read on a placard "Office of the Assistant Manager" is to posit nothing. In every image, even in the one which does not posit that its object exists, there is a positional determination. In the sign, as such, this determination is lacking. When an object serves as a sign it causes us to envision something at the very outset: but we affirm nothing about this something, we limit ourselves to envisioning it. Naturally this something does not manifest itself in the significant material: it is disparate.

In the image-portrait the situation is much more complicated: Peter can be a thousand miles from his portrait (if it happens to be an historical portrait its original may be dead); but it is exactly this "object a thousand miles from us" that we see. All his physical qualities are here before us. The object is posited as absent, but the impression is present. Here we have an irrational synthesis which is difficult to explain. I look, for instance, at a portrait of Charles VIII in the galleries of Florence. I know it is Charles VIII, who is dead. My whole present attitude is full of this fact. Nevertheless, those sensuous and sensual lips, that narrow forehead, immediately arouse a certain affective impression which is directed at *those lips* as they are in the picture. Thus those lips perform a double function simultaneously: on the one hand, they refer to the real lips long since turned to dust, and derive their meaning only from this source; but, on the other hand, they act directly on my feelings, because they are a deception, because the colored spots on the picture appear to the eye as a forehead, as lips. Finally these two functions become grounded, and we have the imaginary state, that the dead Charles VIII is here before us. It is he we see, not the picture, and yet we declare him not to be there: we have reached him only "as an image," "by the mediation" of the picture. Here we see that the relationship that consciousness posits in the imaginative attitude between the portrait and its original is nothing short of magical. Charles VIII is at one and the same time absent and also present. He is present in a state of reduced life, with a mass of determinations (the relief, the mobility, sometime the color, etc.) and as *relative*. He is absent, as absolute. We do not think, in our non-reflective consciousness, that a painter made that portrait, etc. The first bond posited between image and model is a bond of emanation. The original has the ontological primacy. But it becomes incarnated, it enters into the image. This explains the attitude of primitives towards their portraits as well as certain practices of black magic (the effigy of wax pierced by a pin, the holy bisons painted on walls to make the hunt fruitful). This mode of thought has not disappeared. We have it in the structure of the image which is irrational, and, in which, as almost in everything else, we make rational constructions on prelogical foundations.

4. This leads us to make the final and most important distinction between sign and image. Let us say I think of Peter in the picture. This means that I do not think of the picture at all: I think of Peter. But this does not mean that I think of the picture "as an image of Peter." This happens only in reflective consciousness which reveals the function fulfilled by the picture in my present consciousness. For this reflective consciousness Peter and the picture are two distinct objects. But in the imaginative attitude the picture is but a way in which Peter appears to me as absent. The picture thus *delivers* Peter, though Peter is not here. The sign, on the contrary, does not deliver its object. It is constituted as a sign by an

empty intention. It follows that a significant consciousness which is empty by nature, can fulfill itself without destroying itself. I see Peter, and someone says: "That's Peter"; I join the sign Peter to the perception Peter by a synthetic act. The meaning is fulfilled. The consciousness of the image is already full in its own way. Were Peter to appear in person the image would disappear.

. .
. .

We should not, however, imagine that the object of a photo need but exist to be posited as such by consciousness. We know that there is a type of imaginative consciousness in which the object is not posited as existing; and another in which the object is posited as not existing. The preceding descriptions hold for these types with but slight modification. All that is modified is the positional character of consciousness. But it must be insisted that what distinguishes between the different positional types is the thetic character of the intention, and not the existence or non-existence of the object. For instance, I can very well posit a Centaur as existing (but absent). But when I look at the photos in a magazine they "mean nothing to me," that is, I may look at them without any thought that they exist. In that case the persons whose photographs I see are reached through these photographs, but without existential position, exactly like Death and the Knight, who are reached through Durer's engraving, but without my placing them.[1] We can also find cases in which the photograph leaves me so unaffected that I do not even form an image. The photograph forms but a vague object and the persons depicted in it are well constituted as persons, but simply so because of their resemblance to human beings, without any particular intentionality. They float between the

[1] Cf. Husserl. *Ideen zu einer reinen Phänomenologie*, p. 226.

banks of perception, between sign and image, without ever bordering on either of them.

But the imaginative consciousness we produce before a photograph is an act, and this act involves a consciousness which is non-thetic of itself as being spontaneous. We become aware, somehow, of *animating* the photo, of lending it life in order to make an image of it.

3. From Sign to Image: The Consciousness of Imitations

The whimsical Franconay is "doing some impersonations" on the stage of the music hall; I recognize the artist she is imitating: it is Maurice Chevalier. I recognize the imitation: "It is really he," or: "It is poor." What is going on in my consciousness?

Nothing more, some will say, than a comparison by resemblance: the imitation has produced an image of Maurice Chevalier; next I proceed to compare the latter with the former.

This view is not acceptable, since is plunges us right into the illusion of immanence. James' objection carries its full weight here: what is that resemblance which goes out in search of images in the unconscious, the resemblance that precedes the consciousness we have of it?

We might attempt to save this thesis by making several corrections. We might drop resemblance and resort instead to contiguity.

The name "Maurice Chevalier" calls forth in us an image by contiguity. But what about the numerous cases in which the artist suggests without naming? That happens, we might say, because of numerous other signs that can suggest a name: Franconay, without naming Chevalier, might suddenly put on a straw hat. Posters, newspapers, caricatures, have slowly built up a whole arsenal of signs. We only need to draw upon it.

It is true that imitation uses signs which are recognized as such by the spectator. But the union of sign with image, if this is to be understood as an associative tie, does not exist; first, for the reason that the consciousness of imitation, which itself is an imaginative consciousness, involves no mental imagery at all. Furthermore, the image, like the sign, is a consciousness. There can be no external tie between these two consciousnesses. A consciousness does not have an opaque and unconscious surface by which it can be seized and attached to another consciousness. Between two consciousnesses there is no cause and effect relationship. A consciousness is through and through a synthesis, completely withdrawn into itself: it is only at the very heart of this internal synthesis that it can join itself to another preceding or succeeding consciousness by an act of retention or protention. Moreover, if one consciousness is to act on another, it must be retained and re-created by the consciousness on which it is to act. There are no passivities, but internal assimilations and disintegrations at the very heart of an intentional synthesis which is transparent to itself. One consciousness is not the cause of another: it motivates it.

This brings us to the real problem: the consciousness of imitation is a temporal form, that is, it develops its structures in time. It is a consciousness of meaning. But it is a consciousness of special meaning which knows beforehand that it is to become the consciousness of an image. Hence it becomes an imaginative consciousness, but one that retains within itself what there was of the essential in the consciousness of the sign. The synthetic unity of these consciousnesses is an act of a certain duration, in which the consciousness of the sign and that of the image bear to each other the relationship of means to ends. The essential problem is to describe these structures, to show how the sign serves to *motivate* the image, how the former includes the latter in a new synthesis. How there takes place, at the same time, a functional transformation of the perceived object from the state of significant material to that of representative material.

The difference between the consciousness of imitation and the consciousness of the portrait arises from the materials. The material of the portrait calls directly upon the spectator to operate the synthesis, because the painter endowed it with a perfect resemblance of its model. The material of the imitation is a human body. It is rigid, it resists.[1] The impersonator is small, stout, and brunette; a woman who is imitating a man. The result is that the imitation is but an approximation. The object produced by Franconay by means of her body is a feeble form which can be always interpreted in two distinct ways: I am always free to see Maurice Chevalier as an image, or a small woman who is making faces. From this follows the essential role of signs: they must clarify and guide consciousness.

The first orientation of consciousness is on the general situation: it is disposed to interpret everything as an imitation. But it remains empty, it has but one question (who is going to be imitated?), only one directed expectation. From the outset it is directed, through the imitator, upon an undetermined person, conceived as the object X of the imitation.[2] The assignment consciousness makes for itself is twofold: to determine object X in keeping with the signs provided by the impersonator; and to realize the object as an image through the person who is imitating it.

The artist appears. She wears a straw hat; she protrudes the lower lip, she bends her head forward. I cease to perceive, I *read*, that is, I make a significant synthesis. The straw hat is at first a simple sign, just as the cap and the silk kerchief of the real singer are signs that he is about to sing an apache song. That is to say, that at first I do not see the hat of Chevalier *through* the straw hat, but that the hat of the mimic

---

[1] Only imitations without make-up concern us here.

[2] We are of course taking into account the theoretical case in which all the steps of consciousness are clearly distinct. It can also happen that an imitation is as true to life as a portrait (for instance, if the artist painted her face). In that case, we are back to the analyses made in the preceding chapter.

refers to Chevalier, as the cap refers to the "apache sphere." To decipher the signs is to produce the concept "Chevalier." At the same time I am making the judgment: "she is imitating Chevalier." With this judgment the structure of consciousness is transformed. The theme, now, is Chevalier. By its central intention, the consciousness is imaginative, it is a question of realizing my knowledge in the intuitive material furnished me.

This intuitive material is very poor; the imitation reproduces only a few elements which are, moreover, the least intuitive in intuition: namely the relationships consisting of the rakish angle of the straw hat, the angle formed by neck and chin. In addition to this, certain of these relationships are deliberately altered: the angle of the straw hat is exaggerated, since this is the principal sign which must strike us at first and around which all the others are ordered. Thus, whereas a portrait is a faithful rendition of its model in all its complexity and whereas the portrait, like life, calls for a deliberate simplification in order to extricate the characteristic traits, in the imitation it is the characteristic as such which is presented at the very outset. A portrait is, in some respects—at least in appearance—something natural. An imitation is already a studied model, a simplified representation. It is into these simplified representations that consciousness wants to slip an imaginative intuition. Let us add that these very bare simplified representations—so bare, so abstract that they can be immediately read as signs—are engulfed in a mass of details which seem to oppose this intuition. How is Maurice Chevalier to be found in these fat painted cheeks, that black hair, that feminine body, those female clothes?

We must recall here a famous passage from *Matter and Memory*: "*A priori* . . . it does seem as if the clear distinction between individual objects were a luxury of perception. . . . It does seem that we set out neither from the perception of the individual, nor from the conception of the genus, but from some intermediate knowledge, from a confused sense of a *conspicuous quality* or of resemblance." [1]

That black hair we did not notice as being black; that body we did not perceive to be the body of a woman, we did not see those prominent curves. Nevertheless, since it is a matter of descending to the level of intuition, we use their sensible content in what we can find in it to be most general. The hair, the body are perceived as if they were indefinite masses, as filled spaces. They have sensible opaqueness; otherwise they are but a *setting*. Thus, for the first time in our description of the imaginative consciousness do we encounter—and this at the very heart of perception—a fundamental indetermination. We must remember this when, later on, we study mental images. These qualities, which are so vague and which are perceived only in what they contain of the most general, have no value in themselves: they are incorporated into the imagined synthesis. They represent the undetermined body, the undetermined hair of Maurice Chevalier.

These are not enough: we must find some positive determinations. It is not a question of constructing a perfect *analogue* of the body of Chevalier with the body of the impersonator Franconay. I use but a few of the elements that were functioning just now as signs. In the absence of a complete equivalent of the person imitated, I must realize in intuition a certain *expressive nature*, something as the essence of Chevalier delivered to intuition.

First I must lend life to these dry schemes. But let us be careful: if I perceive them for themselves, if I note the junctures of the lips, the color of the straw of the hat, the consciousness of the image vanishes. I must execute the movement of the perception backwards, determine the intuition by beginning with the knowledge and as a consequence of the knowledge. That lip was an erstwhile sign: I turned it into an image. But it is an image only in the degree to which it was

[1] Bergson, *Matière et Mémoire*, p. 172.

a sign. I see it only as a "fat protruding lip." Here we encounter once more an essential trait of the mental image: the phenomenon of quasi-observation. What I perceive is also what I know; the object can teach nothing, and the intuition is but dull, debased knowledge. At the same time, these segregated islets are reunited by vague intuitive zones; the cheeks, the ears, the neck of the actress function as undetermined connective tissue. Here again, it is knowledge which is first; what is perceived corresponds to the vague knowledge that Maurice Chevalier has cheeks, ears, a neck. The details vanish, and what cannot disappear resists the imagined synthesis.

But these different elements of intuition are insufficient to bring about the realization of the "expressive something" of which we spoke. Here a new factor appears: affectivity.

Let us lay down two principles:

1. Every perception is accompanied by an affective reaction.[1]

2. Every feeling is a feeling *of* something, that is, it envisions its object in a certain manner and projects upon it a certain quality. To have sympathy for Peter is to be conscious of Peter as sympathetic.

We can now understand the role of feeling in the consciousness of imitation. When I see Maurice Chevalier the perception involves a certain affective reaction. This feeling projects on the physiognomy of Maurice Chevalier a certain indefinable quality which we might call his "meaning." In the consciousness of imitation this affective reaction is awakened by the intentioned knowledge and becomes incorporated into the intentional synthesis from the very beginning of the signs and the intuitive realization. The affective sense of Chevalier's face will appear correlatively on the face of Franconay. It is this affective meaning which brings about the synthetic union of the various signs, which animates their frozen barrenness, which gives them life and a certain density. It is this, which,

[1] Cf. Abramowski. *Le Subconscient normal.*

endowing the isolated elements of the imitation with an indefinable meaning and the unity of an object, can pass as the true intuitive material of the consciousness of imitation. Finally, it is in fact this object as an image that we see on the body of the impersonator: the signs united by an affective meaning, that is, the *expressive something*. That is the first time, but not the last, that we see feeling supplant the real intuitive elements of perception in order to realize the object as an image.

The imagined synthesis is accompanied by a fully spontaneous consciousness and, we might even say, one that is fully free. This is so because only a formal will can prevent consciousness from gliding from the level of the image to that of the perception. In most cases this gliding occurs all the same, from time to time. It even happens quite often that the synthesis is not completely made: the face and body of the impersonator do not lose all their individuality; but the expressive something "Maurice Chevalier" nevertheless appears on that face, on that female body. A hybrid condition follows, which is altogether neither perception nor image, which should be described by itself. These unstable and momentary states evidently supply the spectator with the most pleasant aspects of imitation. This is no doubt due to the fact that the relationship of the object to the material of the imitation is here one of *possession*. The absent Maurice Chevalier chose the body of a woman to make his appearance.

Thus, primitively, an impersonator is one possessed.[1] Here may lie the explanation of the role of impersonator in the ritual dances of the primitives.

4. From Sign to Image: Schematic Drawings

The image, said Husserl, is a "fulfillment" (Erfüllung) of meaning. But our study of the image shows us that it is rather

[1] We should also speak of the *consciousness of imitating*, which is surely a consciousness *of being possessed*.

a debased meaning, one that has sunk to the level of intuition. It is not a fulfillment, but a change in nature. A study of the consciousness of schematic drawings will confirm us in this view. In these the intuitive element is considerably reduced, and the role of the conscious activity increases in importance: the image is built up by the intention which compensates for its shortcomings as a perception.

The schematic sketch is composed of schema. Caricatures, for instance, can represent a man by a few thin black lines: a black point for the head, two lines for the arms, one for the chest, two for the legs. The distinguishing trait of the sketch is that it occupies an intermediate position between the image and the sign. Its material calls for interpretation. Its one aim is to present relationships. By itself it is nothing. Many of them are meaningless unless one is familiar with the system of conventions which is the key to them; most of them must have an intelligent interpretation; they have no real resemblance to the object they represent. Nevertheless they are not signs because they are not considered to be such. In these few black lines I intend a man who is running (Fig. 1). The

fig. 1

knowledge envisions the image, but is itself not an image; it slips into the sketch and becomes an intuition. But the knowledge does not only involve the acquaintance with the qualities that are directly represented in the sketch. It also comprises, in an undifferentiated mass, all sorts of intentions concerning the diverse physical qualities which can possess the content, including color, facial features, sometimes even the expression. These intentions remain undifferentiated as they reach the schematic figure, but they realize themselves intuitively on it. In these black lines we do not only envision a silhouette, but a complete man, we concentrate in them all his qualities without differentiation: the drawing is filled to the breaking point. But, these qualities are not really *represented*: in fact the black lines *represent* nothing more than some structural relationships and an attitude. But a mere hint of representation is enough for all the knowledge to descend upon it, thereby giving a sort of depth to that flat figure. Draw a man in a kneeling position with arms uplifted and his face assumes the expression of indignant surprise. But you do not *see* it there: it is there in a latent state, like an electric charge.

Most schematic figures produce a definite impression. Visual movements organize the perception, carve out the spatial environment, determine the fields of force, transform the lines into vectors. Let us consider, for example, a diagram of a face (Fig. 2). I may see in it no more than some lines: three seg-

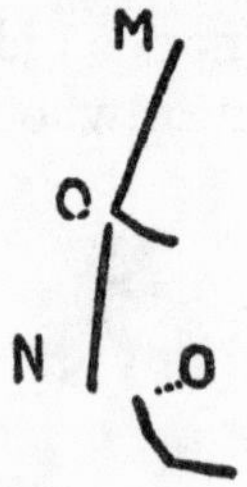

fig. 2

ments which meet at point O; a second point below the O, somewhat to the right, then a meaningless line. In this case I let the lines organize themselves according to the laws of form as studied by Köhler and Wertheimer. The white sheet serves as the common ground, with the three segments getting organized into a fork. My eyes ascend from N to O, and there the movement is widened in following the two divergent lines at once. The isolated point below O forms part of the figure. But the sinuous line I traced below remains isolated and forms a new figure.[1]

Now I read the figure in an entirely different way: I see a face in it. Of the three segments, the one that rises obliquely is interpreted as the contour of the brow, the right segment is an eyebrow, the sloping segment is the line of the nose. The isolated point represents the eye, the sinuous line outlines the mouth and the chin. What happened here? A radical change in the intention took place at the very beginning. We shall not describe that change here, we are quite familiar with it: the perceptual intention becomes an imagined one. But this would not be enough: the figure must lend itself to interpretation. The collection of lines must be animated by a certain attitude of my body, namely, by my body enacting a certain pantomime. Likewise, the white paper on both sides of the figure undergoes a complete change of meaning. The space to the right of the lines is joined to the figure in such a manner that the lines seem to mark the end of it: that is, my eyes take in a certain extent of white space, to the right of the figure, but without positing it as paper. But neither do I think of it as the flesh of a face, but rather as density, as filled space. Furthermore, the movement of my eyes, which began, without much precision, to the right of the figure, somewhat behind the eyebrow, at the level of the tip of the nose, stops abruptly at the lines ONM, which become, by this fact, the limits of an undetermined solid region, while the part of the white paper to the left of the figure remains empty space; because I refuse to take it into account. Of course, I cannot keep from seeing it, when I let my eyes run over the black lines of the figure. But I do not see it *for itself*. In fact, it functions as ground in the perception itself since it is actually also perceived at the moment when my glance attaches itself to the lines con-

[1] It is possible that this way of organizing my perception is true only for me. The reader can determine his own way for himself.

ceived as contours. Thus the space of the sheet becomes a fully occupied space at the right, and a void at the left. At the same time, each line is interpreted for itself by definite movements of the eyes. For example, the nose is "read" from top to bottom, beginning with the eyebrow (since our natural attitude vis-a-vis a nose is to notice "its beginning" and "its end"; and consequently, to think of it as oriented from top to bottom. At the same time we must supply an absent line: the one that joins N to the sinuous line, since we must construct a single figure out of these two separate groups of lines. This we accomplish by carrying our eyes from N to D: we *enact* the missing line, we mimic it with our body. At the same time we proceed to an intentional synthesis from N and from D, that is, we retain N in our successive acts of consciousness, as we retain the different moments of the flight of a bird, so that, arriving at D, we organize N with D as the terminus *a quo* with the terminus *ad quem*. This account is, of course, incomplete but it is enough for our present purpose.

Let us consider, in contrast, another schematic figure which represents a person in profile by means of lines almost like those of the preceding sketch: the right and left spaces join to form an empty ground, and, by contrast, these lines without thickness stop being limits: they take on density, thickness; I recognize in each line a right and left contour. At the same time (at least in what concerns me); the figure is interpreted from bottom to top, etc.

These descriptions can and should be repeated by each reader for himself. The interpretation of a schematic figure depends on knowledge and knowledge varies from person to person. But the results are always the same which is all that interests us. We meet this very unique phenomenon in all cases: knowledge which enacts a symbolic pantomime and a pantomime which is hypostatized, projected into the object. It is this phenomenon which we shall encounter in a somewhat different form in the case of the mental image, and it is this phenomenon which it will be well for us to understand. It will yield us, in the long run, the answer to many problems.

Let us begin with perception. Here is a table, that is, a dense form, a solid, heavy object. I can move my eyes from right to left or from left to right, without causing any change. Likewise if I look at the portrait of Descartes by Frans Hals, I can observe the lips of the philosopher at the line of junction or from the center of the mouth towards the corners: the resemblance they have with the real lips will not thereby be changed. In this clear-cut case we distinguish clearly between the form of the perceived object and the movement of our eyes. In most of the cases, no doubt, we must move our eyeballs and follow the contours with our eyes in order to construct a form. But it matters little whether the movement is made in one way or another, stopped, resumed: when we face the object, which is experienced as a changeless whole, our eye movements can follow an endless number of possible pathways, any one of which is just as good as any other.

This does not mean that an eye movement does not change the perception. When I shift my gaze the relation of the object to the retina is modified. Since movement is relative, there is no sign in the object by which it can be ascertained whether it is the object which shifts in relation to our eyes or our eyes in relation to the object. There are special cases which can confuse us. Most of the time, however, we are not deceived: for first of all it is not the object alone which shifts, but all its surroundings with it; the eye movements are also accompanied by internal sensations (we feel the rolling of our eyeballs in their orbits); all this happens, finally, if not as the product of a voluntary act, at least as that of a mental spontaneity. All that is now needed is knowledge, a very special intention, one might almost say a decision, to refer the movement to our bodies and thereby immobilize the object facing us. This decision is, naturally, not something we might have learned or might have put into play at each moment. It appears when we

assume a perceptual attitude towards our environment, and it is
constitutive of that attitude (with several other intentions
which we need not enumerate here). In itself, it could be said,
the relation of the object to the retina is neutral: it is a relation
of position which leaves unanswered the question concerning
movement.

Now, in the very realm of perceptions certain forms impose
upon us definite eye movements, which may be due to the fact
that their very structure demands of us certain motor reactions, or because of an established habit which is indissolubly
tied to these forms. In such cases the impression of spontaneity
that accompanied the shifting of our eyeballs disappears completely. Since the figure prescribes our movements, the data
of perception are grouped in a new way: we construct new

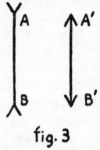

fig. 3

objects to which we refer the change as one of their qualities.
In the Muller-Lyer illusion, for instance, the eye movements
come up against the closed angles at A' and B'; while at the
open angles in A and B the movement can be continued endlessly. The opposing movements are hypostatized at A'B', the
favorable are projected in AB, and we say that AB is longer
than A'B'. But careful observation will show that this is quite
inexact. What appears to us longer in AB is the power of extension. AB reaches upwards and downwards, while A'B' rolls
itself up on itself. What happens is that we project the movement on the segments AB and A'B' while retaining the immo-
bility of the figures. These two contradictory decisions give

the object a novel quality: the stationary movement becomes a potential movement, a force. The segments are transformed into vectors. This simply means that our eye movements, having occurred, are therefore irreversible. All these processes are perceptual: what we did was to confer a new quality on the object, a quality which we *perceived*. The object thus constituted can serve as a sign (a pointing arrow, etc.), but never as an image, at least not as such. We see that what modified the perception, what conferred their direction on the lines, was that the movement ceased to be felt as a spontaneous production. It rather appears to be caused, and we name what causes it the direction of the figure, that is, the same movement projected on the sheet and conceived as cause. What happens here is somewhat like our giving the name of irascibility to the passions of a person projected deep into him and conceived as the cause of their external manifestations.

We now come to schematic images. There is little real compulsion in them. They do not act as rules of movement. It is knowledge which directs motor reactions, and it even happens, as in the case of the face suggested above, that it shatters the natural structure of the forms and brings about a new synthesis. It follows naturally that the eye movements happen *spontaneously*. It would seem impossible, consequently, to objectify them as real properties of the perceived lines. So what happens is that they are objectified as properties *in the form of an image*. We do not fail to notice that the figure seized as a harmony of lines can have another structure, other directions, or no direction at all. But we intend directions upon it as an image. We force the spontaneity of ocular movements into a much greater mental synthesis, which occurs completely as spontaneous: it is this which constitutes the meaning of the figure as an *hypothesis*. *Knowledge*, confronting the lines, provokes movements. These movements are carried out in order to find out whether something "will come out of it." They are at the same time objectified in the form of a "hypothetical direction" on the figure. The question is, therefore, the following: Once the movements are carried out, the direction posited, the figure oriented, will the image crystallize, that is, will it appear as a new and indestructible form, a form which will henceforth provoke by itself the movements that fix it? If the image appears I *see* the man who is running along these several black lines. But I see him as an image, that is, I do not fail to realize that I have projected the movements freely and spontaneously into the lines as vectorial qualities. I know that I create the image at each instant. So that we now see that the representative elements in the consciousness of a sketch are not really the lines, but movements projected on these lines.

Here we find the explanation for the fact that we read so many things in an image whose material is so poor. Actually, our knowledge is not directly realized on these lines which, by themselves, do not speak: it is realized by means of the movements. And, on the one hand, these movements for a single line can be numerous, so that a single line can have many meanings and can serve as representative material of a mass of sensible qualities of the object as an image. On the other hand, the same movement can bring about different knowledges. The line itself is but a support, a substratum.[1]

[1] If one desires an explanation for the enormous disproportion existing between the external representative element and the knowledge therein incorporated, one can consider some examples of the following sort: let us imagine that a well-known person is often represented in newspapers and caricatures by the following three attributes: a straw hat, spectacles, a pipe, and gets to be known to the public by these three objects. If you arrange these three objects into whatever schematic representations (for instance: pipe, hat, glasses) you have signs: from these three attributes we pass to the person whom they are intended to evoke. If you arrange them in their natural order (hat, *under* the hat, glasses, *under* the glasses, pipe, in the distance and the right direction) you have an image; the three attributes *represent* the face of the well-known man. Outside these three designated objects, the only intuitive elements are the order and arrangement of these objects. Through this almost abstract quality we intend the noted man as an image. None of these traits is truly realized on the paper: he is there, in an undifferentiated state, in the space between the hat and the pipe, a space we conceive as *filled with him.*

But can we distinguish between knowledge and movement? As a matter of fact, there is no knowledge which does the directing and a series of movements that obey. But just as we often take account of our thoughts while *speaking*, so we take account of our knowledge while enacting; or rather it is the knowledge which takes cognizance of itself in the form of pantomime. There are no two realities, knowledge and movement: there exists but one thing, the symbolic movement; which is what we wanted to show. Knowledge becomes aware of itself here only as an image; the consciousness of the image is a debased consciousness of knowledge.

5. Faces in the Fire, Spots on Walls, Rocks in Human Form

Here also the concern is with movements which interpret forms, but with a considerable difference in the positional attitudes of consciousness.

When I look at a drawing, I posit in that very glance a world of human intentions of which that drawing is a product. A man drew these lines in order to produce the likeness of a runner. Of course this likeness will appear only with the cooperation of my consciousness. But the artist knows this, he counts on it; he asks for this cooperation by means of his black lines. We must not believe that these lines appear to me first in perception as pure and simple lines, and only afterwards as the elements of a *representation* in the imaginary attitude. They appear as such in the perception itself. Look through an album of sketches and you will not necessarily grasp at a glance the meaning of each line, but you will know what each represents, that it stands for something which is the very justification of its existence. In short, the quality of *representation* is a real property of the lines, I perceive it, in the same way as I do their dimensions and their form. It will be claimed, however, that this is no more than knowledge. But so is the cube: I cannot have a simultaneous intuition of its six sides. Nevertheless, when I look at that piece of shaped wood, it is certainly a cube I see. All imagined consciousness produced by a sketch is therefore built on a position which has real existence, which precedes it and which motivates it on the basis of perception, even though that consciousness itself can present its object as non-existent or even neutralize the question of existence.

When we interpret a spot on the tablecloth, a motif of a tapestry, we do not posit that the spot or motif possesses representative properties. That spot really *represents* nothing; when I perceive it I do so as a spot and nothing else. So that when I assume the imaginative attitude the intuitive basis of my image is nothing that had appeared earlier in perception. These images have for their material a pure appearance, which occurs as such; nothing is posited at the outset; it is a matter, in some way, of an image in the air, without a foundation. We are not so far from the mental image in which the material has so little independence that it appears and disappears with the image. But in the case we are now studying, we still pretend "to see" the image, that is to borrow its material from the world of perception. This appearance we localize; it has matter and form. In a word, the material is not the spot, but a way of surveying it. In the schematic drawing, however, a certain virtuality, a constant power for provoking eye movements is incorporated into the black lines. But in the case of the spot the movements leave no trace on it. Soon as they are finished the spot becomes a spot again and that's the end.

There are two eventualities: in the one, we execute free eye movements without any ulterior motive and look upon the contours of a spot at our pleasure, in following the order that pleases us in bringing together at random this and that part into a synthesis which may be anything at all. This is what happens when our eyes wander over wall paper when we lie inactive during an illness. It then happens that a familiar form springs up from these arabesques, that is, a somewhat coherent synthesis is formed in the course of these movements under my gaze: my eyes have traced a path which remains traced on the tapestry. Then I say: it is a man in a squatting position, it is a bouquet, a dog. That is, I construct a hypothesis on this spontaneously operated synthesis: I attribute a representative value to the oriented form that had just appeared to me. Most of the time I do not even wait for this synthesis to complete itself, but suddenly something crystallizes into something that is about to become an image. "This is beginning to look like a bouquet, or the upper part of a face, etc." Knowledge incorporated itself into my movements and directs them: now I know how I am to finish the process, I know what I am to find.

Or it might happen that some form detaches itself on the background and arouses eye movements by its structure. What we encounter here is almost always the phenomenon Köhler calls faint ambiguous forms, or forms which have an obvious and also a secret figure. The appearance of the latter depends upon a chance eye movement always (as, for instance, in raising the head, a line which we had before noticed only as running from top to bottom on the wall paper is at the moment seen running from bottom upwards, and the rest follows by itself). Here also the form is only outlined: for hardly have forehead and eye appeared when we already know it is a negro. We complete the process ourselves by effecting a harmony between the real data of perception (the lines of the arabesques) and the creative spontaneity of our movements: that is, we supply the nose, mouth and chin ourselves.

But whether the movements arise freely or are induced by certain structures, they are at first meaningless, then suddenly become symbolic because they become incorporated with a certain knowledge. The image is created by the knowledge which is becoming realized on the blot through the mediation of the movements. But the movements occur as free play and the knowledge as a gratuitous hypothesis. So we have here a twofold neutralization of the thesis: the blot is not posited as possessing representative properties, and the object of the image is not posited as existing. The image is, therefore, a pure phantom, a game which would realize itself by means of appearance.

At the basis of this consciousness there is a neutralized thesis. If this thesis is replaced by a positive one by conferring a representative power on the blot, we have the hypnagogic image.

6. Hypnagogic Images, Scenes and Persons Seen in Coffee-Grounds, In a Crystal Ball

By all evidence, hypnagogic visions are images. Leroy [1] describes the attitude of consciousness towards these apparitions in the words "spectacular and passive." This is because the objects that appear in this attitude are not posited as actually existing. Nevertheless, at the bottom of this consciousness there is a positive thesis: if that woman who crosses my visual field when my eyes are closed does not exist, at least her image does. Something appeared before me that represents the very image of a woman. Often the image itself is clearer than the object could ever have been.

"It is strange, but my eye has been transformed into a colored photographic plate and nothing else in this world gives me such an image." [2]

"When I was studying anatomy, I very frequently experienced a hypnogogic vision not rare among medical students. Lying in my bed with closed eyes I would see most vividly and with complete objectivity the preparation on which I had worked during the day: the resemblance seemed perfect, the impression of reality

[1] Leroy, *Les Visions du demi-Sommeil*, Alcan, 1926. One of his subjects says, "It is in sum like a cinematographic representation in color," p. 111.
[2] *Journal des Goncourt*, cited by Leroy, p. 29.

and, if I may say so, of intense *life* which emanated from it was perhaps even deeper than I experienced when facing the real object." [2]

Thus the image is experienced as being "more true than nature," just as a particularly significant portrait is said to be truer than its model. But it is only an image. But consciousness affirms nothing concerning its real nature: whether it is constructed out of actual material, whether it is an illusion, or whether it is an unusually vivid memory. We do not decide this when the image is present. We limit ourselves to affirming that, no matter how it came about, the image is here before us, that it appeared to us, that it is *in* our eyes: what we generally imply when we say "I see." The Goncourts, trying to be more precise, write at the opening of the passage we have already cited: "I have in the retina." However, the position of the image is not built according to the plan of the perception: to perceive a thing is, in effect, to put it in its place among other things. The vision in half-sleep is something unique. In general it is not localized, it is nowhere, occupies no place among other objects, it simply stands out in relief on a hazy ground. In a word, the representation is posited as existing as a representation (without specifying its nature). It is granted, besides the character of objectivity, of clarity, of independence, of richness, of externality, which the mental image never possesses and which ordinarily belong to perception. Its object is not posited as existing.

The hypnagogic image, on the other hand, remains in the realm of quasi-observation. It is this fact which has not been sufficiently shown. No doubt its object occurs with a vivacity that leads us momentarily to believe that its various properties could be studied by careful observation. Leroy implies this when, after describing the vision we reported above, he deplores the "lack of a faculty to evoke voluntarily similar

[2] Leroy, *op. cit.*, p. 28.

visions on the day of an examination." He assumes therefore that by fixing the image and subjecting it to a sort of analysis he could have enumerated its various characteristics.

The fact of the matter is, however, that the object never tells us anything: it appears suddenly in its entirety and does not permit observation. Leroy noticed after a little while that "the abundance of details, the wealth of the vision were illusory." The alleged richness of the image is, therefore, but a *fancy*; and this obviously indicates that all these details of the anatomical preparation which appear with such clarity are not *seen*. Later we shall see that Alain, in his Système des Beaux-Arts, challenges anyone to count the columns of the facade of the Pantheon *in an image*. This challenge holds equally for hypnagogic images.

These images also have a "fantastic" [1] character, which prevents them from ever representing anything with precision. The strict law of individuation does not apply to them.

"While I was busy with my dissections during a part of an afternoon, my preparation underwent constant changes, due not only to my scalpel, but to changes in illumination, in my position, etc. Now, in the presence of my vision of the evening I would not be able to report, even approximately, which moment, which particular aspect, was being reproduced. The illumination especially was always in some way but *theoretical*, extremely bright, more like the colored plates of a beautiful atlas than real light and at times poor lighting of the dissection table." [2]

Furthermore, these visions not only fail to obey the law of individuation, but also the other laws of perception: for instance, those of perspective.

Obs. XXVII: "I am lying down. . . . I see a small woman walking. . . . She is coming towards me. . . . She is not

---

[1] Leroy, *op. cit.*, p. 32.
[2] *Id.*, *ibid*. See also *passim*. For instance: p. 17, Obs. VIII: "a luminous band *whose color I could not recognize*," etc.

getting taller as she approaches me, but the pink of her stockings becomes brighter." [1]

Often it is even impossible to delineate it.

I see clearly two ribs of the parasol, which is nothing unusual,
but the third should be hidden by the cloth and by the body of the
funnel, both of which are opaque, and yet I see it. But I do not
see it transparently: there is something here which can be neither
explained nor delineated.[2]

But it will be said, a moment's observation is quite enough
to determine what they represent. This is not so. In fact, this
essential trait of hypnagogic images has not been sufficiently
stressed: they are never anterior to knowledge. But all of a
sudden one is abruptly struck by the certitude of seeing a rose,
a square, a face. Till then it was not noticed: now *one knows*.
It is regrettable that Leroy failed to study his subjects from
this point of view: his excellent descriptions would have gained
thereby in being absolutely complete. It is but seldom that
remarks like the following are to be found:

"At a certain moment, with eyes closed, I see distinctly a
woman who is sawing wood: *This appears entirely at a single
glance*." [3] Or:

Gradually there appear a certain number of light transverse
lines: the flowers are arranged in fives, so as to bring their upper
ends very close to these threads. *Suddenly I see* that the lines are
really strings and that the flowers have turned into socks that are
drying; and soon I also see the clothes pins of the laundress that
hold them on the strings.[4]

In fact, according to my own observations and those of
many persons I was able to question, a radical distinction must

[1] Leroy, *op. cit.*, p. 58.
[2] *Id.*, *ibid.*, p. 86.
[3] Leroy, *op. cit.*, p. 18. Cf. also p. 45: "Suddenly I *notice that I see* a
carriage stop before me."
[4] This observation shows through and through that in certain cases
knowledge may even precede the image.

be drawn between the way a face appears in perception and the manner the same face occurs in hypnagogic vision. In the former case something appears which is then identified as a face. Alain, among many other philosophers, has amply shown [2] how judgment corrects, organizes and stabilizes perception. This transition from "something" to "this thing" has been often described in novels, especially when they are written in the first person.

"I heard," said Conrad, for instance (I quote from memory), "dull and irregular noises, cracklings: it was the rain."

If we are in the habit of perceiving an object, and if the perception is clear and sharp (especially if it is a visual perception), the interval can be considerably reduced: nevertheless, consciousness must focus upon the object—this focusing being as rapid as one desires—and the object is there before the focusing.

In hypnagogic vision this discrepancy does not exist. There is no focusing. Suddenly knowledge appears, as vivid as a sensory manifestation: one becomes aware of *being in the act* of seeing a face. The appearance of the face and the certitude that it is a face occur together. This certitude, moreover, does not involve familiarity at the moment that the object appeared: careful reflection would rather show that certitude is present at the very moment that the face is noticed. But, in the hypnagogic consciousness the object is posited neither as in the process of appearing nor as already having appeared; one is suddenly aware of seeing a face. It is in the main this positional characteristic which endows the hypnagogic vision with its "fantastic" trait. It appears suddenly and disappears in the same manner.

These few observations enable us to understand that in half-sleep we are dealing with imaginative consciousnesses. The question now arises concerning their material: what, at the heart of these acts of consciousness, is the relation of the inten-

[2] Cf., for instance, *Quatre-vingt-un chapitres sur l'Esprit et les Passions.*

tion to the material. Many writers believe that this material is furnished by entoptic lights.[1] Leroy, without drawing any conclusion, cites in opposition the relative independence of images as regards phosphenes.[2] We shall attempt to show that these objections bear only upon a certain conception regarding the relation of the intention with entoptic lights. For this purpose we must return once more to a general description of the hypnagogic state, as much for the sake of our own personal observations as for these of the authors cited in the footnotes.

We shall begin where Leroy ends and cite his excellent conclusion, now a classic.

What characterizes the hypnagogic vision . . ., is a modification of the total condition of the subject. This is the *hypnagogic condition*; the synthesis of the representations is here different from that of the normal condition; voluntary attention and action, in general, undergo here a special orientation and limitation.[3]

In this statement the only expression open to criticism is *"the condition."* There are no conditions in psychology, but there is an organization of instantaneous consciousnesses into the intentional unity of a longer consciousness: "the hypnagogic condition" is a temporal form that develops its structures during the period called by Lhermitte "l'endormissement" (lulling to sleep). It is this temporal form we need describe.

The hypnagogic state is preceded by some significant changes of sensibility and motivity. Leroy assumes that only visual sensations are abolished. In fact, all other sensations are somewhat blunted. One's body is but vaguely felt, and even more so the contact with the bed sheets and mattress. The spatial position of the body is but poorly localized. Orientation is confused. The perception of time is uncertain.

[1] Cf. Delage: *Le Rêve*. Binet Année psychol. t. I, p. 424–425. Trumbul Ladd. Gellé, "Les Images hypnagogiques," in *Bullet. de l'Instit. gen. psychol.*, 4ᵉ année, No. 1.
[2] Leroy, *op. cit.*, p. 70–74.
[3] Leroy, *op. cit.*, p. 127.

Muscle tonus is in the main relaxed. Tonicity of attitude is almost completely suppressed. The tonicity of some muscles is, however, increased.

For instance, the eyelids are not only shut due to the relaxation of the retractor muscles; but the orbicular muscle must also contract. Likewise, if the large oblique muscles relax, the small oblique muscles contract, resulting in the divergence of the ocular axes; the pupillary orifice takes a position below the bony ceiling of the eye socket. And, finally, the pupillary contraction is likewise due to the contraction of the iris.[1]

The relaxing of the retractor muscles and the large oblique muscles does not immediately follow the closing of the pupils. For a while we review the events of the day. The eyes remain convergent, the pupils are kept closed by the voluntary contraction of the orbicular muscles. Then our thoughts become more vague. At the same time the retractor muscles become distended. Now it takes effort to open the eyes. The large oblique muscles relax and the eyes roll in their orbits. At the least resumption of reflection the large oblique muscles contract and the eyes resume their position. Similarly, on hearing a noise I feel my eyes "becoming fixed," that is, there probably occurs a double reflex of convergence and accommodation. The hypnagogic visions disappear immediately and so, it seems, do the phosphenes.[2] As the muscles relax we become aware of a very unique condition which may be described as paralysis by autosuggestion. Leroy gives a good description of it.

"After an undetermined period it happens that I always lie on my back and feeling myself awake I want to open my eyes. . . . Impossible! But I do feel (I observe this) that my eyelids are stuck together, as they might be for certain persons on awakening, but *I cannot raise them.*" [3]

[1] Gelle, *op. cit.*, p. 66.
[2] All these phenomena are very common; but hypnagogic visions may occur when the eyes are open. Cf. the subject Pierre G., in Leroy.
[3] Leroy, *op. cit.*, p. 115.

The preceding description shows clearly that we are not dealing here with a simple sensation of peripheral origin, like the relaxing of muscle tonus. Moreover, in the case cited by Leroy, there occurs also an active orbicular contraction. To the pure and simple muscular sensation (impression or distention, repose, abandon) there is added the *sui generis* consciousness that it is impossible to *will* these movements, we no longer feel capable of *animating* our body. This is a condition of very slight auto-suggestion, distantly related to hysterical pithiatism and to certain frenzies of influence. We ourselves forged this unbreakable chain. Let a disturbing noise resound and we are at once on the alert. But so long as we remain undisturbed we are muscularly relaxed and instead of simply and purely constituting the hypotonicity, consciousness permits itself to be charmed, in the strict sense of the word, that is, consciousness does not constitute the hypotonicity but *sanctions* it. It will be noticed that here we have an entirely new way of thinking: it is a thought which can be caught in any trap, which sanctions all requests, which assumes an entirely different attitude towards the objects of our wakeful thoughts, in the sense that it is no longer to be absolutely distinguished from them. Leroy shows clearly how it is possible to pass directly from this condition of autosuggestion into the dream itself. Later on we shall see that there is a very general mode of consciousness which bears some close relationships to imagination and which we shall call *imprisoned consciousness*. The dream is, among others, an imprisoned consciousness.

Much stress has been placed upon the disturbances of attention that precede the hypnagogic image. Leroy speaks of a certain breakdown of voluntary attention, of "becoming incapable of applying oneself to more interesting external events, or to pure speculation." [1]

We are here dealing evidently with an indispensable struc-

---

[1] Leroy, *op. cit.,* p. 65.

ture of the hypnagogic consciousness, since these disturbances of attention are met with in pathological cases. In fact, there is a pathology of hypnagogic images. Lhermitte has collected three most interesting cases [1] which he describes as instances of wakeful dreams, but which obviously are hypnagogic visions. Here is the case of a woman of seventy-two who was suddenly struck with a superior peduncular syndrome:

. . . This ailment, in which the mental functions remain undisturbed, was a warning of some very troublesome manifestations. In the afternoon, at sunset, when the shadows gathered in the corners of the room where she was resting, she reported the presence of some animals which were moving noiselessly across the floor; hens, cats, birds, traveling endlessly and indolently; she could count them, she could have named them; but these animals had a strange, bizarre appearance, as in a dream, as if they belonged to a different world from ours. . . . The ailing woman remained perfectly tranquil and composed before this apparition. . . . Despite the association of visual and tactile sensations, it did not occur to her that these might be actual perceptions; she felt certain she was having illusions. The fact to be borne in mind is that she slept very poorly at night, and her nocturnal insomnia caused her to be somewhat sleepy in the afternoon. . . . These apparitions occurred, just as happens in a dream, at the moment when she could see very little because of the fading light."

And he concludes:

What is most clear (in the three cases), is the lack of interest in the present actual situation, a certain degree of disorientation. . . . [2]

It would seem therefore that, in normal as in pathological cases, the constitutive basis of the hypnagogic consciousness is a modification of attention.

[1] Lhermitte. Le Sommeil, p. 142 ff.
[2] Lhermitte, Le Sommeil, p. 148.

Must we admit here the Bergsonian thesis, to which Van Bogaert and Lhermitte turn in connection with the three cases cited above?

These hallucinatory images are in reality due to a weakening of the sense of reality, of attention to life, thanks to which images and representations assume an abnormal clarity.[1]

This view belongs to the illusion of immanence; it assumes implicitly the existence of two complementary worlds, one consisting of things, the other of images, and that when one of them becomes faint the other is thereby illuminated. This is putting images on the same plane with things, giving both the same sort of existence. This explanation is, moreover, valid for the hallucinatory recurrence of memories, but it does not apply at all to completely new images. Finally, and what is of most importance here, it is not only a weakening of attention to life, to the real, that conditions the appearance of hypnagogic images, but above all, the paying of attention *to these images themselves* must be carefully avoided.

Leroy says rightly that "in order to prolong the phenomenon a certain 'absence' of voluntary attention is necessary, as in the case of its generation." [2]

And Baillarger: "The phenomenon disappears as soon as active attention is turned on it."

Without saying so expressly, Leroy considers this absence of attention to be a distraction.

"A certain *automatism* must be able to function for the phenomenon to develop," he says.[3]

Consciousness is supposed to be a modificatory power, possessing a certain efficacy which withdraws from the game and permits the phenomena to unroll in a blind succession. Leroy distinguishes, in fact, between consciousness which is "con-

[1] *Id., ibid.,* p. 147.
[2] Leroy, *op. cit.,* p. 59.
[3] *Id., ibid.,* p. 57.

templative" and hypnagogic phenomena which are automatic. But this notion of a psychological automatism whose apparent clarity has deceived so many authors, is a philosophical absurdity. Hypnagogic phenomena are not "contemplated by consciousness": *they are of consciousness.* Now, consciousness cannot be an automatism: at the utmost it can ape an automatism, associate itself with automatic forms; that is the case here. But in that case, we must speak of a kind of bondage. This inattentive consciousness is not distracted: it is *fascinated.*

This does not mean, in fact, that consciousness is not fully centered on its object: but not in the manner of attention. All phenomena of attention have a motor basis (convergence, accommodation, contraction of the visual field, etc.). These different movements are for the time being impossible: to produce them we must emerge from the condition of paralysis in which we find ourselves, in which case we return to the wakeful state. Now it is these movements that permit the subject to orient himself in relation to the object and to observe it; it is these movements that give the subject his independence. Even the attention we pay to a purely cenesthetique sensation implies a bodily orientation in relation to that sensation; and even the attention given a thought implies a sort of spatial localization. To pay attention to something and to localize that something are but two terms for one and the same operation. From it there results a sort of objectification of the subject in relation to the object (be it a sensation or a thought). In falling asleep the motor basis of attention is weak. From it there results a different type of presence for the object. It is there, but without externality; we cannot observe it, that is, build hypotheses and control them. What is lacking is precisely a contemplative power of consciousness, a certain way of keeping oneself at a distance from one's images, from one's own thoughts and so permit them their own logical development, instead of depositing upon them all of one's own weight, of throwing oneself into the balance, of being judge and accused, of using one's own power of synthesis to make a synthesis of whatever sort with no matter what. A coach appeared before me which *was* the categorical imperative. Here we see the fascinated consciousness: it produces an image of a carriage in the midst of thinking about Kantian morality, it is no longer free to keep things distinct, but yields to the blandishments of the moment and forms an absurd synthesis in conferring a *meaning* on its new image which permits the retention of the unity of thinking. But this consciousness is of course not in bondage to objects but to itself. We shall study elsewhere, in connection with the dream, these participatory modes of thought. But we may chance the conclusion right now that we do not contemplate the hypnagogic image but are fascinated by it.

So here am I, trunk bent, muscles relaxed, eyes closed, lying on my side; I feel myself paralyzed by a sort of autosuggestion; I can no longer follow my thoughts: they are swamped by a crowd of impressions which divert them and charm them, or else they stagnate and repeat themselves indefinitely. At each moment I am caught by something from which I cannot free myself, which enchains me, which whirls me in a circle of prelogical thoughts, and disappears. The paralysis of my limbs and the fascination of my thoughts are but the two aspects of a novel structure: consciousness in bondage. The ground is prepared for hypnagogic images: I am in a unique condition, comparable to that of certain psychaesthenics, it is the first lowering of potential, the first deterioration of consciousness preceding the dream. The hypnagogic images do not represent a level of second degree: they appear on this ground, or they do not appear at all. What happens here is similar to certain psychoses which possess a simple and also a delirious form. Hypnagogic images belong to the delirious form. I am still able to reflect, that is, to become conscious of being conscious. But to maintain the integrity of these primary consciousnesses it is necessary that the reflexive consciousnesses are in turn charmed, that they do not place before them the acts of primary consciousnesses in order to observe them and describe them. They must share their illusions, posit the objects which they posit, follow them into bondage. In fact, a certain complaisance is called for on my part. It remains in my power to shake off this enchantment, to knock down these paper walls and to return to the wakeful world. This is the reason why the transitory, unstable hypnagogic state is, in a sense, an artificial state. It is "the dream which cannot shape itself." Consciousness does not wish to congeal completely, in the sense in which we say that cream will not congeal. Hypnagogic images appear with a certain nervousness, a certain resistance to sleepiness, just like so many interrupted moments of just falling asleep. When we are at rest, when perfectly composed, we glide imperceptibly from a condition of simple attention into sleep. As a general rule, however, we *want* to fall asleep, that is, we are aware of drifting into sleep. This consciousness delays the process by creating a certain condition of conscious attraction which is exactly the hypnagogic condition.

In this condition of willing bondage I have the power to decide whether or not to permit myself to be fascinated by the field of phosphenes. If I become fascinated then hypnagogic images will appear.

My eyes are closed. A field of relatively stable bright spots of various colors and brightness appears. Movements begin, vague eddies, which create luminous forms without definite contours. But in order to describe forms the eyes must be able to follow their contours. Now, since entoptic lights are in the eyes, it is not possible for the eyeballs to assume a position in relation to these lights. Nevertheless we are constantly being urged to give contours to these lights. It even happens, at the beginning of sleep, that we attempt to follow them with our eyes. This is a vain attempt: the movement should be made *along* the spot, which cannot be done since the spot changes position with the movement. These movements give rise to indefinite and indefinable phosphorescent crossings. Then, all of a sudden, there appear forms with clear contours.

About half an hour after going to bed I see a number of brilliant pointed stars and bizarre forms every time I close my eyes, from among which I particularly recall those that had appeared most frequently, whether on a small or large scale: a broken line formed irregular teeth of a saw, the whole comprising an irregular circular space.[1]

These forms arose somewhat ahead of the entoptic spots: there was a slight displacement of the hypnagogic field in relation to the entoptic field. The first forms appeared on the edges, underneath, above, to the right, to the left: never—at least in the beginning—in the center of the field. As we have shown above, after having tried in vain to observe the entoptic field for a moment, one suddenly *finds oneself in the act of seeing* these contours. These forms are not posited as really existing outside of us, nor even as existing in the entoptic field: but only as being seen at that moment. In a word, I do not *see* the teeth of the saw (I only see phosphenes), but I *know* that what it sees *is* a figure of the teeth of a saw. Likewise, in the rather prolonged dream (onirism) of mental confusion, the patient knows that the sheets he is seeing are griping pains. Nothing new has appeared, no image is projected on the entoptic lights, but, in apprehending them, they are apprehended *as* teeth of a saw or *as* stars. The slight displacement of the hypnagogic field in relation to the entoptic field appears to me to be an illusion; it arises simply from the fact that we do not see the entoptic spots as having the form of the teeth of a saw, but that, at the outset of the entoptic lights, we perceive the teeth of a saw. The visual field stands out with precision, is oriented, is restricted as it becomes the hypnagogic field. In sum, the phosphenes function at the time they occur

[1] Leroy, *op. cit.*, p. 12.

as intuitive material of an apprehension of the teeth of a saw. There is an intention towards the teeth of the saw which gets hold of them and which they fulfill intuitively. But naturally this intention is of a very special order: it undoubtedly resembles the one that sees a face in a blot or a flame, but the latter is free and aware of its spontaneity. But in the hypnagogic consciousness the intention is chained: it has been unhooked, disconnected, aroused by a need to define the phosphene forms; it came to apprehend them: they offered no resistance—because in fact they have no form—but neither did they lend themselves to it: and consciousness constructed a new object through them. Does it posit the existence of these lines, these curves? No: every thesis concerning their existence is completely suspended. It posits only having seen them, that they are "its representation." It had to see forms since it was looking for them; the idea took on body immediately and inevitably as a visual form having an actual reality. Such is the radical deceptive nature of the hypnagogic image: it realizes as a subjective phenomenon, along the line of a perception, what is in fact but an empty intention. The real qualities of the entoptic material act as supports of intentions which greatly enrich it. For instance, I see three beautiful violet flashes. I *know* that I see this violet, but I do not see it, or rather, I know that I am seeing something which *is* violet. That something, as I can account for it after the disappearance of the image, is the luminosity of the entoptic spot. I have therefore apprehended the luminosity as violet; the luminosity *enacted the role* of violet, etc.

Images as such (persons, animals, etc.) come next. Cases are reported in which geometric figures appeared before anything else, but I have been able to observe that most of the time these arabesques of the hypnagogic field are hardly noticed. In fact, it seems to me that they are always the first to appear. They mark the limits of a three-dimensional space from the entoptic field; they posit a frame. The more complex

images *are abrupt convictions concerning the geometric forms.*
It is almost like what we experience in wakeful thought when
we say: these lines arouse an image in me. But here thought
is enchained, and cannot move back upon itself. To think
that lines evoke a face is to see a face in the lines. Captive
thought is compelled to realize all its intentions. I have been
able to follow their appearance and disappearance very frequently. In this connection nothing is more instructive than
what is known as unsuccessful visions. For instance, I see a
colored mass or an image having a certain form and a vague
resemblance prompts me to think "eagle." If some noise or
some thought disturbs me suddenly the interpretation vanishes midway and I am able to realize that the interpretation
was about to be "taken in," that is, to become a sensory experience, to be deceived. The essential feature of the chained
consciousness seems to us to be fatality. Determinism—which
can in no way be applied to the facts of consciousness—posits
that when such a phenomenon occurs such another must necessarily follow. Fatalism posits that such an event should happen and that it is this coming event that determines the series
that is to lead up to it. It is not determinism but fatalism which
is the converse of freedom. It might even be said that fatalism,
incomprehensible in the physical world, is perfectly in its
place in the realm of consciousness. Alain has shown this
clearly.[1] In captive consciousness, in fact, it is the representation of the possible that is lacking, that is, the faculty of suspended judgment. But all thought captures and enchains consciousness—and consciousness toys with it and completes it
at the same time that it thinks it. Had that sudden noise failed
to arouse me, my interpretation of "eagle" would have matured
into the form "I see an eagle." It becomes a certainty when
taken for a finished act of consciousness. Thus the sudden
changes of the essence of hypnagogic objects represents so
many sudden changes of belief:

[1] Cf., for instance: *Mars ou la Guerre Jugée.*

"Suddenly I see that the lines in question are so many strings." [1]

The same text also shows clearly how thoughts crystallize into intuitive certainty:

"And soon I also see the clothes-pins that fasten the stockings to the strings." [2]

The strings and stockings call forth the idea of clothes-pins. But this idea is not thought of as a pure idea; it becomes a certainty at once: what I see calls for clothes-pins. Here we see clearly how knowledge is corrupted in intuition.

It is of course necessary to explain the incessant changes that occur in hypnagogic images. It is, in fact, a world of perpetual motion: figures are being transformed, succeed each other rapidly, a line becomes a string, a string becomes a fact, etc. Each figure is also full of changing and rotating movements, which are but whirling wheels of fire, rapidly falling shooting stars, faces that move towards and away from each other. These movements seem to us to be explainable in terms of three factors: on the one hand, the very course of chaired thought which is never short of interpretation; evidence pursues evidence; a dazzling certainty of seeing a face is followed by evident certainty of seeing a skeleton, etc. In the second place, the very changes of the entoptic field furnish an ever-renewed intuitive foundation for certainties that are ever new. Whether these lights are due to a spontaneous activity of the optic nerve, circulatory phenomena, or to the automatic action of the eyelids on the eyeballs, or to all of these working together, these causes are constantly changing, and with them also their effects. At the foundation of these figures which are rapidly revolving on themselves or which unroll in spirals, there is, we believe, a certain continuous scintillation of certain entoptic spots. The third factor would naturally be the movement of the eyeballs. It is in this way that I would explain

[1] Leroy, *op. cit.*, p. 37.
[2] Cf. *supra*.

certain paradoxical phenomena of hypnagogic vision, as, for instance, the fact that a star seemingly gliding downwards and across my entire visual field appears at the same time to *remain always at the same height* in relation to my optic axes.

But we are not concerned here with the problem of determining the structure of a hypnagogic consciousness in all its details. We only wanted to show that this consciousness is an imaginary consciousness and that it is very much like the consciousnesses that find images in a blot or in a flame. In the one, as in the other case, the material is plastic: in the one are arabesques, faint forms, in the other lights without contours. In the one, as in the other, the mind is relaxed; often the position is the same: often the subject, lying down and being unable to sleep, amuses himself by following the arabesques of the wall paper with his eyes. It is in this condition that the largest variety of images are discovered. It is also such a condition that marks the beginning of fascination. Often the arabesques assume a strange aspect, lines are gathered into a sort of motionless whirlpool, forms are grasped in motion, directions which join them side by side and then disappear. Our attention is caught by certain unities and all the rest of the visual field remains vague and shifting. It is at this moment that the new forms, the faces, appear. In the case of a severe fever these faces and personages can have a quasi-hallucinatory vividness. But there is always a very great difference between these two types of consciousness: in the arabesque it is not posited that the real purpose of the object is to represent something real, an animal or a face. There is in it no existential position. In consciousness there is a feeling of spontaneity. There is a playful activity which is conscious of itself as such. In the hypnagogic image this consciousness of play has disappeared. The image is not posited as an object, but as a representation. One sees if not a cat at least a representation of one; or, to be more exact, *one is about to see a non-existent cat*. No doubt, there remains in the hypnagogic consciousness, in spite of all, a vague feeling of spontaneity, of complaisance towards oneself. One has the feeling of being able to stop everything at will. But what is involved is a non-thetic consciousness which is in some way contradicted by the manner of positing the object. Besides, it is because consciousness feels itself but slightly enchained that it posits its object as non-existent. It pretends to see a cat; but since it is aware in spite of all of the origin of the vision, it does not pretend that this correlative exists. Whence this paradox: I really do see something, but what I see *is nothing*. This is the reason why this chained consciousness takes the form of an image: because it does not reach its own end. In the dream the captivity is complete, so the cat is posited as an object. In the hypnagogic image we have a primitive attitude of consciousness very much like the one we assume towards a Durer engraving: on the one hand I *see* Death, we might say; on the other this Death that I see does not exist. The same is true in the case that concerns us. Only that in the imaginative consciousness of the engraving the material retains its independence, that is, it could be the object of a perception. But in the hypnagogic consciousness the material is practically inseparable from the consciousness we have of it, since it is radically transformed as consciousness seizes hold of it, and this not only in its functions, but in its very structure. No doubt, in the imaginative apprehension of an engraving the flat part became a relief, the colorless became the colored, the empty became the full, etc. But, at least, most of the qualities of the engraving grasped as an image stayed with it when it became the object of a perception. In the hypnagogic consciousness there is almost no relationship between the image and its intuitive support. So that, when the imaginative consciousness is disintegrated, it takes a great deal of effort to rediscover in the perceptual attitude the elements which acted as material.

Although the imaginative consciousness that arises from spots and arabesques differs fundamentally in *conviction* from the hypnagogic consciousness, there nevertheless exist some intermediaries between them. We have seen, in fact, that in the former there is an onset of fascination. It is our opinion that this fascination could be complete, when certain unusual objects are fixated for a long time under special psychological conditions. The crystal ball of the magician, the coffee grounds of the clairvoyant seem to us to belong to this class of objects. In all probability, a naive subject favorably inclined sees pictures in the crystal ball. Here, in fact, is an object very much like entoptic spots: nothing definite, nothing specific in that crystal ball. The eye can fixate on no particular thing, it is held by no form. When the vision appears, incited by this constant unbalance, it presents itself spontaneously as an image, and the subject will report that it is the image he wanted. This shows us that entoptic spots are far from being the only possible material of hypnagogic visions. On the contrary, it would be possible to establish a whole class of objects capable of functioning as the intuitive basis of these images. All that is needed is that they constitute faint forms, disintegrate when under observation and yet continue to reshape themselves endlessly, forms in which the gaze loses itself (whether the eye meets nothing as in the crystal ball, or whether it constantly meets pin points as in coffee grounds), in short, forms that possess the powers of exciting the attention endlessly and of deceiving it endlessly. Now let the subject be sleepy, that is, in a state of suggestibility, and the hypnagogic image will appear.

7. From the Portrait to the Mental Image

We shall now proceed to a description of the mental image, which completes our series. But first it would be well to review the ground we have covered.

The deeper intention has not changed. In the different cases we have studied the problem always was that of animating a certain material in order to turn it into the *representation* of an absent or of a non-existent object. The material was never the perfect analogue of the object to be represented: a certain knowledge came along to interpret it and to fill in the gaps. It is these correlative elements, material and knowledge, which have evolved from case to case.

A. *The Material*—The material of a portrait is a quasi-face. No doubt that the portrait is first of all a neutral element which can function as the support of a perceptual as well as of an imaginative consciousness. But this indifference is mainly a theoretical one. As a matter of fact, the spontaneity of consciousness is strongly aroused: these forms, these colors, so strongly organized, proclaim themselves as being almost the image of Peter. If a notion strikes me to *perceive* these elements, they resist. A picture offers itself spontaneously *in relief* to the imaginative consciousness, and the perceptual consciousness would have much trouble to see it as a flat surface. This quasi-face is moreover accessible to observation: naturally I do not refer the new qualities I see in it to the object I am looking at, to this painted canvas. I project them far beyond the picture, on the true Peter. The result is that every judgment I make is a probability (while in true observation the judgments are certainties). When I say "Peter's eyes are blue," I imply: "provided this painting represents him at all faithfully."

The material of my image is an object which is strictly individual: this painting is unique in time and space. To this should be added the fact that the traits of the quasi-image also possess this intrinsic individuality: that quasi-smile cannot be equaled by any other. But this individuality appears only to the perceptual consciousness. In passing from perception to the image the material acquires a certain generality. We are likely to remark: "Yes, *he does smile* like this," implying that this smile is but typical of the way Peter smiles. We apprehend these various qualities of the material as representatives, each one of which stands for a mass of qualities that Peter now possesses or used to possess: This pink color becomes the *pink* of his cheeks; this green light is the *green* of his eyes. What we are looking for by means of the photograph is not Peter as he might have looked to us the day before yesterday or on such a day of last year: it is *Peter in general*, a prototype which serves as a thematic unity of all of Peter's individual traits.[1]

As the imaginative consciousness rises in degree the material becomes increasingly impoverished. At first, and in spite of some differences, what was seen in perception passes as such into the image: what does change—and radically so—is in the meaning of the material which first sends us back to itself, and then on to another object. Even in the case of imitation, what appears to imaginative consciousness is not at all like what is seen in perception. The material is impoverished as it passes from the one to the other: a number of qualities drop out. This means, then, that the intuitive basis of my image can never be that of a perception. This means that there is an essential poverty in the material of the image, namely, that the object intentioned through the material grows in generality. When Franconay impersonates Chevalier, it is no longer even "Chevalier in his brown costume," "Chevalier with the green eyes," etc., that I see in her. It is Chevalier, that's all. In the schematic drawing, I project into its black lines "the runner-while-running," that is, a prototype of all possible runners. It is difficult, at this level, to differentiate clearly between *the idea* of the runner and his picture. We shall see later on that this can be done, but the object of the idea and that of the image—although experienced in different ways—are identical. From that moment on we are in the presence of a phenomenon of quasi-observation, that is, the material (the face of the impersonator, the lines of the schematic

[1] If the image is to depict the individual as he looked on some one occasion, as "that which can never come back," the artist would have to inscribe it. For instance, the artist who makes a sketch for a newspaper says that it is "The criminal *at the moment* when the jury renders its verdict."

drawing) comes to mean only what we put into it. The farther removed that the material of the imaginative consciousness is from the material of perception, the more that it becomes penetrated with knowledge, the more does its resemblance to the objective picture become attenuated. A new phenomenon appears: that of *equivalence*. The intuitive material is chosen for its equivalent relationships to the material of the object. The movement is hypostatized as the equivalent of the form, and the luminosity as the equivalent of the color. What this means is that knowledge plays an increasingly more important role as it replaces intuition on the very soil of intuition. At the same time the truly imaginative intention is less and less incited by the material of the image. To launch it a system of signs is needed (imitation), or a collection of conventions and knowledge (schematic image), or the free play of mind (spots on the wall, arabesques), or a fascinated consciousness (hypnagogic images). In a word, as knowledge increases in importance, intention gains in spontaneity.

B. *Knowledge*—Knowledge is not substituted in its ideational form for the faltering material. As knowledge it cannot fill in the gaps of intuition. It must undergo a debasement to which we shall have to return. It becomes intuitive in the form of pantomine; it flows in the movements. A new phenomenon appears: *the symbolic movement*, which, by its very nature as movement, belongs to intuition, and, by its meaning, belongs to pure thought. But it can happen that knowledge becomes directly incorporated with other sensible qualities, as in the case of hypnagogic images. We shall see that this degradation of knowledge is not exclusively an imaginative phenomenon and that it is also to be found in simple perception.

8. The Mental Image

Absurd experiments have been conducted to show that the image has a sensory content:

Perky seated O before a screen in a well lighted room and asked him to project on the screen the visual image of an object, such as a banana. As soon as O started to project his imaginary banana on the screen an assistant in an adjoining room threw a very faint picture of a banana on the screen and very gradually increased its intensity till O reported that he had a good image. Intent on his effort to conjure up a good image O mistook the picture for his own.[1]

The more recent experiments by Schraub are of the same stamp: "Sounds of known loudness are produced, and the subject is instructed to reproduce them mentally. The subject is instructed to compare each of these mental sounds with the given sounds which are reproduced, and which are increased or decreased in loudness until they are no louder than the subject's image of them." [2]

These researches can make sense only if the image is a faint perception. But it *is an image*, and any comparison as regards loudness between it and perception is therefore impossible. One does not know who is more lacking in understanding, the experimenter who asks such questions or the subject who responds to them so submissively.

Above we defined the image as "an act that envisions as an actual body an absent or a non-existent object by means of a physical or mental content, but which appears only through an 'analogical representative' of the envisioned object." In the case of the mental image the content has no objectivity. We see a portrait, a caricature, a blot: but we do not *see* a mental image. To see an object is to localize it in space, between this table and that carpet, at a certain height, to my right or left. But mental images do not mingle with surrounding objects, which we try to explain by saying that present sensations act as "reducers." But why should there be a reduction, why not rather a building-up?

[1] Woodworth, R. S., *Experimental Psychology*, p. 45.
[2] Dwelshauvers, *Traité de Psychologie*, p. 368.

The fact of the matter is that the mental image does envision a *real thing*, which exists among other things in the world of perception; but it envisions that thing by means of a mental content. That content must, of course, meet certain conditions: in the image consciousness we apprehend *an object* as an "analogue" of another object. Pictures, caricatures, impersonations, spots on the walls, entoptic lights: all these *representatives* have as common trait that they are objects for consciousness. The purely mental *content* of the mental image cannot escape this law: a consciousness which faces the thing it envisions is a perceptual consciousness; a consciousness which envisions the thing as empty is a pure consciousness of meaning. This necessity for the material of the mental image to be already constituted as an object for consciousness we shall call the *transcendence* of the representative. But transcendence does not mean externality: it is the represented object that is external, and not its mental "analogue." The illusion of immanence consists in transferring externality, space and all the sensible qualities of the thing to the transcendent psychic content. It does not possess these qualities: it represents them, but *in its own way*.

It would now seem that all we need do is to describe this analogical content just as we described the material contents of the consciousness of the portrait or of the impersonation. But here we meet with a great difficulty: in the cases we have previously described, when the truly imaginative consciousness wanes, there remains a sensible residue which is describable; namely the painted canvas or the spot on the wall. In repeating certain movements or in permitting the lines and the colors of the painting to act upon us, we could at least reconstruct "the analogue" without too much trouble, from this sensible residue, and do so without actually forming the imaginative consciousness over again. The material of my imaginative consciousness of the portrait was obviously this painted canvas. It must be admitted that reflective description does not tell us directly anything concerning the representative material of the mental image. This is due to the fact that when the imaginative consciousness is destroyed its transcendent content is destroyed with it; no describable residue remains, we are confronted by another synthetic consciousness which has nothing in common with the first. We cannot therefore hope to get at this content by introspection. We must choose: either we form the image, and get to know the content only by its function as analogue (whether we form a non-reflective or reflective consciousness), we apprehend on it the qualities of the envisioned object; or we do not form the image, in which case we no longer have the content, nothing remains of it. In a word, we know—since this is an essential necessity—that in the mental image there is a psychic factor which functions as analogue but when we wish to ascertain more clearly the nature and components of this factor we are reduced to conjectures.

We must, therefore, leave the sure ground of phenomenological description and turn to experimental psychology. That is, form hypotheses and seek evidences in observation and experiment, just as is done in the experimental sciences. Such evidences never permit us to go beyond the domain of the probable.

Part II

THE PROBABLE

The Nature of the Analogue in the Mental Image

1. Knowledge

THE IMAGE is defined by its intention. It is the intention that determines that the image of Peter is consciousness of Peter. If this intention is taken at its origin, that is, when it springs up from our spontaneity, it already implies a certain knowledge, no matter how naked and despoiled it may appear to be, and which is, hypothetically, the consciousness of Peter. I admit that this knowledge is but a simple empty anticipation, a direction: but it is in every way a direction *towards Peter*, an expectation *of Peter*. In a word, "the pure intention" is a combination of contradictory terms, since it is always *intention towards something*. But in the image the intention does not confine itself to envisioning Peter in an undetermined manner: it envisions him as blond, tall, with a turned up or aquiline nose, etc. It must therefore become charged with knowledge, it must traverse a certain layer of consciousness which we might call the layer of knowledge. So that, in the imaginative consciousness, knowledge and intention can be distinguished only by abstraction. The intention is defined only by the knowledge because it is only what we know in some sort of way that we represent to ourselves as an image and conversely, the knowledge here is not simply a knowledge, it is an act, it is what I want to represent to myself. I do not restrict myself to the knowledge that Peter is blond, this knowledge is a requirement: it is what I must realize as an intuition. This knowledge is, naturally, not something which is added to an already constituted image in order to clarify it: it is the active structure of the image.

An image could not exist without a knowledge that constitutes it. This is the basic reason for the phenomenon of quasi-observation. But the knowledge can exist in the free state, that is, constitute a consciousness only to itself.

"I maintain," writes Bühler, "that as a rule every object can be fully and exactly thought of without the help of an image. I can think in a fully determined manner and without representation of any individual nuance of the blue color of a painting hanging in my room, provided it be possible for this object to be given to me by some means other than sensations." [1]

What are we to understand by knowledge in a free state? Does it really envision the object? One of Bühler's subjects will answer the questions for us:

Do you know how many primary colors there are in the Madonna of the Sistine Chapel? Yes. At first I had an image of the Madonna in her cloak, then that of two other figures, especially that of Saint Barbara in yellow. Thus I had the red, the yellow, the green. Then I asked myself whether "the blue" was also there, and I had the impression, without an image, that it was represented there.

The knowledge envisioned the blue as being represented in the painting as the fourth of the primary colors. Messer's subject gave a similar report.

The word *Mountain* suggests to a subject "the consciousness" (without a word) of a direction towards something determined which could be ascended."

This shows that the mountain is not conceived as an intuitive reality but as a certain *guide* (*règle*). Bühler's classification is a good confirmation of this. He divides the "Bewusstheiten" into three categories: namely, *consciousnesses of guides*, of *relationship*, and of *intentions*. The last term, which is very inappropriate, finally gets to mean consciousness of order, arrangement, system. In short, knowledge in a pure state pre-

[1] Bühler, *Tatsachen und Probleme zu einer Psychologie der Denkvorgänge.* I, Ueber Gedanken, 321, Arch. F. ges. Psych., 1907.

sents itself as a consciousness of *relations*. This is naturally an empty consciousness, since the sensible material is thought of only by compulsion of the outcome, that is, as a support for the relations. For instance, the blue of the painting is thought of only as "fourth primary color." The knowledge can be as detailed as is desired; it can embrace a number of diverse relationships in a complex synthesis; it can envision concrete relationships between the individual objects (for instance, M. Lebrun can be given to me as "The first officer of France"); it can precede or accompany the judgment; it can even be joined to a sign or group of signs: but in spite of all this, it remains a consciousness empty of meaning.

But, says Husserl,[1] this empty consciousness can fill itself. But not with words: words are only the support of knowledge. It is the image [2] which is the intuitive "filling in" (Erfullung) of the meaning. If I think "sparrow," for instance, I may at first have only a word and an empty meaning in my mind. If the image appears, a new synthesis is formed and the empty meaning becomes a consciousness full *of sparrow*.

We admit that this theory is disagreeable to us. First, what could the image be without the synthesis of meaning? We cannot admit that the image comes "to fill in" an empty consciousness: it *is* itself a consciousness. It seems that in this theory Husserl was the victim of the illusion of immanence, but what interests us above all is what we might call the question of the debasement of knowledge. Is it entirely certain that knowledge, in passing from the free state to that of intentional structure, undergoes no other change than a filling in? Is it not rather the object of a radical change? Psychologists who have investigated—by the method of experimental introspection—the relationships between the image and the thought process have discovered in their subjects some strange conditions, namely, that alongside the pure knowledge designated as

---

[1] Husserl, *Logische Untersuchungen*, t. II, ch. I; t. III, ch. I.
[2] Naturally, in the absence of perception.

"Bewusstheiten," "Bewusstseinlagen," "Spharenbewusstsein," etc., there appear some strange states which, although containing no representative element whatsoever, are nevertheless reported by the subjects as images.

In Schwiete we find some very significant reports:

1. Subject I: "open."

"I had an undetermined image of an 'opening.'"

2. Subject II: "unlike."

"I saw two undetermined and unlike objects." [3]

Here we have an opening which is an opening of nothing, and which, moreover, does not even have a definite form. Nevertheless it is an opening as an image. Here are two objects without even spatial characteristics, that is, objects that have no intuitive quality whatsoever by which they could differ from each other but which are nevertheless *grasped in an image as being unlike*. The question arises here as to how the image differs from a pure knowledge. And it nevertheless manifests itself as an image.

Burloud is even more outright. He writes *à propos* the works of Messer:

"At the lowest degree, a spatial direction, a direction of outwardness." At the word Atlas subject II had a visual representation of a place on a map. "It was rather in a direction beyond the Mediterranean Sea. . . ." The subjects are often uncertain whether to call it an image or a thought. At the word *nail* subject I reported the presence in his consciousness of something visual or conceptual but of such a nature that it could give rise to a visual impression. "I thought of something long, pointed." These conditions are indicated by expressions like: a knowledge, a simple tendency to a visual representation, the term of a visual representation, etc.[1]

We repeat that as knowledge enters into the constitution of

[3] Schwiete, *Ueber die psychische Representation der Begriffe*. Arch. f. gen. Psych. Bd. XIX, p. 475.

[1] Burloud: *La pensée d'après les recherches expérimentales de Watt, etc.* Alcan, 1927, p. 68.

the image it undergoes a radical modification. This it undergoes even before the image is built up. There are consciousnesses of a special type that are empty, altogether like consciousness of pure meaning. They affirm their intimate relationship with the sensible from the very outset. They present themselves as "something visual *or conceptual but of such a nature that it could give rise to a visual impression.*" We are far from the "Bewusstheiten" of Bühler. It is still knowledge which is involved, but knowledge that is debased.

Could not this knowledge, which presents itself as "the germ of a visual representation," be the dynamic scheme of Bergson? The latter does, in fact, present itself as determined in its intimate structure by its relation with future images. . . . "At one time it consists in an expectation of images, in an intellectual attitude destined to prepare the arrival of a certain precise image as in the case of memory, at another time it organizes a more or less prolonged game between the images which are capable of inserting themselves into it, as in the case of creative imagination. It is to the open condition what the image is to the closed condition. It presents in terms of *becoming,* dynamically, what images give us as ready made, in the static condition."[1]

When Bergson conceived his theory the dynamic scheme was a great advance on associationism. Today psychology has freed itself even more from the influence of Taine. Thought, irreducible to sensation, becomes defined by meaning and intentionality. It is an act. In the light of these new theories the dynamic scheme appears to be an effort which is as yet very timid and which misses its goal. No doubt it is already a synthetic organization which is better than a simple association of images. But in Bergson we seek in vain for a positive description of the intentionality that constitutes it. Such is the constant ambiguity of the Bergsonian dynamism: melodic syntheses— but without a synthetic act; organizations without an organ-

[1] Bergson, *L'Energie spirituelle,* p. 199.

izing power. Such is also the dynamic scheme—dynamic it is
without doubt, of the nature of a force, of a whirlpool. But it
is clearly in no way an act: it is a thing.

This basic deficiency gives rise to all the ambiguity of its
nature. Now it appears to be a transitory form which can take
a representation.

"To work intellectually consists in conducting *a single representation* through different levels of consciousness in a direction which goes from the abstract to the concrete, from schema
to the image." [1]

Now it is an organizing power which effaces itself behind
what it has organized.

". . . It is a representation of a different order always
capable of realizing itself in images but always distinct from
them. . . . Present and active in the work of evoking the
images, behind the images it has evoked, having done its
work." [2]

It is likewise impossible to grasp the exact role of feeling in
the constitution of these schemes. About this Bergson writes:

"When I wish to recall a proper name I address myself first
to the general impression I have kept of it; it is this impression
which will enact the role of 'dynamic schema.' " [1] And further:
"I begin with the general impression I retain of it. It was an
impression of strangeness, but not of an undetermined strangeness. There was in it something of a note of barbarism and
rapine." [2]

But these impressions are not, however, purely affective since
Bergson calls his schema [3] "an undivided schema with a certain
affective coloration."

The fact of the matter is that Bergson did not try hard
enough to describe his schema clearly. What interests him

[1] Bergson, *L'Energie spirituelle*, p. 188 (italics ours).
[2] *Id., ibid.*
[1] *Id., ibid.*, p. 193.
[2] *Id., ibid.*, p. 175.
[3] *Id., ibid.*, p. 178.

most is to rediscover in it the qualities which he develops in all his descriptions of consciousness: The schema is a *becoming*;[4] moreover, his elements *interpenetrate each other*.[5] It is this interpenetration and this melodic progression that sets off the schema from the image "by fixed contours," "*by juxtaposed parts*." It is the life, the very movement of consciousness. It "delineates what has been." Here we encounter once more the great Bergsonian themes and the classical oppositions of the system; the schema is the ever-changing, the living; the image is the static, the dead, the space which subtends the movement.

It is precisely this opposition that seems to us unfortunate and which prevents us from accepting Bergson's description in toto. We maintained at the very outset that knowledge does not disappear once the consciousness of the image is established; it is not "effaced" behind images. It is not "always capable of realizing itself as images but always distinct from them." It represents the active structure of the imaginative consciousness. We cannot accept this radical distinction between the image and the schema. If this were so then we would have to *learn* our images as we do our perceptions; and to do this we would have to observe them; to observe them we would have to have schemes, and so on to infinity.

This conception of the image as "a representation . . . of which the parts are juxtaposed" appears to us, moreover, to belong to the illusion of immanence. The parts are juxtaposed *in the objects*. But the image is an inner synthesis marked by a real interpenetration of its elements, like the persons of our dreams who can be at once a man and a woman, a child and an old man.[1] Leroy has expressed the view that our wakeful images may perhaps also possess this polymorphism. This we shall show in the following chapter. At all events, a whole

---

[4] Bergson, *L'Energie spirituelle*. Cf. pp. 199–200.
[5] *Id., ibid*. Cf., for instance, pp. 189, 178: "An undivided schema," etc.
[1] Cf. Freud, *Traumdeutung*, p. 67, the dream of Irma.

category of images, those Flach [1] calls symbolic schemes, manifest in their original wholeness a mass of things which discursive thought must analyse and iuxtapose.

"To understand the meaning oi the word: Baudelaire."

"In the open space, on a completely dark background, I saw immediately a splash of blue-green color, like that of vitriol, and as if thrown there with a single and broad stroke of the brush. The splash was longer than broad—perhaps twice as long as broad. It dawned on me immediately that this color must express morbidity, the sort of decadence that character- izes Baudelaire. I speculate whether this image can be applied to Wilde or Huysmans: impossible. I feel a resistance which is as strong as if someone proposed something to me which was contrary to logic. This image holds only for Baudelaire and from this moment on will be representative of this poet to me."

It is therefore best that we drop such vague expressions as "becoming," "dynamism," etc. This psychology of "sympathy with life" has had its day. Bergson did see that there does exist a certain state of knowledge which is "waiting for images." But this expectation of images is homogeneous with the image itself. This expectation is moreover very unique; what the knowledge is waiting for is to transform itself into an image. Instead of the expression "dynamic scheme" we still prefer that of Spaier,[2] "the dawn of an image," because it shows so well that there is a continuity between the empty imaginative knowledge and the full imaginative consciousness.

Subject II: "Ah it is. . . . I stopped because I knew what I wanted to say before the word 'rich' came, I felt an inner release, an *ah*! a sort of inner movement like a swiftly rising noise of a siren." I feel that it will come, it is coming, I know that I understood. "Then the word surged up."

[1] A. Flach, "Ueber Symbolische Schemata im Produktiven Denkprozess," *Arch. f. ge. Psych.* B. II, pp. 369, 599.
[2] Spaier, "L'Image mentale d'après les expériences d'introspection," *Revue philosophique*, 1914.

And Spaier adds:

"There exists therefore a tendency not to go all the way to the end: an attempt is made to keep the image itself from going faster, one is satisfied with the dawn. . . ."

We believe that there is a greater difference between an imaginative knowledge and a knowledge of pure meaning than between an imaginative knowledge and an image in its full bloom. This difference we must examine more thoroughly, that is, we must determine exactly the nature of the debasement the knowledge undergoes in passing from the state of pure "meaning" to the imaginative state. For this purpose we want to examine somewhat more closely those pure cases in which the imaginative knowledge appears in the pure state, that is as free consciousness.

The reports of the Wurtzburg psychologists are significant in this connection: among the subjects two types of free consciousnesses are to be found.

Type I: CIRCLE. At first a general consciousness (allgemeines Bewusstsein) corresponding to the concept: geometric figure. The word was not present.

Type II: PATIENCE-FORBEARANCE. A special consciousness of a Biblical environment.

HAUGHTY KING. "(I feel myself) transported into another sort of reality, one of ballads and old legends. . . . A direction towards the past of Germany where the haughty monarch would play an important role." [1]

The consciousness of "circle" is general, that of "patience forbearance" is particular. But the difference does not lie there. The consciousnesses of Type I can, as a matter of fact, also be particular. But what is grasped in the former is a rule; in the latter it is a thing. This we must examine closely by means of another example.

[1] Messer, *Experimental psychologische Untersuchungen des Denkens*, Arch. f. ges. Psych., 1906, VIII, pp. 1–224. Messer arbitrarily characterizes the acts of consciousness of Type II by affectivity.

I am reading a novel. I am greatly interested in the hero, who is, let us say, about to break out of prison. I read with great eagerness the least detail of his preparation for flight. But writers are agreed that reading is accompanied by few images.[2] In fact, most subjects have few of them and they are also incomplete. It should even be added that images appear apart from the reading process itself, that is, when the reader is thinking of the events of the preceding chapter, when he is dreaming over the book, etc. In short, the images appear when we cease reading or when our attention begins to wander. But when the reader is engrossed, there are no mental images. We have demonstrated this on ourselves over and over again and it has also been confirmed for us by several persons. A flow of images is characteristic of disturbed and frequently interrupted reading.

Nevertheless it cannot be that the imaginative element is wholly absent in reading. Without it how are we to account for the intensity of our emotions? We take sides, we become indignant; and some even weep. In reading, as in the theatre, we are actually in the presence of a world and we attribute to that world just as much of existence as we do to that of the theater; that is, a complete existence in the unreal. Verbal signs are not the intermediaries between the pure meanings and our consciousness, as they are, for instance, in the case of mathematics: they represent the area of contact between us and this imaginary world. In order to describe correctly the phenomenon of reading it must be said that the reader is *in the presence* of a world. It is this fact which clearly demonstrates—if the matter were to be proven—the existence of what Binet calls "latent images."

"We often have more definite images than we think: in reading a play, for instance, we have images of position, of stage-setting; without being aware of it we construct a set of scenery. For instance, we must have the plan of the scene

[2] Cf. for example Binet, *Etude expérimentale de l'intelligence*, p. 97.

of action drawn up for us to become aware of our own setting, by a feeling of inner resistance." [1]

We cannot, of course, accept this thesis: for us an image is a consciousness and "a latent consciousness" would be a contradiction of terms. Nevertheless we must admit that something does enact the role of these alleged latent images: namely, imaginative knowledge.

The consciousness of reading is a consciousness *sui generis*, which has its structure. When we are reading a poster or a phrase isloated from its context we simply produce a consciousness of meaning, a lexis. If we are reading a scholarly work we produce a consciousness in which the intention adheres every moment to the sign. Our thought, our knowledge slip into the words and we become aware of it *on the words, as an objective quality of the words*. These objective qualities do not, of course, remain separated but fuse from word to word, from phrase to phrase, from page to page; hardly have we opened a book when we have before us an objective sphere of meaning.

Thus far there is nothing new. It is always a matter of meaningful knowledge. But if the book is a novel everything changes: the sphere of objective meaning becomes a world of unreality. To read a novel is to assume a general attitude of consciousness: this attitude is roughly like that of a spectator who sees the curtain rising in the theater. He is preparing to discover a whole world which is not that of perception, but neither is it the world of mental images. To be present at a theatrical performance is to apprehend the characters *on* the actors, and the forest of "As You Like It" *on* the cardboard trees. To read is to realise *on* the signs a contact with a world of unreality. In that world there are plants, animals, fields, towns, men: at first those that are described in the book, then a horde of others that are not mentioned but which are in the background and which give that world

[1] Cited by Delacroix in *Traité de Psychologie de Dumas*, t. II, p. 118.

its solidity. (For instance, in a chapter describing a ball, all the guests who are present but about whom nothing is said and who "make up the number.") These concrete beings are the objects of my thoughts: their unreal existence is the correlative of the syntheses which I operate with the help of the words. That is, I operate these syntheses as perceptual syntheses and not as meaningful syntheses.

If I read: "They will enter Peter's office," this simple notation becomes the subdued theme of all subsequent syntheses. When I read the account of their quarrel I localize their quarrel *in the office.* Here is the phrase "they left slamming the door." I know that it is the door of Peter's office; I know that Peter's office is on the third floor of a new building and that this building is in the suburbs of Paris. Naturally there is nothing of all this in the single phrase I had just read. I must be familiar with the preceding chapters in order to know all this. Therefore everything that exceeds, includes, orients and localizes the naked meaning of the phrase I am reading is the object of a knowledge. But this knowledge is not a pure "meaning." It is not as meaning that I think "office," "third floor," "building," "suburb of Paris." I think of them *in terms of things.* To understand the difference all we need do is read this phrase in a report: "The syndicate of owners of buildings in Paris" and this one in a novel: "He walked down the three stories of the building in haste." What has changed? Not the content itself of the knowledge "building": but the way it is known. In the first case the content of the knowledge is envisaged by consciousness as a rule; in the second as an object. No doubt but that the knowledge is always an empty consciousness of an order, a rule. But at times the knowledge envisages the order first and the object through the order, and very vaguely as "that which supports the order," that is, still as a relationship—and at times envisages the objest first and the order only in so far as it is constitutive of the object.

But what are we to understand here by object? Must we

believe with Bühler that "I can think of any nuance whatever
of the blue color of a painting in a fully-determined way
without representation"? To believe this is to commit a basic
error, which is not only psychological but ontological. The
individual nuance "blue" and the knowledge belong to two
different orders of existence. The blue color of this portrait
is something inexpressible. Kant had already shown the irreducible difference between sensation and thought. What constitutes the individuality of this particular blue, which is here,
before me, corresponds exactly to the sensible character of the
sensation. Pure thought cannot therefore envision it as such.
It thinks of it as something external, as the substratum of a
relationship, as, for instance, "the fourth primary color of the
Sistine Madonna" or as "occupying such a position in the
scale of colors." The attempt to catch it directly is to attempt
to see it. But in order to attempt to see this unique and concrete
blue as blue, we must already possess it as such, or how could
we know what it is we want to see? Consequently, knowledge
can catch the object only through its essence, that is, through
the order of its qualities. But the imaginative knowledge does
not envision this order in itself. It *cannot* yet envision the
blue, it no longer *desires* to envision "the fourth primary color
of the Sistine Madonna." It envisions *something* which is this
fourth color. The relation passes behind the thing. But the
thing is as yet only "something." That is, a certain position
lacking opacity and externality—opacity and externality which
are precisely determined by the relations which were made
to pass behind their bulkiness. This is well shown by the
example we have already cited:

"At the word *nail* the subject reports the presence in his
consciousness of something visual—or conceptual but of such
a nature that it could arouse a visual impression: I thought
of something long and pointed."

If the knowledge does not present itself as conceptual it is
because it affirms itself to itself as waiting for the visual. For

want of something better it presents its content as *something* long and pointed.

It is obvious that what is involved here is a radical modification of the intention. The pure knowledge is pre-objective, at least when not associated with a word. That is, that formal essence and objective essence are undifferentiated in it. At times it appears in the form of what one of Binet's subjects calls "one feeling like another," and, in this form, it represents a sort of vague account to the subject as to his own capacities ("Yes, I know," "I could know," "It is in that direction that we must look")—and at times it includes the knowledge of certain objective relations (long, pointed, the fourth primary color, geometric figures); in a word, it is an ambiguous consciousness which occurs at the same time as a consciousness empty of a relational structure of the object and as consciousness full of a state of the subject.

Imaginative knowledge, on the contrary, is a consciousness which seeks to transcend itself, to posit the relation as an *outside*. But not in affirming its truth; in which case we would have only a *judgment*. But in positing its content as existing *through* a certain bulkiness of the real which serves as its representative. This real does not, of course, itself appear in its undifferentiated and very general form of "something." It is only envisioned. Imaginative knowledge presents itself therefore as an effort to determine this "something" as a will to reach the intuitive, as an expectation of images.

Let us return to the consciousness of the reader. The phrases of the novel have become filled with imaginative knowledge; it is this knowledge I grasp on the words, and not simple meanings: the syntheses, which, as we have seen, constitute an objective sphere of meaning from page to page, are not mere syntheses of relationships; they are syntheses of *something* which possesses this or that quality with *something* which possesses this and that characteristic. The relationships do not arrange themselves as if to compose the meaning of a concept; the rule of their synthesis is that the relationships between them must be like the relationship that exists between the different qualities of an object. For instance, Peter's office becomes *something* which is *in* the building; and the building becomes *something* which is *on* Emile-Zola Street.[1]

There follows a curious change in the role of signs. These, as we know, are perceived in the aggregate in the form of words, and each word has its own physiognomy. We can say roughly that for the reader of a novel the words play the role of signs whose principal characteristics we described in the preceding chapter. But imaginative knowledge has too strong a tendency towards an intuition which will fill it up, not to attempt to make the sign enact the role of representative of the object; when this happens it uses the sign as if it were a drawing. The physiognomy of the word becomes the representative of the physiognomy of the object. A real contamination takes place. When I read "this beautiful person," the words no doubt *mean*, above all, a certain young woman, the heroine of the novel. But to a certain degree they *represent* the beauty of the young woman; they enact the role of this *something* which is a beautiful young woman. This occurs more often than we believe. Dwelshauvers[2] cites some strange examples which confirm our thesis. He presents pairs of words to the subject who is to report whether the two terms agree or disagree. Of course the attitude of the subject is very different from that of a reader of a novel. Nevertheless the words do play the role of representatives, and rather frequently.

On presenting the pair "Sympathy-Pity," the subject reacts with the implicit thought that there is no agreement between them. Immediately after his reaction he analyses his response and gives no reason for it. At the end of the series of experiments, in recalling this reaction, the subject seems to remember

---

[1] We are, of course, omitting the role of feeling in the consciousness of reading.

[2] Dwelshauvers, *Traité de psychologie*, Payot, 1925, pp. 122–124.

that the letter T stood out more prominently than the other letters in the word Sympathy than in the word Pity. A feeling of disagreement arose between these letters and the aspect of the words.

So the question here is therefore no longer one concerning empty imaginative knowledge: the word often plays the role of representative without ceasing to act as a sign so that in reading we have a hybrid consciousness, half-meaningful and half-imaginative.

Imaginative knowledge is not necessarily preceded by pure knowledge. In many cases (as, for instance, in the reading of novels) the objects of the knowledge are at first presented as correlatives of an imaginative knowledge. Pure knowledge, that is, the mere consciousness of relations comes next. In certain cases, which we shall study later, pure knowledge presents itself as an ideal which is never reached. In such a case the consciousness becomes the prisoner of its imaginative attitude.

Things present themselves at first as presences. If we begin with knowledge the image will arise as a result of thought trying to make contact with the presences. This birth of the image coincides with a debasement of the knowledge which no longer envisions the relationships as such but as substantial *qualities* of things. These empty imaginative knowledges—which Spaier calls the dawn of images—occur very frequently in the life of consciousness. They come and go without becoming images, but not without having placed us on the brink of the image, properly so called. The subject is not at all sure whether he had a "vivid image," the "dawn of an image," or a concept.

2. Affectivity

It is necessary that some remarks on the fundamental nature of feeling be made at the very outset. Writings like those of

Brentano, Husserl and Scheler have established in Germany a certain conception of feeling which French psychologists would do well to study. The fact of the matter is that as regards the subject of feeling French psychology still belongs to the period of Ribot.[1] In the new treatise by Dumas we find the old and wearisome arguments concerning the peripheral theory and the central theory. Since James and Nahlowsky the physiology of feeling has made some advances. But the nature of feeling itself is not known any better.[2] Dwelshauvers gives a good summary of the general opinion when he speaks of an affective state as being "of life." This expression, like the comments upon it, have the effect of cutting off the feeling from its object. Feeling is presented as a sort of purely subjective and ineffable agitation which possesses an individual tonality but which is shut up in the subject who experiences it. Basically, feeling is no more than the becoming conscious of organic changes. It is pure subjectivity, pure innernesss. This is the source of all those theories which consider feeling to be a primitive stage of mental development: a stage for which the world of things does not yet exist—any more than does the correlative world of persons. There exist only living states, a flux of subjective, inexpressible qualities. At most feeling is confused with coanaesthesia. It is no doubt recognized that affective states are usually associated with representations. These associations are, however, established from the outside. It is not a living synthesis of representation and feeling: we remain in the mechanical realm of associations. Transfer, condensation, derivation, sublimation: so many devices of an associational psychology. Literature is no more advanced: in reaction against the old and basic theory of Pascal regard-

---

[1] Ribot, *Psychologie des Sentiments.*

[2] We must make an exception of the works of M. M. Janet (de l'Angoisse à l'Extase) and Wallon who attempt to present feeling as a special class of behavior. The behavorial view, which is certainly an advance, is, however, obscure and contradictory. Cf. my little book: *Esquisse d'une théorie des Emotions* (Hermann, 1939).

ing love-esteem the writers of the XIXth century turned feelings into a mass of whimsical apparitions which occasionally became united by chance with representations but which fundamentally have no real relation with their objects. And what is even more, feelings have no objects. For Proust and his disciples the tie between my love and the beloved person is at bottom but a tie of contiguity. Among psychologists and novelists we have a sort of solipsism of affectivity. The reason for these strange conceptions lies in the fact that feeling has been isolated from its meaning.

There are, as a matter of fact, no affective *states*, that is, inert contents which are carried by the stream of consciousness and attach themselves to representation by chance of contiguity. Reflection yields us affective *consciousnesses*. Joy, sorrow, melancholy are consciousnesses. And we must apply to them the great law of consciousness: that all consciousness is consciousness *of* something. In a word, feelings have special intentionalities, they represent one way—among others—of self-*transcendence*. Hatred is hatred *of* someone, love is love *of* someone. James said: remove the physiological manifestations of hatred, of indignation and all you have remaining is abstract judgments without feeling. Today we can answer: try to bring about in yourself the subjective phenomena of hatred, of indignation, without having those phenomena oriented *on* some hated person, on an unjust act, and you can tremble, pound your fists, blush, but your internal condition will be devoid of indignation, of hatred. To hate Paul is to intention Paul as a transcendent object of a consciousness. But neither must we commit the intellectualistic error by believing that Paul is present as the object of an intellectual representation. The feeling envisions an object but it does so in its own way which is affective. Classical psychology (and even La Rochefoucauld) holds that the feeling appears to consciousness as a certain subjective tonality. This is to confuse the reflective with non-reflective consciousness. The feeling appears as such to reflective consciousness, the meaning of which is precisely to be conscious *of* this feeling. But the feeling of hatred is not the consciousness *of* hatred: it is the consciousness *of* Paul as hateful; love is not, primarily, consciousness of love: it is consciousness of the charms of the beloved. To become conscious of Paul as hateful, annoying, sympathetic, disturbing, winning, repulsive, etc., is to confer upon him a new quality, to construct him along a new dimension. These qualities are in a sense, not properties of the object, so that basically, the very term "quality" is inappropriate. It would be better to say that the qualities constitute the sense of the object, that they are its affective *structure*: they permeate the entire object; when they disappear—as in cases of depersonalization—the perception remains intact, things do not seem to be changed, but the world is singularly impoverished nevertheless. In a sense, the feeling presents itself therefore as a species of knowledge. If I love the long, white and delicate hands of that woman, this love, which is directed on these hands, can be considered to be one of the ways they appeared to my consciousness. It is a feeling which envisions their *delicacy*, their *whiteness*, the animation of their movement: what would a love mean if it were not a love *of* these qualities? It is therefore a certain way that delicacy, whiteness and vivacity have of appearing to me. But it is not an intellectual knowledge. To love delicate hands is, we might say, a certain way *of loving* these hands *delicately*. Still, love does not intention the delicacy of the fingers which is a representative quality: it projects a certain tonality on the object which may be called the affective sense of that delicacy, of that whiteness. Lawrence excels in suggesting, while he seems to be doing no more than to be describing the form and the color of objects, these subdued affective structures which constitute their deepest reality. Here is an example of an English woman who was fascinated by the strange charm of the Indians.

"It was always the one man who spoke. He was young,

with quick, large, bright black eyes that glanced sideways at her. He had a soft black moustache on his dark face, and a sparse tuft of beard, loose hairs on his chin. His long black hair, full of life, hung unrestrained on his shoulders. Dark as he was, he did not look as if he had washed lately." [1]

The representative retains a sort of primacy. The animated, white and delicate hands appear first as a purely representative complex and then bring about an affective consciousness which confers upon them a new meaning. So we can raise the question, as to what it is that happens, under these conditions, when we produce an affective consciousness in the absence of the object which it envisions.

We are at first inclined to exaggerate the primacy of the representative, to feel that there must always be a representation to arouse the feeling. Nothing is further from the truth. In the first place, a feeling can be aroused by another feeling. Furthermore, even when the feeling is aroused by a representation it does not imply that the feeling will envision that representation. If I enter the room where my friend Peter lived, the sight of the familiar furniture can no doubt lead me to produce an affective consciousness directly aimed at them. But it can also arouse a feeling which will envision Peter himself, to the exclusion of every other object. So the entire problem is still before us.

I assume therefore that in the absence of a certain person it is the feeling which was inspired in me by her beautiful hand that reappears. Let us suppose, for the sake of greater clarity, that the feeling is pure of all knowledge. This is obviously an unusual case, but one which we have the right to imagine.

This feeling is not a pure subjective content, it does not escape the law of all consciousness: it transcends itself, analysis reveals in it a primary content which animates intentions of a

<hr>

[1] Lawrence, *The Woman Who Rode Away*. See also the descriptions of the game-warden in *Lady Chatterley's Loves,* that of Don Cipriano in the *Feathered Serpent* and those of the captain in the *Captain's Doll*.

very special type; in short, it is an affective consciousness *of* those hands. Only this consciousness does not posit the hands it envisions, *as hands*, that is, as a synthesis of representations. Knowledge and sensible representations are lacking (by hypothesis). The consciousness is rather of something fine, graceful, pure, with a nuance of strictly individual fineness and purity. What is unique for me in those hands—and which cannot express itself in a knowledge, even imaginative—namely, the tint of the skin at the finger tips, the shape of the fingernails, the small wrinkles around the phalanx, all this does, no doubt, *appear* to me. But these details do not present themselves in their representative aspect. I become aware of them as an undifferentiated mass which defies all description. And this affective mass has a character which lacks clear and complete knowledge: the mass is *present*. What this means is, that the feeling is present so that the affective structure of the objects builds itself up together with a determined affective consciousness. A feeling is thus not an empty consciousness: it is already a possession. Those hands present themselves to me *under their affective form*.

Let us suppose now that my feeling is not simply an affective recall of those hands; let us suppose that I also desire them. The desire is at first naturally the consciousness of the desired object: else how could I desire. But—if we suppose it to be empty of all knowledge—it cannot entail the knowledge of its object, it cannot, by itself alone, posit it as a representation. The desire must then superadd itself, in a new synthesis, to the affective consciousness of its object. So, in one sense, the desire is already possession, for in order to desire *these hands* the desire must posit them in their affective form, and it is upon this affective equivalent that the desire is directed. But it does not know them as *hands*. It is in this way that I happen to feel the birth in me of a very definite desire after a wearisome and sleepless night. Affectively, the object of this desire is strictly determined, on this point we cannot be deceived: only I do not *know* what it is. Do I wish to drink something refreshing and sweet; do I wish to sleep, or is it sexual desire? In vain, all I do is exhaust myself with suppositions. It must be, as a matter of fact, that I am a victim of an illusion: a consciousness is born due to fatigue and takes the form of a desire. Naturally this desire posits an object; but this object exists only as the correlative of a certain affective consciousness: it is neither drink, sleep nor anything real and all effort to define it is by nature doomed to fail.

In a word, *desire* is a blind effort to possess on the level of representation what I already possess on the affective level; through the affective synthesis it envisions a "beyond" which it pursues without being able to know it; it directs itself upon the affective "something" which is now given to it and apprehends it as the *representative* of the desired thing. So the structure of an affective consciousness of desire is already that of an imaginative consciousness, since here, as in the image, a present synthesis functions as a substitute for an absent representative synthesis.

Under the name of "theory of constellations" or "law of interest," a certain psychological theory to be found even in the books of Ribot views feeling as operating a choice between constellations of images and drawing into consciousness those that will fix it. Thus Hesnard can write: "Every affective wave in a creature capable of consciousness, tends to stir up an image which justifies it; every feeling linked with an external object tends to justify itself, to express itself by the inner representation of that object."

The image is thus considered to be a mental formation which differs radically from affective states, but most affective states are supposed to be accompanied by images, which represent for the desire that which is desired. This theory is guilty of the errors of confusing the image with its object, the illusion of immanence, negation of the affective intentionality, and complete misunderstanding of the nature of consciousness. In fact, as we have just seen, the image is a sort of ideal for feeling, it represents a limited state for the affective consciousness, the state in which desire is also knowledge. If the image presents itself as the lower limit towards which knowledge tends when it becomes debased, then it also presents itself as the upper limit towards which affectivity tends when it seeks to know itself. Is the image, then, not a synthesis of affectivity and knowledge?

In order to understand fully the nature of this type of synthesis we must renounce all comparisons drawn from physical intermixtures: a consciousness of knowledge which is at the same time a consciousness of feeling is not *part* knowledge and *part* feeling. A consciousness is always transparent to itself: and it therefore must be at the same time entirely knowledge and entirely affectivity.

Let us return to those beautiful white hands: if I produce a cognitive-affective consciousness instead of a pure affective consciousness, those hands are at one and the same time the object of a knowledge and of feeling, or rather they are posited by an affectivity which is knowledge, by a knowledge which is feeling. Desire posits an object which is the affective equivalent of those hands: something transcendent, something which is not myself is given as the correlative of my consciousness. But at the same time, this something gets to fill in an imaginative knowledge, that is, that I am invaded by the knowledge that this something stands for "two hands." This assurance comes upon me suddenly: in relation to this affective object I find myself in the attitude of quasi-observation. Those hands are really there: the knowledge that penetrates them gives them to me as "the hands of such a person, white hands, etc.," and at the same time the feeling reproduces most poignantly what there is of the ineffable in the sensations of whiteness, of fineness, etc.; it gives that empty knowledge the opacity of which we spoke in the preceding chapter. I *know* that the object which is there, transcendent, confronting my consciousness stands for two white and delicate hands; at the same time I *feel* that whiteness and that delicacy, and particularly the *nature of hands* always so intimate, so personal. But, at the same time, I am aware that these hands have not as yet come into existence. What is before me is a substitute for these concrete hands, full but unable to exist by itself. When that substitute is present it delivers the hands to me completely, but at the same time it lies in its nature to *claim* these hands which it posits, so that I am aware of envisioning them through it. Let us recall *the essential characteristic of the mental image: it is a certain way an object has of being absent within its very presence.*[1] Here we encounter this characteristic once more and as a matter of fact, this affective-cognitive synthesis we have just described is none other than the fundamental structure of the image consciousness. No doubt but that we shall encounter more complex forms of the imaginative consciousness, and others from which the affective element is almost excluded: but if we want to grasp the image at its source we must begin with this structure. Besides, many images contain nothing more. This is the case with all those images whose object is a color, a flavor, a landscape, a facial expression, in short, for those images that envision in the main sensible qualities other than form and movement. "I cannot see," says Stendhal,[2] "the physiognomy of things. I have but my childhood memories. I see images, I recall effects on my heart, but for causes and phsyiognomies, nothing. I see a train of very clear images, but with no other physiognomy than the one they had for my vision. Moreover, I see that physiognomy only as a memory of the effect it produced on me."

3. Movements

Many authors have stressed the close relationship that exists between images and movements. Guillaume has shown in his

[1] Cf. Part II, Ch. I.
[2] Stendahl, *Vie de Henri Brulard.*

treatise [2] how the image becomes gradually the "motor cause of movements" and at the same time "the element of control." The experiments of Dwelshauvers [3] seem to show that there are no images without several slight movements (trembling of the fingers, etc.). But all these observations only tend to present the image as a condition for movement. But what we wish to know is whether movements, that is, kinaesthetic sensations, do not play an essential role in the make-up of the image.

Some of Pieron's interesting investigations afford us a point of departure.[1] He showed his subjects a figure made up of a tangle of lines and asked them to draw the figure from memory. Here are some of his conclusions:

Mr. Sp. . . . Beginning with the fourth presentation he observes methodically. He wishes to make some verbal remarks for which he has no time, so he uses the movements of his eyes and reproduces the lines in keeping with these movements. By observing his behavior, he notices that as his eye movements are following the lines, and while his hands are reproducing the lines with slight synergical movements . . . several words uttered softly ("there!" "good") punctuate certain stops that correspond to an observation, to a remark not explicitly formulated. . . .

Mr. To. . . . On the first presentation he is surprised by the very large number of lines and the difficulty of seeing them well; when the text is removed he has the impression that he has an image of it and attempts to draw it very fast but it disappears so quickly that he cannot use it. The first few times he only observes the heavy lines, and on the second presentation he does not recognize the test. He knows, because he made a mental note of it, that here and there are some light lines, but whose direction he no longer knows. Little by little he increases his understanding with several observations, several remarks (here an acute angle, there two lines almost parallel, a line somewhat heavier than another . . . etc.). When observed, he seems to follow the lines by head

---

[2] Guillaume, *L'Imitation chez l'enfant,* pp. 1–27.
[3] Dwelshauvers, *Les Mécanismes subconscients,* 1925.
[1] Art., cit., p. 134, fig. I.

movements with very slight displacements of the eyes and by movements of the hand.

Mr. Fa. . . . He tries to make some geometrical remarks, and soon notices a small triangle on the left side of the test but does not succeed in finding the necessary "hang" of it. He counts the lines, observes the convergence, the parallelisms, etc. . . . He squints at the lines. . . . In his reproduction at the end of a week the deforming influence of the geometrical schematization is noticeable: the principal lines are grouped in a diamond-shaped form. . . .

Thus these observers who wish to reproduce the figure indicate the occurrence of movements or mnemotechnical remarks which in the end become the guides for the performing of certain movements. Later on, when the subjects will form an imaginative consciousness of that figure, these movements, whether carried out sketchily or completely, will serve as a basis for the image.

Now the object was presented to them by visual perceptions. Since, as a general rule, we are directly informed of the movements of our body by a special type of sensations, namely, kinaesthetic sensations, a question arises: "How can kinaesthetic sensations function as material for an imaginative consciousness which envisions an object furnished by visual perceptions?"

There is no doubt concerning the fact itself: Dwelshauvers demonstrated it by a whole series of experiments.[1]

"There exist," he concludes, "mental images which are the conscious translation of muscular attitudes. These attitudes are not perceived by the subject, but they give rise to an image in the consciousness of the subject which is very different from the attitudes themselves. In other words, it happens that the genesis of our mental images is as follows: 1. Idea of a move-

---

[1] Cf. Dwelshauvers, *L'Enregistrement objectif de l'image mentale.* VIIth Intern. Congress of Psychology and *Les Mécanismes Subsconscients.* Alcan édit.

ment to be carried out. 2. Muscular attitude objectifying that idea, that motor intention without the subject's awareness of his motor reaction, of his attitude as such. 3. An image aroused in consciousness as the recording of the motor reaction and qualitatively different from the elements themselves of that reaction."

But no explanation has been given of these unquestionable phenomena. Dwelshauver's account of them is far from satisfactory. We shall try to show what the facts are and if possible to explain them.

My eyes are open, I am watching the index finger of my right hand, which is describing curves, geometrical figures, in the air. I *see* these curves to a certain extent at the tip of my finger. From the very first, as a matter of fact, a certain persistence of retinal impression is responsible for the fact that a certain course (direction) still exists after my index finger is removed. But this is not all: the different positions of my finger do not present themselves successively and isolated. No doubt each position is a concrete and irreducible event. But these events do not associate themselves externally as simple contents of consciousness. They are internally united through the synthetic acts of mind. Husserl has given a remarkable description [1] of these particular intentions of which, beginning with the living and concrete "now" direct themselves towards the immediate past in order to retain it and towards the immediate future in order to seize it. He calls them "retentions" and "protentions." This *retention*, which constitutes for itself the continuity of the movement, is not itself an image. It is an empty intention which is directed towards the phase of the movement that has just been destroyed; we will describe it, in psychological language, as a knowledge centered on the present visual sensation and which causes that *now* to appear as being also an *after* of a certain quality, an *after* which does not follow

[1] Husserl, *Leçons phénoménologiques sur la conscience interne du temps.*

any sensation but only the one that has just disappeared. The protention, on its part, is an *expectation* which presents that very same sensation as being also a *before*. Naturally this latter is not as rigorously determined as a "before" as it is as an "after," since—excepting in the special case when we perform a predetermined movement—the sensation that is going to follow is not entirely known; but this final sensation is already pretraced by a very precise expectation: I expect a *visual-sensation-produced-by-a-movement-of-my-index-finger* beginning from a *definite position*. Retention and protention constitute, in every respect, the sense of the present visual impression: without these synthetic acts we could hardly even speak of an impression; this *before* and this *after* which are the correlatives of these acts do not occur as empty forms, as homogeneous and indifferent frameworks: they are concrete and individual relations which the actual sensation sustains with the concrete and individual impressions which have preceded it and which will follow it.

But we must be explicit: all consciousness is consciousness of something. We mentioned a while ago that retention and protention envision impressions for the sake of simplification. But what they really envision is objects that are constructed by means of these impressions, that is, the trajectory of my index finger. This trajectory appears naturally as a static form; it presents itself as the *pathway* traversed by my finger and, more vaguely, beyond its actual position, as the pathway still to be traversed. The pathway that has been traversed—or a part of it—presents itself moreover as a vague luminous trail, produced by the persistence of impressions on the retina.

These visual impressions that constitute an immobile form are joined, by strictly kinaesthetic sensations (skin, muscles, tendons, articulation) which accompany them mutely. These represent more feeble elements that are completely dominated and even denatured by the forms and clear perceptions of vision. They are doubtless the support of the intentions and protentions: but these secondary intentions are rigorously sub-ordinated to the retentions and protentions that envision the impressions of vision. Since, otherwise, there is no kinaesthetic persistence, they are immediately effaced.

Now I close my eyes and with my finger carry out movements like the preceding. We might believe that the kinaesthetic impressions, now freed from visual domination, will appear with force and clarity. But there are none. No doubt the visual sensation has disappeared, but we insist that so has the kinaesthetic sensation. What arises in our consciousness is the trajectory of the movement *as a form in the making*. If I trace the figure eight with the tip of my index finger, what appears before me is an *eight* in the making, somewhat like the letters of a cinematographic advertisement forming themselves on the screen. This form is, of course, given *at the tip of my finger*. But it does not appear as a kinaesthetic form. It appears as a visual figure.

But we have seen that this visual figure is not the result of visual sensations: it presents itself as that which I could see at the tip of my finger if I were to open my eyes; it is a visual form as an image. We might be inclined to say, with Dwel-shauvers, that the movement *evokes* the image. But this interpretation is not acceptable; the image is directly apprehended at the tip of my finger from the very beginning. Moreover, since we cannot admit that the movement evokes the image while itself remaining unconscious [1]—the kinaesthetic sensations, according to this hypothesis, should subsist alongside the image they evoke. Now, these kinaesthetic sensations are even less independent than when they are hidden by the authentic visual impressions: they are as if swallowed by the image and, if any attempt is made to recover them their appearance is accompanied by the disappearance of the image. Shall we then just say that the kinaesthetic sensations function as analogical

[1] It seems to us that a similar conception sometimes held—at least seemingly so—by Dwelshauvers, is purely and simply without any meaning.

substitutes for the visual form? That would already be more to the point, besides, we have already met up with such a case when we were studying the role of visual movements in the apprehension of schematic drawings. But this view gives us little light on the analogical substitute. It is somewhat as if we were told that goats function as analogical substitutes for seaplanes. Besides, if we observe ourselves, we will notice that the image persists even if movement is arrested, that is, it survives the last kinaesthetic impression, and seems to remain for a few moments in the very localities covered by my finger. It is, therefore, desirable that we investigate more closely the mechanism of the substitution lest we deceive ourself with mere words.

The problem would be, in fact, insoluble if the impressions that constitute the perception of movement were to present themselves all at once. It is their very nature to present themselves only one after the other. Moreover, none of them presents itself as an isolated content: each of them presents itself as *the actual state of the movement*. We have seen, in fact, that each visual impression was like the point of application of a retention and a protention which determined its place in the continuity of forms described by the movement. The kinaesthetic impressions are also unified by the acts of retention and protention. If these acts only aim to retain and to foresee the states that have disappeared or that are to come from the movement under their forms as kinaesthetic impressions, we would have in the end a kinaesthetic perception, that is, the grasp by consciousness of a motor form that actually exists.

But this is not what happens most often. Generally the visual impressions prevail over the vague and feeble kinaesthetic impressions. Even when absent, they impose themselves and I even look for them; only they can serve as regulators: Dwelshauvers has shown that subjects who are asked to trace two equal lines with eyes closed guide themselves by visual representations of their extremities. What happens most often, consequently, is that the retention and the protention retain and anticipate the past and future aspects of the movement as if these were actually perceived by the organs of vision. This is, of course, a case of pure knowledge of a debased sort which we described above. We must nonetheless admit that consciousness assumes a *sui-generis* attitude from the beginning: all retention is, here, at the same time a conversion of the kinaesthetic into the visual, and this conversional retention deserves a phenomenological description by itself. It is easier to imagine what protention may be because the future impression does not need to be converted; consciousness expects a visual sensation at each moment from the beginning of the present sensible content.

What does the concrete impression, the support of the intentions, become? It is, of course, kinaesthetic; and cannot therefore present itself visually. But it is nevertheless apprehended as an "after" of a very special quality, namely, the result, the final point of a past which presents itself visually. At the same time it presents itself as the actual moment of a series of contents which stretch into the future. Thus, on the one hand, it is the only concrete element of the intentioned form, conferring on that form its characteristic of being present, which supplies the debased knowledge with "the something" it envisions. But, on the other hand, it derives its sense, its range, its value, from the intentions that aim at visual impressions: it was itself expected, received as a visual impression. Of course this is not enough to turn it into a visual sensation but no more is needed to give it a visual "meaning": this kinaesthetic impression provided with a visual meaning therefore functions as the analogue of a visual form, and when it glides into the past it will do so as a visual impression. Nevertheless time flows on, the movement reaches its end. The retentional knowledge has increased considerably; and it is by virtue of this knowledge that the greater part of the visual trajectory is envisioned. But it always uses the present sensation for its point of support; it is this present sensation alone that gives it a sort of reality. When the last impression will have disappeared the intentional knowledge will remain, as a track, an imaginative knowledge conscious of having been filled, and then, because of lack of support, this last trace disappears and becomes a total retention.

Up to now we have worked on the supposition that the gestures of my hands occurred by chance: in which case the knowledge is exactly contemporaneous with the movement. But we can conceive of cases when the knowledge occurs *before* the movement. In such cases the movement performs the function of making the knowledge explicit. At first the form is empty and incompletely differentiated. Gradually the potential knowledge changes into retention; it becomes clear and precise; at the same time it envisions a concrete impression which is about to *come* into existence. The relationship between the protention and the retention becomes one of equivalence, then it reverses itself. This slow clarification of the knowledge, which cannot operate unless a present sensation slips into the past on that occasion, ends up by giving a direction to the movement: the phenomenon as a whole is irreversible. This is what happens when I decide to trace the figure eight with my finger. It is also what happens in the symbolic schemes of Flach.[1] These determinations of pure space (straight lines, curves, angles, loops, etc.) are produced, in our opinion, by kinaesthetic impressions which function as analogue and which are stimulated by the displacement of the eyeballs. The forms—which are initially envisioned by a vague knowledge which gains in precision as the knowledge is reversed from future to past present themselves naturally as static. That figure eight traced by my finger is there, in space: it is not moving, it only exists. But my intention can change in accordance with the case: I can deliberately envision the form as such. In this case the concrete impression, the "now," is apprehended only

[1] See Part Three, Chapter I.

as that which converted the protention into a retention, or rather—since our consciousness is directed towards the object—that which causes the form to pass from a potential into an actual. I can also envision more particularly the instantaneous concrete impression: retention and protention—although they continue to play their primary role—appear here as subordinated to the impression. This impression will occur as the *mobile* which moves along a figure actually existing. There are intermediate cases (which are in the majority) in which it is the moving body which, as it is displaced by the form, transforms the form from a potential into an actual. This description also holds for what I shall call the passive perception of movement, or the perception of the figure traced by someone's finger on my palm or cheek. Here also there is visualization of movement. We were able to confirm this by a small investigation of our own: the subject closed his eyes and was asked to guess the form we were tracing on the palm of his hand: "It is a Z," one subject told us, "I see the form at the tip of your index finger."

In the cases we have just studied, the moving object describes the figure completely. But if the subject knows in advance what figure the moving body is going to trace he is often satisfied with a mere motor direction, or what psychologists have called "outline movement," "preparatory movement," "incipient movement." These phrases are very obscure, the last one in particular. It is our opinion, however, that these phenomena can be very simply explained. Let us first remind ourselves that all consciousness of movement or of a figure traced by a movement is constituted—excepting at the initial and terminal moments—by a concrete impression, a sensible intention, which separates a retention from a protention. To *realize* an empty knowledge of movement or form, is, therefore, basically to create two directions at the heart of this knowledge, one by which it turns to the past in order to retain it, the other by which it envisions the future in order to anticipate it. To bring about this differentiation in the bosom of knowledge calls for nothing more than an instantaneous impression or, since instantaneity is a limited idea, at least for a very brief period of real movement. This movement does not necessarily happen as the initial phase of the movement. Let us suppose, for example, that I want to produce an image of the figure eight. My intention at first involves an undifferentiated

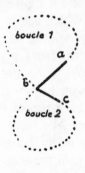

fig. 4

imaginative knowledge of eight. This knowledge contains that of a *loop* which appears for a moment by virtue of the empty imaginative intention, after which I make a slight movement of the eyes, from a to b, in synthetic connection with the empty knowledge of the preceding moment and which will give me, let us say, one of the parts of the eight. At that moment, what was pure imaginative knowledge of the loop becomes a retention as it glides into the past. But although the movement does not last long, its meaning does survive it: it stops at b, and at b it presents itself as the "beginning of a loop" and, quite apart from this concrete impression, a protention of the loop shoots forward towards the future. This means that I grasp the described movement as completing itself alongside *a part* of the loop, which is enough to transform the pure imaginative knowledge of the loop into the retentional state and, at the same time, I project a loop beyond b: the loops are presented as unreal existences *beyond* and *on this side* of my real movement. Beginning at b I make a new eye movement from b to c. The movement bc occurs at one and the same time as prolonging loop 1 and as carrying itself out and along the length of loop 2, which then becomes the object of an imaginative protention, that is, that loop 2 becomes the *meaning* of my movement; I can grasp that movement only to the degree in which it operates alongside an imaginative loop. The result is that, having in reality operated the angular movement abc (Fig. 4) I have apprehended that movement in overloading it with a retentional meaning of "eight." Were I to apprehend the movement as a real movement, it would appear to me as a movement operated *alongside* an eight as an image, but if I envisioned eight as a static form through the movement, it will naturally be this form only that will be unreally visualized on the real kinaesthetic impression.

It is time to draw some conclusions from these several observations. We shall see presently that movement can play the role of analogue for an imaginative consciousness. This is so because when a movement is given by another sense than sight, the consciousness that apprehends it is already imaginative and not perceptual. No doubt this imaginative consciousness is more simple than those we are about to study: but it is basic. That is to say, that basically it becomes or can become a fourfold substitution:

1. A series of kinaesthetic (or tactile) impressions can function as analogue for a series of visual impressions.

2. A movement (given as a kinaesthetic series) can function as analogue for the trajectory that the moving body describes or is assumed to describe, which means that a kinaesthetic series can function as analogical substitute of a visual form.

3. A very small phase of the movement (as, for instance, a very slight muscular contraction) may suffice to *represent* the entire movement.

4. The muscle that contracts is not always the one that would enter into play if the intentioned imaginary movement had really occurred.

We now come to the problem that interests us: how can the movement become the analogical substitute of the object for the imaginative consciousness? The answer is obvious: since the structure of the consciousness of movement is imaginative, it undergoes no modification when the image is richer. The kinaesthetic impression which already *represents* a visual form will simply function as *representative* of more complex objects: more will be *demanded* of it, since the knowledge envisions a greater number of qualities. We have seen in Chapter IV of Part II how an increasingly greater knowledge flows into the "symbolic movements" which we perform in observing a schematic drawing. The same happens here; namely, that the role of the movement has not changed, from the one case to the other: in the former it functioned as analogue *on* the lines of the drawing; in the latter the lines are absent and the movement is no longer revealed to us by visual sensations; but its role remained the same. In a word, when we form an image of an object, the kinaesthetic impressions which will accompany certain contractions, certain voluntary displacements of organs, can always serve as substitutes for a visual form. But this visual form will now have a wider meaning: it could be the form of my fist, of an ink-pot, of a letter of the alphabet; in short, the form of an object. To illustrate this point: Some years ago the writer got a clear impression of eye movements as he tried to imagine a swing in rapid motion. He next tried to imagine the moving swing while keeping his eyes still. In order to do so he fixed his eyes on the number of a page of a book. What happened then was that his eyes either moved in spite of his effort at control or that he could get no image of the moving swing. The case is a very simple one; and we have already discussed it above. What is involved here is neither a pure static form nor a pure shifting of a moving body. The moving body must be conceived (represented by the present kinaesthetic impression) as causing the figure to pass (the arc of a circle) from potential to actual. But the moving body was not simply an undetermined moving body: it was moreover apprehended as the analogue of a swing.

So we discover two analogical materials for an imaginative consciousness: the kinaesthetic impression with its retinue of protentions and retentions, and the affective object. But these two materials serve the same purpose. The affective substitute is transcendent but not external, it shows the object in its fullest and inexpressible nature. The kinaesthetic substitute is at the same time transcendent and external: it yields nothing that is very deep but it is through it that we apprehend the form of the object as a differentiated quality, that is what "externalizes" the object as an image, that localizes it, that indicates its direction and its movements, if these occur. These two types of analogue can therefore well exist concurrently as correlatives of the same act of consciousness. Three cases can present themselves:

1. The analogical correlative of the imaginative knowledge is the affective object. We have described that structure in the preceding chapter and will return to it.[1]

2. The correlative of the knowledge is the movement. We are therefore dealing mostly with the determinations of pure space. Of this we shall speak later in connection with symbolic schemes and synaesthesias.[2]

3. The complete image includes an affective analogue which presents the object in its basic nature and a kinaesthetic analogue that externalizes it and gives it a sort of visual reality. At the same time, the kinaesthetic analogue, produced by several movements which are easy to retain, constitutes an excellent mnemotechnical means. A subject to whom we showed

[1] Cf. Chapter V, Part 3.
[2] Cf. Part 4.

a picture of "the Return of Soldiers from the Crimean War" described it afterwards very correctly. When he was asked whether he had interpreted it or described it, he said: "In the main I reconstructed in accordance with the movement of the lines."

Shortly before this he had reported: "I represented the picture to myself in the main by an upward movement."

This movement was in fact very characteristic because of the large number of bayonets in the picture, all of them parallel. The subject later reported having in mind a figure formed by vertical lines joined together towards the bottom by semicircles. This figure represented the picture for him. The figure was evidently of kinaesthetic origin and drew all its meaning from the knowledge. But it would be inexact to say that the affective object possesses any externality: it is but transcendent. There is therefore no spatial relation between the two substitutes. A special act of consciousness is needed to affirm that each of the two substitutes manifests the same object in its own way. It is naturally the unity of consciousness which causes the unity of the image.

If our analysis is correct and if the non-visual apprehension of the movement itself has an imaginative structure, it should follow that our consciousness is always, or nearly always, accompanied by a mass of poorly differentiated representations, so that the subject cannot tell whether they are kinaesthetic apprehensions or images. This is actually what the experiments of the Würzburg psychologists seem to confirm.

"Something of this symbolism," writes Burloud,[1] "is discovered in the motor representations that accompany mental work. The representations are so obscure that the subjects are not always cetrain whether these are images or sensations of movement. In the experimental reports we find mention of eye and head movements; "a sort of symbolic sensation of nodding of

[1] *Loc. cit.*, pp. 71-72.

the head in approbation"; "a convulsive pressure of the jaw concomitant with symbolic sensations (or representations) as when one turns the head away from something, in suppressing a thought"; "a motor incertitude in the hands and the posture of the body" as when in doubt; all these phenomena jostle each other in intellectual processes as in emotional processes. Subjects are most often unable to state whether what they experience is consciousness of an attitude or attitudes of consciousness."

So, in the consciousness which is clearly imaginary there is a zone of semi-darkness where almost imperceptible states, empty imaginative cognitions which are almost images, and symbolic apprehensions of movement appear and disappear rapidly. Let one of these cognitions fix itself for a moment on one of these movements, and the imaginative consciousness is born."[1]

4. The Role of the Word in the Mental Image

Words are not images: the function of the acoustic or optic phenomenon which we call the word has no resemblance whatsoever to the physical phenomenon, the picture. The only common trait between the consciousness of a sign and that of an image is that each envisions, in its own way, an object through another object. But in the one the intercalated object functions as *analogue*, that is, fills consciousness *in place of*

[1] We have tried to explain the motor basis of the image by using only real movements, movements really performed. Today we are familiar with the hypothesis of incipient, exquisite, restrained movements, motor impressions whose origin is not in muscular contractions, presented by Mourgue in his book *Neurobiologie des Hallucinations.*

If this interesting theory is confirmed it is evident that nothing we have said will need to be modified. All we need do is admit that the imaginative intention holds for these non-peripheral motor impressions. But we did not deem it to be our duty to give an account here of these new conceptions since they are not as yet sufficiently confirmed. We have therefore followed the famous theory of William James on the peripheral origin of the feeling of tension.

another object, which is, in short, present by proxy; in the other type of consciousness it is restricted to directing consciousness on certain objects which continue to be absent. The consciousness of the sign can thus remain empty, whereas the consciousness of the image knows a certain fullness together with a certain nothingness. This distinction applies fully to the mental image and inner speech. In this domain we find nothing but confusion. While M. L. Meyerson, in keeping with the opinion of numerous psychologists, turnéd the image into a vaguely-defined sign, which is lacking in equilibrium, and which has a meaning only for the individual, others look upon the endophesic work as a "verbal image"; so that the sign is an image and the image a sign. This view results in deep confusion. If I produce an image of a horse while thinking of a horse, the image is alleged to be a sign for my thoughts. But a sign of what? Are words not enough for the purpose? We might as well say that when I have some thoughts about a horse at which I am looking the horse is a sign for my thoughts about the horse. And, let us not forget that in the mental image we are in the presence of a horse. Only that this horse has a sort of nothingness. It is present, as we say, by proxy. The fact of the matter is that the theory of image-sign arises from the illusion of immanence. It is assumed that the mental image of a horse is a copy of a horse (something of a lesser horse). And between this well-constituted lesser horse, and the horse of flesh and bone there could be but an external relationship: the relationship of a sign to the thing signified. We have tried to show, on the contrary, that there is an internal relationship between the horse and its image, what we have called a relationship of possession: by means of the analogue it is the horse itself that appears to consciousness. We shall have to return to this, since it is obvious that the role assigned the image in mental life has been various, depending on whether it is looked upon as being an undisciplined sign, an outlaw outside the system defined by society or a certain way in which an absent object presents itself to us. At all events, we can conclude from now on that in the mental image the function of the analogue has nothing in common with the function of the verbal sign in the consciousness of the word.

But it would be a mistake to identify the consciousness of the word with that of the image. The words of silent speech are not images; there are really no verbal images, for a word that has become an image is no longer a sign. This is the way we would interpret the case in which the subject reported "seeing words written in printed letters," "seeing words written in his own handwriting." Since, as we shall see, it is in fact impossible to read *on* a mental image, we should be able to admit that internal speech is accompanied in these subjects, now and then, by true visual or auditory images whose mission it is to "presentify" ("presentifier") the leaves of a notebook, the pages of a book or the total physiognomy of a word, a phrase, etc. But no real internal language is present: it is exclusively propulsive.[1] A simple illustration will clarify this point for us: it often happens that we get to know our own thoughts as we put them into words; language prolongs them, finishes and specifies them; what was a vague "airy consciousness," a more or less undetermined idea becomes a clear and precise proposition by being spoken. So that whether our language is overt or "internal" our thoughts become more and better defined by means of it than we ourselves were able to make them; it *teaches us* something. But the mental image teaches nothing: this is the principle of quasi-observation. It cannot be said that an image clarifies our knowledge in any manner whatsoever for the very reason that it is the knowledge that constitutes the image. If language then teaches us something it can do this only because of its externality. It is because

---

[1] We believe that the alleged "visuals" or "auditories" are only people who do not know how to observe very well and who have not noticed the real word which is the movement behind the image.

the mechanisms according to which sounds and phrases are arranged are partly independent of our consciousness, that we are able to read our thoughts on the phrases. But in a phrase, as in an image, there is lacking that resistance which makes thought clear and precise: the image is modified to suit our knowledge and lacking this resistance the knowledge remains what it is, namely, more or less undifferentiated. Thus a phrase as an image is never a complete phrase because it is not an observable phenomenon and, reciprocally, a phrase of language spoken internally cannot be an image: the sign always retains a certain externality.

The image (mental or otherwise) represents a filled consciousness which can in no way form a part of a large consciousness. But the consciousness of the sign is empty. No doubt but that the sign has an externality which has no affective analogue but the intentionality of meaning does not revert to the sign: it is through the sign that it refers to another object which has but an external relationship to the sign. Consequently, a meaningful consciousness can very well *fulfill itself*, that is, enter by virtue of structure into a new synthesis—a consciousness of perception or of an image. We have seen that when knowledge combines with affectivity it undergoes a debasement which is precisely what permits it to fulfill itself. But this does not mean that the words to which it could be linked disappear. They continue to enact their role in the imaginary consciousness: they form the articulation of the knowledge, it is due to them that the knowledge emerges from its first vagueness and is able to go out in search of a plurality of differentiating qualities in the analogue. The independent mental contents of the words are therefore not merely a purely associative tie attached from the outside to the image, as Taine believed. The words are, of course, not indispensable to its structure and there are many images without words. Furthermore, they do not constitute a part of consciousness as such, their externality throws them in the direction of the analogue.

But, in the first place, since all knowledge tends to express itself through words, all images have a sort of verbal tendency. Then, again, when the word is given to the imaginary consciousness, it becomes integrated to the analogue, in the synthesis of the transcendent object. Just as when I see the moon and I think the word "moon," the word flows into the perceived object as one of its qualities, so if I produce only the imaginary consciousness of the moon the word will attach itself to the image. Does this mean that it will function as an analogue? This is not necessary; often the word maintains its function as a sign. But it can also happen that it becomes contaminated by the interpolated object and that it also presents itself as a representative. Nevertheless, it is to be noted that it can not occur as a representative of the real word (visual or auditory) because it is itself a real word produced by the real movements of the vocal chords. The word of silent speech is not an image, it is a physical object functioning as a sign. It will therefore appear as a representative of a quality of the thing. When I produce the imaginary consciousness of the moon this word "moon" can very well present itself as if it were a real quality of the object, the quality of *being the moon*. In this case the word, which is a system of movements, can confer upon the image that externality which it ordinarily demands of the movements of the eyes, the head or the arms. The word will even represent the central kernel of the analogue, which we could have already anticipated from what we said concerning the role that the word plays in the reading of a novel. In a more complete study it would be fitting to define the relationships that exist between the old function of the word as a sign and its new function as a representative. But this is not the place to undertake such an investigation. It is enough for us to note that if we give the name of image to the whole system of the imaginative consciousness and its objects, it is a mistake to say that the word adds itself to it externally; it is internal.

5. How the Thing Appears in the Mental Image

The image, like the perception, can indicate clearly the relationship of the object to an act of consciousness. In the second part of this work we have tried to describe how the object, when absent, presents itself through a presence. In the mental image the object is envisioned as a synthesis of perceptions, that is, in its bodily and sensible form; but it appears through an affective analogue. Will this not bring about some basic modifications in the manner of its appearance? This is what we must examine now.

If subjects are questioned concerning their images most of them will declare, if the images are "visual," that they *see* them, and if the images are "auditory" that they *hear* them.[1] What do they mean? We must not believe that to see means here to see *with the eyes*. To account for this all we need do is compare the belief of a subject in the hypnagogic image and in the mental image. In the former, when we believe that we see an image, the term must be understood in its literal meaning. The image is an external object, the hypnagogic field is a part—or at least that is what the subject believes—of the real world (of real space). But subjects who affirm most positively that they "see" their mental images readily admit that there is nothing in their images of the nature of the hypnagogic image. Their images are not localized in space. They have no *relationship* to this chair or table before which I am seated. Since the literal sense of the word "to see" is "to see in space" the subjects could not mean to say that the images are given to them visually. Nor do they imply that the images occur as neural processes or processes of the visual centers. Taine realized, in fact, that if the image is produced by the functioning of cerebral centers, as in the case of perception, it

---

[1] It should be noted, however, that all subjects (even those unfamiliar with psychology) distinguish between the perceived object and the imagined object.

should belong with other perceptions. And his theory of a reducing agent is the only logical point in this theory. Unfortunately, however, it is not borne out by the facts. By its very nature the image is without spatial localization. How then are we to understand the frequent reports of subjects that "I see my images"? To see an image of a dog, for instance, involves the possessing "in" consciousness of a certain mental content composed of visual sensations (the color of the coat, shape of the body, etc.), but these sensations can not be externalized and can be given by some other means than the visual organs. But if these traits are removed what is there left of sensations? Here we are obviously confronted by a contradiction. And it will not do to expose this contradiction: it seems to belong to the very nature of the image. It must be described and, if possible, explained.

We have seen, in the second part of this work, that one of the essential factors of the imaginative consciousness was that of belief. This belief envisions the object of the image. All imaginative consciousness has a certain positional quality in relation to its object. In fact, an imaginative consciousness is a consciousness of an object *as an image* and not consciousness *of an image*. But if we form a second consciousness, or a reflective consciousness, on top of this imaginative consciousness, a second kind of belief appears: the belief in the existence of the image. It is then that I say: I have an image of a dog; I "see" the Pantheon. The contradiction of which we just spoke is a phenomenon of belief which is placed in the realm of reflection. What does one mean when one reports "having an image"? One means that one has an intervening object before his consciousness which functions as a substitute of the thing. This belief, if it does not go beyond a belief, is justified: the object exists, it is the analogue. But the reflective belief moreover posits the image as a picture. What does this signify?

Let us suppose that my imaginative consciousness envisions the Pantheon. In so far as this consciousness is knowledge, it envisions the Pantheon in its sensible nature, that is, as a Greek temple, of a gray color, with a certain number of columns and a triangular facade. On the other hand, the envisioned Pantheon is present in a certain manner; it presents itself in its affective reality. On this affective presence my intentionality of knowl-edge apprehends the qualities cited above. It is as if I thought: "this object before me, I *know* that it has columns, a facade, a gray color. All this is present as a certain form: what I *sense* there is the Pantheon, with its columns, its facade, its gray color." But the Pantheon exists *elsewhere* and it presents itself as existing elsewhere: what is present is, in some way, its absence.

Thus, for a few moments, I was as if in the presence of the Pantheon and the Pantheon is nevertheless not here: this is the phenomenon of possession we have already described. But is it not rather natural that I should try to reconstruct this im-pression logically; for is it not absurd to say that I was in the presence of the absent Pantheon? These absent presences are repugnant to my reason. Should we not rather say that an object like the Pantheon was present and that this object was the image? In this way what is absent remains absent, and what is present retains completely its characteristic of presence. The image will naturally be the analogue. It *represented* the sen-sible qualities of the absent object without possessing them: one will say that it *had* them, without *being* the absent object. Nothing is clearer, better constructed, than this illusion: to *represent* this gray color, that is to fulfill without satisfying this consciousness which is reaching for the gray, is this not to present to it the least of gray, a gray without externality, a phantom gray one which retains nothing more of the sensible than its nondescript nature of gray. Such is the origin of the illusion of immanence: in transferring to the analogue the qualities of the thing it represents, a miniature Pantheon is constructed for the imaginative consciousness and the reflec-tive consciousness presents the imaginative conscious as a consciousness *of* that miniature. The result of this construction is a mirage: I believe that the object of my consciousness is a complex of real sensible qualities but which are not externalized, whereas these qualities are perfectly externalized but *imaginary*. I believe that I could conduct myself before this complex of sensible qualities as if it were any sensible object whatsoever; I believe myself able to read a printed page which is before me as an image, count the columns of the Pantheon, describe, and observe. I fall here into the illusion which constitutes the hypnagogic image, even though my belief is less powerful and tenacious: *I can do nothing* with this object which I believe able to describe, decipher, enumerate. The visible object is there, but I cannot see it—it is tangible and I cannot touch it—audible and I cannot hear it.

"Many persons," writes Alain, "report having an image in their memory of the Pantheon and being able to evoke it quite readily. I ask them to please count the columns that support the facade; and they not only fail to do so but even to try it. However, this is the easiest thing to do the moment they have the real Pantheon before their eyes. What then do they see when they imagine the Pantheon? Do they see anything?" [1]

From this Alain draws the conclusion that the image does not exist. In this we can not follow him: we only wanted to show the paradoxical nature of the image, to draw attention to these columns which are actually the object of my consciousness and which *I cannot even attempt to count*.

This happens because the object occurs in the image in a very particular way. The Pantheon could not appear to the imaginative consciousness in the same manner as it does to a perceptual consciousness. It is not true that the image is a "representation whose parts are juxtaposed," as Bergson would have it. Of course, as knowledge, an imaginative consciousness does envision the external object in its externality, that is, as composed of juxtaposed parts; but as affectivity, the imagina-

[1] Alain, *Système des Beaux-Arts*. (N.R.F.) New edition, p. 342.

tive consciousness presents the object to itself as entirely un-differentiated. At times I envision the whiteness of the columns, the gray of the facade as separate qualities; at times I know that the facade is one thing and the columns another—and at times I present to myself a whiteness which is gray, columns which are a facade, a temple without parts. The object thus presents itself in images now as something indivisible, each quality of which extends from part to part across all the others, and now as an organization of distinct properties, a system of fragmentary views on this primitive mass. It involves an inherent contradiction, a radical defect in make-up: the unique quality of the mirage which we exposed above consists of the fact that we accept this contradiction without taking note of it, that is, without positing it for what it is.

But what should open our eyes are the frequent confusions we are compelled to commit. The reason is, in effect, that because it is not sustained by discrete representations the knowledge is contaminated by the syncretism of the affective object if it has not been acquired by a systematic observation, if it is not made explicit by means of words.

In one experiment 369 persons were shown [1] a picture of a young boy with dark hair with a dark coat and blue trousers. They were then asked to report the color of the different objects. Here are the answers:

1. For the blue trousers:

Boys		Girls	
Blue	15 times	Green	8 times
Brown	20 times	Brown	19 times
Yellow	5 times	Yellow	3 times
Grey	4 times	Grey	7 times
		Red	3 times
		Black	3 times

[1] Dauber, *Die Gleichförmigkeit des psychischen Geschehens und die Zeugenaussagen.* Fort. der Psych. I (2), 1913, pp. 83–131.

2. For the dark coat:

Boys		Girls	
Blue	28 times	Blue	21 times
Green	18 times	Green	12 times
Grey	13 times	Grey	19 times
Red	20 times	Red	9 times
Yellow	2 times		

It is impossible to suppose that the colors "blue" and "brown" exist as juxtaposed representations in the memory of the subjects: otherwise, these curious errors could not be accounted for. But here the vague knowledge is carried along by affectivity. The way in which the object "appears blue" in an image does not exclude a certain way of "appearing dark" which remains blended in the first of a sort of harmonic resonance. Besides, the blue generally seems to have masked the dark, because of circumstances. The former is present but recessive. The cognition permits itself to be decided by the strongest affective sonority. The others remain in the first like an harmonic resonance. In the works of Gorphe [1] and Abramowski,[2] numerous examples of the same sort are to be found.

In a perception everything presents itself as being what it is. By this we must understand that the thing occupies a rigorously defined position in time and space and that each of its qualities is rigorously fixed: this is the principle of individuation. We must also understand that the thing cannot be itself and something else at the same time and in the same relationship. These two conditions are but imperfectly fulfilled by the object as an image. No doubt that the knowledge can expressly envision the thing in this or that of its aspects. But we must draw a distinction here: the knowledge does indeed always envision a certain object (or a certain class of objects) to the exclusion of all others, and, consequently, it envisions the

[1] Gorphe, *La Critique du Témoignage.*
[2] Abramowski, *Le Subconscient Normal.*

object always as one and the same. But it is extremely rare that it envisions the object as a unique appearance in an indivisible moment of time. From this last point of view there can be an accord between the knowledge and the affectivity, whereas from the point of view of identity the affectivity must yield or the conflict arises.

1. *The object of the image does not obey the law of individuation.*

As we noted at the end of Part I [1] the object does not appear in its instantaneous aspect either as a picture, as an imitation, or as an hypnagogic image. This instantaneous aspect cannot be presented by the mental image for an even better reason: for in the latter case as in the former ones the knowledge envisions, for example, Peter with "*his* red cheeks," "*his* cheerful smile," etc. Affectivity for its part, can never render an affective equivalent for an instantaneous appearance of the object. So that the Peter who appears to me as an image is neither envisioned nor presented as the Peter whom I could perceive at the same instant, if he were present: the Peter who is presented by the mental image is a synthesis which draws together within itself a certain duration, and often even contradictory aspects; this is also the explanation for the moving character which certain images retain long after their object of flesh and bone has lost the power of moving us.

So knowledge envisions and affectivity delivers the object with a certain coefficient of generality. But this does not necessarily prevent the conflicts at the very heart of the imaginative consciousness, because the generality with which the object is envisioned by the knowledge is not necessarily that with which it appears through the affective *analogue*. For instance, my intention of knowledge can envision Peter as I saw him this morning while my affective intention can present to me through the analogue Peter as he has been appearing to me for more than a week. Nevertheless, since there occurs an

[1] Cf. Part I, Ch. VII: *From the Portrait to the Mental Image.*

identifying fusion of the two intentionalities, the Peter of the past week is presented as being the Peter whom I saw this morning. His sadness of the beginning of the week, the ill humor that made him so disagreeable yesterday, are all condensed in the affective analogue and consequently everything is presented as being the Peter of this morning.

There can occur an even more serious displacement: the Peter whom my knowledge envisions is the one who had his coffee and rolls this morning in his dressing gown; while the one presented to me by the analogue is the Peter whom I saw the day before yesterday in a blue overcoat on the Place du Châtelet. But this Peter in an overcoat is, nevertheless, presented as being the Peter in his dressing gown. It is the conflict within the imaginative consciousness which can explain the paradox that astonished us at the close of the second part of this work; the object of the image of Peter, we said, is the Peter of flesh and bone who is actually in Berlin. But on the other hand, the image I now have of Peter shows him to me in his home, in his room in Paris, seated in his easy-chair which I know so well. So we can raise the question whether it is the Peter who lives actually in Berlin who is the object of the image or the Peter who lived last year in Paris? And if we insist that it is the Peter who lives in Berlin we must explain the paradox why and how the imagined consciousness envisions the Peter of Berlin through the Peter who lived last year in Paris. What we could not explain previously is now more clear to us: the knowledge envisions the object through what is furnished it by the analogue. And the knowledge is *belief*: belief of finding oneself before Peter who is dressed in this or that way. But the analogue is *presence*. Hence the contradictory syntheses.

2. *The object of the image does not of necessity appear as obeying the law of identity.*

The knowledge envisions a certain object; the affectivity can furnish an analogue which stands for several objects: in fact, things often possess unexpected affective equivalents among themselves and the same affective content can thus supply a number of things in an undifferentiated state. This is the reason why, in a dream, one person can be several persons at once. This undifferentiated multiplicity of the image is less apparent in the wakeful state because in the formations of the wakeful state the knowledge imposes its mark on affectivity more clearly. Leroy had, however, already stated that "the ordinary visual representations of the wakeful state which are often so difficult to describe and even more difficult to draw, without our being able to give a clear account why, should imply contradictions of the same kind." [1]

Every one of us, for example, has been able to observe in himself some instance of what I shall call *facial contaminations*. A face appears to us in an image; we ask ourselves where we could have seen it, but in vain. Finally, when the solution appears, we understand: it was two undifferentiated faces, that of an employee of the bank we visited yesterday and that of a policeman we see every day at a certain intersection. The two faces were present completely, through each other, because of a certain resemblance from which there resulted this curious formation contrary to the law of identity: the contamination. Many images are thus contaminations. The other day, for instance, as I tried to recall a red stone building located at Saint-Etienne, an image appeared and I suddenly realized that it stood for two buildings: the one of stone in Saint-Etienne and the other of brick in Paris.

Even when this contamination does not occur it often happens that the object of the image appears in a form which it could not possibly have in perception. If I represent to myself a thimble it is present in an image at one and the same time as a view from the outside and also from the inside. If I grasp the arm of this easy chair in my hand, a hand as an image will loom up grasping the arm of the chair as an image. But I "see" this hand which is closed on the opaque arm from the

[1] Leroy, *Les Visions du demi-sommeil.*

inside, I see the palm and the inside of the fingers, as if the arm were made of glass. If I place my hand on my knee I translate into a visual image the fact that I clasp at once the material against my palm and against my knee and the knee through the material: I have an image of the hand (both sides of it), of the material (both sides of it) and of the knee. Such examples could be cited endlessly. This we shall not do. But it shows us that the image, intermediate between the concept and the perception, gives us the object in its sensible aspect but in a manner that prevents it on principle from being perceptible. The image envisions the object most of the time in its entirety all at once. What we try to recover in the image is not this or that aspect of a person but the person himself, as a synthesis of all his aspects. Thus, when children draw a person in profile they nevertheless give him two eyes. So it is with the person we evoke, we grasp him in a particular place, on a particular day, and even dressed in a particular way and in a particular attitude. But this particular intention is accompanied by a mass of others which contradict it and alter it. So that this person, without ceasing to have this or that attitude, finishes by being a complex of a mass of attitudes and aspects which it is impossible to analyse. What is successive in perception is simultaneous in the image: and this could not be otherwise since the object as an image is given at once by all our intellectual and affective experience.

At the close of these chapters, which have tried to show the elements of the imaginative synthesis, we should warn the reader not to interpret our ideas incorrectly. In pointing out the main factors of the image we had no intention whatever of reducing the image to the mere sum of these factors. In fact, we called attention above to the irreducible reality of the consciousness of the image. It is only as an abstraction that movements, knowledge and feeling can be separated. And the analysis here is so far from being a real dismemberment that it is only a probability. Never can an image be effectively reduced to its elements, for the reason that an image, like all mental syntheses, is something different from and more than the sum of its elements. What counts here is the new meaning that penetrates the whole: I want to be with Peter, I want to believe he is here, my whole consciousness is directed to him, it is "fascinated" in some way. And this spontaneity, this "intention towards" Peter causes this new phenomenon to flash forth, which is comparable to nothing else: the consciousness of the image. This consciousness represents a mental *form*. When consciousness assumes this form it gives rise for a moment to a stable appearance, then the form, carried by the current, disintegrates and vanishes. Far from denying then, as do Alain, Montier, the Behaviorists, and many others, the specificity of the image, we give it a greater dignity, because of the fact that we do not make of it a reborn sensation but on the contrary an essential structure of consciousness, and even more than that, a mental function. Correlatively, we affirm the existence of a special class of objects of consciousness: imaginary objects.

Our view of imagination is thus far removed from diluting it in the totality of the mental life, while our conception of the image is even farther removed from considering it to be but the automatic reappearance of a sensible content. For us the image represents a certain type of consciousness which is completely independent of the perceptual type, and correlatively, a type of existence *sui generis* for its objects. And we also restore to *imagination* as such, which disappeared when psychologists ceased to believe in faculties, an importance which cannot be exaggerated, as one of the four or five great mental functions. It is this function which we shall now try to describe.

Part III

___

THE ROLE OF THE IMAGE IN MENTAL LIFE

1. The Symbol [1]

THE IMAGE serves neither as illustration or support for thought. It is in no way different from thought. An imaginative consciousness includes a knowledge, intentions, and can include words and judgments. And by this we do not mean that a judgment can be made *on* the image, but that, in the very structure of the image judgments can enter in a special form, namely, in the imaginative form. For instance, if I want to represent to myself the stairway of a house which I have not mounted for a long time I at first "see" a stairway of white stone. Several steps will appear before me in a fog. But I am not satisfied, something is missing. I hesitate for a moment, I burrow in my memories, but without emerging from the imaginative attitude, then, all of a sudden, with the clear impression of engaging myself, of assuming my responsibilities, I cause to appear before me a rug with copper rods on the stone steps. A thought process occurred here, a free and spontaneous decision was made. But this decision did not pass through a stage of pure knowledge or of a simple verbal formulation. The act in which I was engaged, the act of affirmation, was precisely an imaginative act. My assertion consisted exactly of conferring on the object of my image the quality "recovery of a cover." And this quality I caused to appear *on* the object. But this act is evidently a judgment since, as the researches of the Wurzburg school have so well shown, the essential characteristic of the judgment is the *decision*. Into the imaginative consciousness there enters there-

[1] In this and the following chapters it will be convenient for us to use some constructions and expressions which appear to endow the unreal object with the power of causality over consciousness. This is to be taken only metaphorically. It is easy to reconstruct the veritable processes. For instance, an image has no persuasive power but we persuade ourselves by the very act by which we construct the image.

fore a particular sort of judgment: imaginative assertions. In a word (later on we shall see that even reasoning may occur in imagery, that is, necessary connections of imaginative consciousnesses) the ideational elements of an imaginative consciousness are the same as those of the consciousnesses to which the name of thoughts is usually given. The difference lies essentially in a general attitude. What we ordinarily designate as *thinking* is a consciousness which affirms this or that quality of its object but without realizing the qualities on the object. The *image*, on the contrary, is a consciousness that aims to produce its object: it is therefore constituted by a certain way of judging and feeling of which we do not become conscious as such but which we apprehend *on* the intentional object as this or that of its qualities. In a word: the function of the image is *symbolic*.

For the past several years much has been written, about symbolic thinking, no doubt under the influence of psychoanalysis. What struck one in these writings was the conception of the image as a material trace, an inanimate element, which later plays the role of symbol. Most psychologists look upon thinking as a selective and organizing activity which fishes for its images in the unconscious to arrange them and combine them according to circumstances: the thought stays strictly on the outside of the images it gathers together, which may be compared to a checker player who moves his pieces on the checker board so as to bring about a certain combination. Each combination is a symbol.

We cannot accept a conception according to which the symbolic function is added to the image from the outside. It seems to us, and we hope that we have already made it somewhat obvious, that the image is symbolic in essence and in its very structure, that the symbolic structure of the image cannot be suppressed without destroying the image itself.

But what exactly is a symbol? How is the symbol to be distinguished from the sign or the illustration? A critical analysis of the outstanding but little-known works of Flach on "the symbolic schemes in the thought process" [1] will enable us to answer this question.

"I have noticed," writes Flach, "that from time to time, when I wanted to clarify the data of a problem or even to understand some propositions which were definitely useful for my thinking, there came to the fore some more or less vivid representations but which always brought along with them the solution of the problem, the comprehension of the phrase."

These representations appear with the act of comprehension, properly so called. They do not accompany the mere memory of a proposition or of a problem. They cannot be voluntarily produced. If an attempt is made to produce them, all that comes to the fore is what Flach calls "illustrations of thinking," [2] that is, the "thin engraving" of Binet. If a scheme is to appear it must be aimed at directly—all of the subject's effort must be directed to the understanding of a word or a proposition. But are all acts of comprehension accompanied by schemes? Flach does not think so. He notes that there are no schemes in very weak mental effort. "We obtained no schemes when work was very easy or when subjects could solve the problem by recourse to memory. In such cases we found at times a verbal-motor reaction and at times simple illustrations."

These schemes possess an essential trait: they "have no meaning in themselves but only a symbolic one." If a subject makes a sketch of the scheme that has just appeared to him the sketch appears deprived of meaning in the eyes of an uninformed observer. That is, these images possess *all the basic traits* called for by an exact representation of thinking in its concrete structure—and *only these traits*.

This is what distinguishes them from other sorts of images,

---

[1] A Flach, Ueber Symbolische Schemata im produktiven Denkprozess, *Arch. f. Ges. Psych.* Bd. LII, p. 369 et seq.
[2] Denkillustrierungen.

called by Flach, as we have seen "illustrations of thinking" and which he defines as follows:

"By this I understand that what they make sensible is an illustration of the object whose relationships with thought are fortuitous, external, and of a purely associative order."

We can guess that in the illustrations there is at one and the same time more or less than in thinking.

"Experiment 53: the subject asked to give a short and essential account of Zola at a horse race. The experimenter asks whether the subject knows what relationship this representation has with the account asked for and the subject answers that one day he read a detailed description of a journey in *Nana* and that since then the image regularly arises at the name of Zola."

But note, on the other hand, several symbolic schemes (sketches, diagrams, outlines) from the accounts of the experiments of Flach. Flach presented his subjects with common terms, generally abstract ones, which they were to try to understand:

"7. Exchange: I gave my thoughts the form of a ribbon (bands). Here is a ribbon which represents the circular process of the exchange. The movement of the curve is a spiral because in the exchange the one acquires what the other loses. The inequality of the curves should explain the gain and the loss involved in every exchange. The ribbon appeared on the field."

This schema, says Flach, is interesting as being the one which represents in logic two concepts whose extensions (or comprehensions) have a common part. But here it is a question in logic of a particular determination that is involved.

"14. Compromise: It is the association of two men. I had the representation of two bodies gliding towards each other, sideways. Their form was vague but it was two bodies—one on the right, the other on the left—which sucked up each other. The body was solid and had some protuberances which it pushed ahead and which disappeared in each other. Then, there was only *one* body. But what is surprising is that the body did not increase much in size. It was a bit larger than each of the parts but smaller than the two combined. It was a greyish green, had a dirty greyish green color. At the same time I made the movement with my hands."

"22. Baudelaire: I saw immediately, in the open space, on an absolutely dark bottom, a spot of blue-green color, of the color of vitriol and as if thrown there with one wide stroke of the brush. The spot was longer than broad—perhaps twice as long as broad. Immediately I knew that this color must express morbidity, the kind of decadence which characterizes Baudelaire. I study whether this image can be applied to Wilde or Huysmans. Impossible: I feel a strong resistance, as if something contrary to logic were proposed to me. This image belongs only to Baudelaire and, from this moment on, will represent that poet to me."

"27. Proletariat: I had a strange image, a flat and black area and, underneath, a sea flowing dimly, an endless wave, something like a dark and thick mass rolling with unwieldy vagueness. What did the mass signify? Extension in the entire world; something like a latent dynamism."

The schemes in general have but one meaning, that of the thought they symbolize:

"This intuitive image expresses nothing else than a system of conceptual relationships which are grasped while the subject sees them as determined relations between the sensory data. These relations, as sensory data, present themselves as *a priori* determinations of space.

"In symbolic schemes a thought is always grasped, due to the fact that the conceptual relationships that constitute it are lived intuitively and, as far as I could ascertain, as spatial data. Whereas in the cases illustrating thought, space has the role of a receptacle, a background, or a substratum and functions as a stage on which they are placed, yet when it is a matter of symbolic representations, it has, on the contrary, a clarifying role: spatial determinations and figurations do not exist. They are but the supports and essential concretization of abstract relationships. It is by the spatialization of these relationships that the abstract content of thought is seized. By means of simple limitations, of condensations, by indications of the directions or by a particular rhythm of a region of space, an abstract thought can specify its content. Here is an example: When we asked: what do you understand by altruism, the subject had the representation of a direction, the fact of going towards another thing which is not given. . . ."

Flach adds that we must distinguish between the preceding cases "and those in which an ideal abstract content is as if localized in a determined region of space without the thought being characterized by that localization. These localizations are then nothing else than contact points for the thought, which they tie to spatial determinations and which can thus rest on them as on real objects."

What remains to explain is the source of these symbolic schemes. It is on this point, we must admit, that Flach is most unsatisfactory. He restricts himself, or nearly so, to looking upon the symbolic scheme as a creation of "Sphaerenbewusstsein." [1]

"It is, as a whole, on the level of the consciousness of direction without words, the stage in which we endeavor to give expression to and define in words the essence of an objective content that we have precisely lived subjectively (internalized) and that we nevertheless possess in some way the more or less intuitive condition. Then it often happens that, in its main outlines, thought emerges as a scheme from its all-inclusive wrapper."

But why does the symbolic scheme appear and in which

[1] "Consciousness of spheres." An expression used especially by psychologists of the Würzburg school and which designates a certain condition of pure knowledge, prior to the image—and, by extension, thought, as understood by the psychologist.

cases? How does it build itself up? What is its relationship
to pure knowledge, to the pure act of comprehension? What
does it mean for a comprehension to realize itself by the intermediary of a symbol? And just what is the symbolic function
of the scheme. These are the questions Flach leaves unanswered. We must then take up again after him the study of
these symbolic schemes and see what further conclusions we
can draw about them.

We have seen that acts of ready comprehension or consciousness of pure meaning are not accompanied by schemes.
The scheme accompanies the effort of intellection, properly
so-called, and it presents in the form of a spatial object the
results of this effort. Nevertheless, it would have been interesting to know whether all the acts, beginning with a certain
degree of difficulty are translated into a scheme, or whether
there can occur intellections (understanding, perception)
without images. The results of Mesmer's experiments enable
us to complete the work of Flach on this point; there are
many cases in which understanding occurs without imagery,
by simple words, *in* the words; examples can also be found of
a direct and pure understanding without imagery or words.
But in the latter case it rather seems that the understanding
stopped on the way, that one stopped short of a complete
development. But what fails to reach the end is not the
imaginative phase: in every case we have been able to study the
subjects are aware of having been short on words. We can
therefore affirm that there are two classes of comprehension:
a pure comprehension (whether or not supported by signs)
and an *imaginative comprehension* (which also may or may not
make use of words). Since we cannot admit that this division
is the effect of chance we must suppose that there is a functional difference between the two types of comprehension.
Numerous observations have, in fact, permitted us to con-

clude that the use of the one or the other of these comprehensions was not governed by the object. I have often verified, for instance, that, depending on the circumstances, I could understand the same phrase by means of schemes or without any help at all. These observations permit us to formulate a first problem more clearly: granted that there are two ways of understanding and that these two ways can be applied regardless of the object of consciousness, what are the motives which can lead consciousness to operate an understanding in one or the other of these ways? These motives must be looked for in the very structure of antecedent consciousnesses and not in the objects. In a word, an imaginative comprehension is always a part of a temporal form to be described, in which consciousness takes a certain position in relation to its object. It is this position we must ascertain; we can ask ourselves for which intentional attitude of consciousness comprehension will operate in the imaginative way and what is the functional relation of the symbolic scheme to that attitude. But it is not easy to determine immediately the nature of that attitude and we must at first make a deeper study of the idea of symbolic schemes.

We see at once that the symbolic scheme is constructed out of the elements which we described in the second part of this book. A knowledge, which we must still investigate, penetrates and unites into a synthetic act a kinaesthetic analogue to which at times there is joined an effective analogue. These determinations of psychological space are none other, in fact, than impressions of movement apprehended imaginatively. Everything we said concerning movements in our preceding section is applicable to experiments 7 and 13 as we reported above. Experiments 14 and 21 which we also cited, show very clearly the way in which the affective analogue is added in a new synthesis to the kinaesthetic analogue. The purpose of the latter is to express as clearly as possible the rational structure, the concept to be understood. The non-kinaesthetic element of the analogue is more difficult to characterize. It nevertheless translates the personal reaction of the subject to the concept; but it translates it as a quality of the concept since it occurs itself as a quality of the scheme. In this connection experiment 14 is very instructive:

". . . It was moldy green, it had a dirty moldy green color." According to Flach himself, this person had to give a "dirty" color to her scheme because she was compelled by her surroundings to incessantly renew an arrangement which appeared to her immoral and humiliating. Whatever one may think of this interpretation which is psychoanalytical, it is quite typical that the art of Baudelaire is symbolized by a blot the color of vitriol. As we noted above, the affective analogue presents itself as representing ineffable sensations. In the two cases we cited, it serves as a substitute of a color. The rational elements of the concept, on the contrary, are translated into a form, that is, a movement.

With the scheme thus constituted, we should ask ourselves whether it is true that it is the sense of the concept or of the proposition to be understood that is read *on* the scheme. Flach claims repeatedly that "the essential characteristic of these schemes is that the thinking proceeds *on* these images, *beginning* with these images. . . . The image appears first and only then the thinking . . . which indicates that I thought on the occasion of that image."

And, in truth, several statements of his subjects ("Thought followed immediately, which I read in the image . . ."), seem to confirm this. But is this possible? What this view comes to when clearly expressed is this: first the symbolic image appears, when the subject tries to understand—and the subject deciphers this image and finds in it just the meaning he is looking for. The essence of the effort to understand would thus consist of constructing the schemes.

Now we must note that according to this hypothesis when the subject constructs the scheme he does not yet understand it. And we ask how, under these circumstances, was he able to produce a symbolic representation which can have, according to Flach's own terms, "all the basic traits of the idea he is to understand." This could happen only provided an unconscious understanding preceded the conscious understanding. But in that case, if the image occurs first and is then deciphered, how can the subject interpret it correctly? We have seen, in fact, that an uninformed observer is unable to understand a symbolic schema without an explanation unless he is shown a sketch of it. We are then called upon to suppose that the unconscious understanding is transformed behind the scheme into conscious understanding. But in that case the role of the scheme is superfluous. But shall we claim, as does Flach, that in the scheme the idea is "lived intuitively" before it is understood? But, we repeat that the construction of the scheme implies the comprehension of the idea. We do not mean to say, of course, that understanding occurs first and then construction. But it is very evident that comprehension is realized in and by construction. The structure of the concept to be understood serves as the rule for the elaboration of the scheme and one becomes conscious of this rule by the very fact of applying it. So that once the scheme is constructed there is nothing more to understand. What could have deceived some subjects and Flach himself is that, if we do not limit ourselves to understand for ourselves only, if we desire to transmit the result of our thinking by discourse, we must transport ourselves on another level and express by means of verbal signs what we had grasped as spatial relations. This transcription which naturally takes understanding for granted nevertheless calls for some effort of adaptation which, in certain cases, could be mistaken for understanding itself.

Everything we have just said could be expressed more simply: in accordance with the phenomenological description of Part I we could say that it is impossible to find in the image anything more than what was put into it; in other words, the image teaches nothing. Consequently, it is impossible that understanding operates on the already constructed image. A similar conclusion follows from the illusion of immanence. The image cannot, as a matter of fact, have for its function helping understanding. But understanding can in certain cases adopt the imaginative structure. The image-object appears in such a case as the simple intentional correlative of the very act of comprehension.

But at what point will understanding assume the symbolic form? To answer this question it is enough to remind ourselves of the typical make-up of a symbolic scheme. A scheme is either a form in movement, or a static form. Both cases involve a visual imaginative apprehension of kinaesthetic sensations. We saw in the preceding part how this apprehension works. We saw that the sensible element as such is framed by a protention and a retention. By protention we are finally thrown back to a knowledge which presents itself as protention and which is transformed into retention as the movement flows out. The constitution of the symbolic scheme therefore sends us back to the knowledge as to its origin. What knowledge is involved here?

Understanding is not pure reproduction of a meaning. It is an act. In making itself manifest, this act envisions a certain object and this object is, in general, a truth of judgment or a conceptual structure. But this act does not start from nothing. For instance, I may try to understand the word "man" but not its corresponding German "Mensch" unless I know German. Every word in terms of which I can make an effort to understand is therefore shot through and through with a knowledge which is nothing other than the recollection of past understandings. We know that Descartes draws a distinction between ideas and the recollection of ideas. Knowledge is in some manner a recollection of ideas. It is empty, it implies past and future understandings but is itself not an understanding. It is evident that when Flach presented his subjects with words they were to understand, the understanding began with this knowledge: it proceeded from the knowledge to the act. It is then at the level of the knowledge that the nature of understanding is decided. In accordance with the intention of the knowledge, this comprehension will be imaginative or not, that is, the knowledge will or will not change into a protention followed by a symbolic movement. In a word, the essential factor we have to describe is that intentionality which appears in the knowledge and which finally constructs the symbolic scheme. Why does it debase the knowledge?

Does it do so in order to facilitate the understanding? This we have already answered above: the image teaches nothing. The understanding attains its end *as an image*, but not *by* the image. In the next chapter we shall see, moreover, that the scheme, far from helping intellection, often checks and deflects it. But if we return to an analysis of Flach's experiments it may help us to understand the function of the image.

Let us give an account of experiment 27. The subject who is asked to give the meaning of the word "proletariat," sees "a flat and black area, and, below it, a sea rolling vaguely." What can lead us astray here, and what seems to have deceived Flach, is a faulty interpretation of the idea of symbol. Flach seems to believe in fact that this scheme is the *symbol* of proletariat, that is, that his subject, in producing this symbol, intends to represent his idea by means of lines and colors. This image will therefore present itself as a schematic representation of the content of the idea "proletariat," as a means of making the inventory of that content. In other words, the image would still be a sign. But to this view we can object, first, that it is impossible to see the reason why the subject should want to make such a construction. Secondly, and above all, we need but produce one of these schemes for ourselves and observe it to convince ourselves that the schemes in no way perform the role of sign and representative. No doubt there is a representative in the scheme: it is the affective-motor analogue by means of which we apprehend the form and its color. But the scheme itself is no longer an analogue: it itself is an object having a meaning. That "flat and dark area" with that "vaguely rolling sea" is neither a sign nor a symbol for the proletariat. It *is* the proletariat in person. Here we reach the real meaning of the symbolic scheme: the scheme is the object of our thought giving itself to our consciousness. So the function of the scheme as such is in no way to help the understanding; it functions neither as expression nor as support, nor as exemplification. We expressly declare, using an indispensable neologism, that the role of the scheme is that of *presentifier*.

At the beginning of Part II we defined *pure knowledge* as consciousness of a rule. But let us add, it is "an ambiguous consciousness which is given as both a consciousness without any relational structure of the object and as a consciousness full of a state of the subject." In a word, just as we called it pre-objective, it can be called pre-reflexive. It brings to the subject instructions concerning its own capacities: "Yes, I know . . . , I could know," etc.) but this does not appear fully as a spontaneous activity of ideation and the relation which makes the object of the knowledge appears at times as an objective relation and at times as a rule for obtaining ideas. This state without equilibrium can become debased into imaginative knowledge: in which case all reflection disappears. It can also become a pure reflective consciousness, that is, posit itself for itself as consciousness of a rule. In that case the meaning of a word will be grasped on the reflective level as the content of a concept and the meaning of a phrase as judgment. On this level, reasoning still appears as a succession of ideas which are generated from the very depth of their innerness, the premises appear as the operating rules for forming the conclusion and the psychic motivation clothes the following form: "If I posit that A implies B and that B implies C, then, in order to be consistent, I must posit that A implies C." It is in considering the reflexive nature of classical reasoning that formal logic defined itself as the study of the condition "of the agreement of mind with itself." All this mental activity moves on the reflective level, the ideas appear as ideas at the same time that they are forming themselves. Consciousness is separated from the object while it is reasoning. It can rejoin it at the level of the conclusion, provided it converts this latter into a non-reflective affirmation. This reflexive ideation is not accompanied by images. In the first place, images are here useless; secondly, if they should appear as image consciousnesses of image and not as object consciousnesses, they would lose their meaning.

But ideation can operate entirely on the non-reflective plane: all that is needed is that the pure knowledge become debased into imaginative knowledge, that is lose its pre-reflective character in order to become unhesitatingly non-reflective. In that case, all thought becomes consciousness of things and not consciousnesses of itself. To understand a word is no longer to apprehend a concept: it is to realize an essence, the comprehension of the judgment bears upon this objective content which the Germans call *Sachverhalt*. This non-reflective plane may be called the *plane of presences* because of the attitude assumed by consciousness: it behaves in fact as if it were *in the presence* of the objects which it judges; that is to say, it seeks to apprehend that thing and to formulate ideas on it as on an external object. To understand a word at that moment amounts to constructing before consciousness the corresponding thing. To understand "proletariat" consists in constructing the proletariat, and making it appear to consciousness. The form in which this something will appear will naturally be a spatial form, because a consciousness can effectuate a presence only as a spatial form. But this spatialization is not desired for its own sake. In reality what operates here in consciousness is the natural confusion between transcendence and externality. Instructed to understand the word "proletariat" or the phrase "nature imitates art" we attempt to refer to the things themselves in order to contemplate them; in other words, the first step of consciousness is to turn to intuition. The understanding of the word occurs therefore as a sudden appearance of the object. So that the spatial determinations are not signs or images of the structural relations which constituted the thing: they are apprehended as these relations themselves. They are these relations constituted by a knowledge which incorporated itself into a series of movements. But, naturally, the object is not really constituted, it is there only "as an image" and consequently it presents itself as absent. Correlatively the attitude of consciousness is not that of observation but of quasi-observation, that is, the presence of the object as an image teaches him nothing since the constitution of the object as an image is already the understanding. Nevertheless the final thoughts will occur as reactions of consciousness to the transcendent object, that is, as the results of contemplation, as they unroll by a normal track from the original comprehension. We shall shortly investigate the mechanism of this thought as an image and see that, if the construction of the scheme changes nothing in the phenomenon of comprehension, the final thoughts are changed in their essence by the fact that they have been motivated by an original thought as an image.

2. Symbolic Schemes and Illustrations of Thought

Before defining the symbolic scheme Flach distinguishes between them as follows:

1. *Simple illustrations of thoughts* which can appear, according to him, together with a symbolic scheme but which can never express more than one example.

2. *Schematic representation* of Messer ("it was neither lion

nor tiger, I was aware of a hairy skin."). The symbolic scheme is not the image of a definite concrete object from which something is missing: schematic representations are therefore illustrations of somewhat hazy thoughts containing something indefinite.

3. *Diagrams* which represent schematically, for instance, the days of the week, the months of the year.

"What the diagram has in common with the symbolic scheme is the fact that the diagram represents spatially an abstract and unextended object. But there is nothing else here than a definite localization in space. This localization serves as a mooring, an attachment, an orientation for our memory, but plays no role in our thought."

4. *Synaesthesias and synopsies*, that is, images aroused regularly by hearing proper names, vowels, etc.

5. *Auto-symbolic phenomena.* This is the name Silberer gives [1] to hypnagogic visions that symbolize an immediately preceding thought. Flach recognizes two types of hypnagogic symbolization. The first contains symbols which are close to symbolic schemes. In the second there are simple illustrations of thought.

The essential distinction Flach draws between illustrations, schematic representations, diagrams, synaesthesias, auto-symbolic phenomena, on the one hand, and symbolic schemes, on the other, comes in the main to this: The former do not express thought, they are connected with ideation by external ties and are moreover quite loose (what is roughly known as ties of *association*), the latter are a direct product of thought and its exact expression on the level of the image. This amounts to admitting that there are images which have a symbolic function and others that have no function of any sort, whether as survivals, fortuitous connections, or stereotypes. Below the level of symbolic schemes Flach places the "engravings" of Binet.

[1] Herbert Silberer, *Der Traum,* Stuttgart, 1919.

We do not share his opinion. The image is a consciousness. If this principle is accepted what meaning does the association of ideas retain? Association occurs as a causal linkage between two contents. But there can be no causal linkage between two consciousnesses: one consciousness cannot be aroused *from the outside* by another consciousness: but it arises by itself by its own intentionality, and the only tie that can connect it with the previous consciousness is that of *motivation*. Consequently we must no longer speak of automatisms and stereotypes. Binet and the Würzburg psychologists tend to construct the image, over against thought, as a phenomenon deprived of meaning. But if the image is a consciousness, it must have its own meaning, as does every other sort of consciousness. Its appearance in the course of thought is never the effect of a chance connection: it plays a role. This role is undoubtedly easier to determine in the case of the symbolic scheme than in that of the engraving. But if our premises are correct, there must be a function for all images which do not occur as schemes.

Diagrams are quite readily reduced to symbolic schemes. Flach almost admits this when, after having distinguished most diagrams from symbolic schemes and having denied them any other function than that of an "orientation for our memory" makes an exception of diagrams whose structure be-trays a dominant preoccupation of the subject. *A propos* of a diagram representing the month of the year, for instance, when the subject was asked why three months were missing, the answer was: "because in my childhood there were three months of anxiety out of every year."

This diagram is evidently symbolic. But is this not the case with every diagram, although somewhat more di creetly so? For many subjects the months are completely given but arranged in an ascending, descending, broken, bent, straight, etc., order. All these arrangements have a meaning which corresponds most often to the way in which the year is divided by the professional vocation of the subject. In a word, the diagrams which represent the months or the days of the week for the subject express regularly the way in which the succession of the months or the days appear to the subject; that is, the year or the week appears in its concrete structure. The same is true for syntheses, that is, for those cases, for instance, in which a vowel arouses in the subject a certain color. Synaesthesia never occurs as the product of a pure association. The color occurs as the *sense* of the vowel.

"A man forty years of age, who experiences very definite colors for a, o and u, but not for i; he understands that if need be the sound can be seen white or yellow, but he feels that in order to find it red one must have a distorted mind or a perverted imagination." [1]

When Flourney tries to explain synaesthesias by what he calls "identity of emotional basis," he does not take into account the sort of logical resistance one experiences when one attempts to change the color aroused by a vowel. This happens because the color occurs as the sound "in person" just as the "vague sea" occurs as the proletariat in person. Naturally what we have here is a consciousness which is more affective than intellectual and the image attributes the personal reaction of the subject to the vowel. Besides, it is hard to see why Flach, who admits the symbolic meaning of the color in his discussion of Experiment 14 ("arrangement . . . he had a dirty color, greenish grey") or of experiment 21 ("Baudelaire . . . a spot of blue-green color, of the color of vitriol") will not admit this in the case of synaesthesia. Moreover, what difference is there between experiment 21 "Baudelaire" and a simple synaesthesia, other than in complexity? No doubt that the symbolic scheme is generally built up as a spatial determination. But this is simply due to the fact that purely intellectual

[1] Cited by Flourney, *Des phénomènes de syopsie,* p. 65.

comprehensions are more readily translated into movements. Knowledge, as we have seen, directly impregnates kinaesthetic sensations. But there is also a comprehension "of the heart," and it is this comprehension that expresses itself by synopsies.

Finally, it is fitting to show that images which present all the features of "engraving" can play the role of a symbolic scheme. This Flach himself recognized: when one of his subjects was asked to furnish him with a brief description of the philosophy of Fichte, he pictured "the self creating the nonself in order to go beyond it" as a worker pounding a wall with a hammer; and Flach is compelled to admit that this illustration of thought is functionally similar to a scheme.

So if we brush aside the phenomenon of auto-symbolism, which is so uncertain and difficult to investigate, a first examination leads to the following conclusions: first, that the realm of the symbolic scheme is wider than Flach assumes and we must admit into it all the neighboring phenomena which Flach tried to side-track; secondly, the distinction between scheme and engraving is not well marked: these are rather limited cases connected by transitory forms; they should not therefore be looked upon as exercising radically different functions.

We must, however, face the fact that when a scheme is compared to an illustration considerable differences are found between these two sorts of images. Let us suppose I am asked to define the historical period known as the Renaissance in a few words. It may happen that I produce an indefinite image of movement, something like a stream of water which expands and wanes; I may also see the opening out of a flower. In both cases we call my image a symbolic scheme. There is no doubt more in the second case than in the first: in addition to a symbolic meaning, the image has another meaning which can be grasped from without, as for instance, if the subject makes a drawing of his image. But this supplementary meaning is not thought of for its own sake: in the degree to which it is conscious it is still a quality I confer upon the subject.

But I can also produce another sort of image: for instance: on hearing the word Renaissance, I may "see" the David of Michelangelo. The essential difference in this case is that David *is not* the Renaissance. We should also note that this difference cannot be verified from without. Only the subject can say whether the image is symbolic of the Renaissance or whether, in some way, it is a *lateral* image; only he can inform us if the David of Michelangelo is thought of for itself or as a symbol. Let us suppose that the David of Michelangelo is apprehended for itself. In this very apprehension there must be a particular intention, since it is the apprehension itself which could be symbolic. The symbolizing apprehension gives David the meaning of "Renaissance"; the non-symbolizing apprehension constitutes it as the "statue of Michelangelo to be found in such and such a museum in Florence, etc." If my first aim was to give a brief definition of what I understood by "Renaissance," I must recognize that my thought deviated. But this deviation could not arise on the level of the constituted image; it is on the level of the knowledge, at the very level of the process of ideation that the change of direction operates; and, this change, far from being aroused by the appearance of the image, is the indispensable condition for its appearance. It is therefore a spontaneous deviation which thought gives to itself and which cannot be the effect of chance or of some external compulsion; this deviation must have a functional meaning. Why has a thought which seeks to discover the content of the concept "Renaissance" made this hook, why has it delayed to form the image of that statue?

It is advisable that we undertake a description of how this image appears to me. We notice, first, that it occurs as linked by the unity of the same quest to the anterior productions of consciousness; in a word, this David does not present itself simply as such but as a step towards the understanding of the term "Renaissance." And this very term of step is a rubric for the total of the contradictory meanings of the statue. In one sense, in fact, it presents itself as a unity among others, the collection of which constitutes the total extension of the term being studied. It is a point of departure for a systematic review of all the works of art I may know which were produced at the time of the Renaissance. But, from another side, the image attempts to hold us upon itself: in this very David I could find the solution of the problem I am investigating. David, without presenting himself explicitly as the Renaissance, pretends vaguely to conceal in himself the meaning of that period, as happens, for instance, when we say that by visiting the castle in Berlin one will understand the meaning of the Prussia of Bismarck. At the end of this pretention and, by a sort of participation, the envisioned statue can appear as *being* the Renaissance.

Only, this way of *being* the Renaissance cannot have the purity of that of a symbolic scheme. In the scheme, in fact, the spatial determinations have no other meaning than that of the concept they represent, or if, perchance, they have a meaning of their own (flower, the worker pounding with a hammer), this meaning has value only within the limits of the concept symbolized and as a more subtle means to make it appear. For David, on the contrary, the manner of appearing as David is wholly independent of the Renaissance. The very meaning of David *as David* goes back to a mass of ideas which cannot be of service here. This statue by Michelangelo presents itself to me as the David I have seen in the course of my journey in Italy, as the work of a sculptor some of whose other works I also know, as an artistic production which I can class among others, etc., and, finally, as a unique event in my life, from the beginning of which I can reconstruct a whole atmosphere, a whole past epoch. All this is, of course, not specified, it is an affective meaning which could be developed. But it is enough for this David who, in some way, *is* or *tends to be* "the Renaissance" to appear also as something which can divert my thought and carry me far from my actual task, in short, as the correlative of a consciousness which can lose its equilibrium and slip perhaps into revery. So that the statue seems rather *to be* the Renaissance by a mystic tie of participation.

At the end of this brief description we arrive at the conclusion that the image as an illustration is produced as the first groping of a lower thought, and that the ambiguities concerning its meaning are due to the uncertainties of a thought which has as yet not risen to a clear vision of a concept. It seems to us, in fact, that our first response to an abstract question, even though it may correct itself immediately, is always—at least as an answer to the question—a lower response, at once prelogical and empirical. This response is at the same time without unity because the thought is uncertain and hesitates between several means—all of them insufficient—to produce a concept. Socrates asked Hippias: "What is Beauty?" and Hippias answered: "It is a beautiful woman, a beautiful horse, etc." This answer seems to us to make not only an historical step in the development of human thought but also a necessary step (as well as the habit of reflection can curtail it) in the production of a concrete individual thought. This first response of thought naturally takes on the form of an image. Many persons, when questioned about the nature of Beauty, form an image of Venus de Milo, and this is as if they answered: "Beauty is the Venus de Milo."

But this is only one of the aspects of the image as an illustration: it is formed in addition by an unintelligent thought, which rapidly attempts to cast the greatest amount of knowledges on the question presented; it is as if we were to say: "Beauty? Well: the Venus de Milo, for instance . . . ," without going any further because of the contradictory tendencies which make up the image. So here we see a second way that thought has of representing a concept for itself: it is simply the sum of the unities of the class it designates.

But the very fact that these knowledges (Venus de Milo, David, etc.) present themselves under an imagined form and not purely verbal indicates more and better. Place someone in a hall in a museum in which there are several masterpieces of the Renaissance and ask him to give you a short account of that artistic epoch and it is a safe bet that before answering he will cast a quick glance at one of the statues and paintings. Why? This he could not answer himself: it is an attempt to observe, to return to the thing itself and to examine it; it is the primary data of experience, a way of confirming a naive empiricism which is also one of the lower stages of thought. In the absence of these masterpieces the reaction would be the same: the statue of David *would be evoked*, that is, thought would assume the form of imaginative consciousness. Only thought itself does not know whether the object it presents to itself in such haste *is* beauty or only a *sample* of beautiful things or whether one could derive an idea of the concept "beauty" by examining it. The result of these uncertainties is an image which sets itself up for its own sake and also as a step in understanding. From this point on thought will suddenly leave this course by means of real understanding, and by a creative effort will consider the Renaissance itself as present in person: it is then that the scheme appears. It is then not the role of the image that changes, which is always the correlative of a consciousness; but the nature of the thought. From the onset of the image as an illustration, two roads are always possible: one by which thought loses itself in revery as it abandons its first assignment, and another which leads it to understanding as such. It is this ever-possible annihilation of thought at the level of the image that has impressed some psychologists like Binet and led them to the conclusion that the image was an obstruction for thought. But it is thought itself that is responsible for this unbalance of thought, and not the image.

3. Image and Thought

We shall not seek to know whether all non-reflective thought assumes the form of the image. We are satisfied with having shown that the image is like an incarnation of non-reflective thought. Imaginative consciousness represents a certain type of thought: a thought which is constituted in and by its object. Every new thought concerning this object will present itself, in the imaginative consciousness, as a new determination apprehended on the object. But it is naturally only quasi-apprehensions that are involved here. The thought does not, in fact, establish itself on the object; it rather *appears as the object*. If the development of an idea occurs in the form of a series of imaginative consciousnesses that are synthetically linked, it will imbue the object as an image with a sort of vitality. It will appear now under one aspect, now under another, now with this determination, now with some other. To judge that a coachman whose face one imagines vaguely had a moustache is to see his face appear as having a moustache. There is an imaginative form of the judgment which is nothing else than the addition to the object of new qualities, accompanied by the feeling of venturing, promising, or of assuming responsibilities. These few observations enable us to suggest a solution of the problem of the relationships of the image to the concept. If we think imaginatively of some individual objects it will be these objects themselves that will appear to our consciousness. They will appear as they are, that is as spatial realities with determinations of form, color, etc. But they will never have the individuality and unity which characterize objects of perception. There will be some distortions, a sort of deep-seated vagueness, lack of definiteness: we tried to expound this essential structure of the image in

Part III of this book. At the same time, the object presents itself as not being here in body, as an *absent object*. Whatever it may be, it is the form that thought takes on in order to appear to our consciousness. If we think right now of a class like "horse," "man," etc., it is the class itself that will appear to us. It is, of course, but rarely that we think of a class all alone. Most of the time our thoughts are of the relationships between classes. We can say rightly that the thought of an isolated concept is always the result of artificial practices. But such thought is, however, always possible and it-can occur in three ways: in the first, do not know direction of the looked-for concept or we approach it indirectly. In this case our first approximations will present themselves under the form of individual objects belonging to the extension of that concept. If I try to think the concept "man," I could orient myself by producing the image of a particular man or the image of the geography that represents the white man, etc. In the preceding chapter we attempted to give an account of this type of thought. But it is also possible that our thought grasps the concept itself directly. In this second case the concept could appear as an object in space. But this object will not be individualized, it will not be this or that man, but *man*, the class turned into a man. The object of our imaginative consciousness will naturally be an undetermined man, who has nothing in common with the composite image of Galton, but whose indetermination will be the essence itself. It will be like the fleeting consciousness of having a man before one without either being able, or even wanting, to know his appearance, his color, his height, etc. This way of getting to the concept in extension is, no doubt, a very low level of thought. But if, in the third place, we get to the concept all at once in comprehension, that is, as a system of relations, it will then appear to us as a collection of pure spatial determinations which will have no other function than *to present it;* that is, it will take the form of a symbolic scheme. But some concepts like "man," "horse," etc. are too charged with the sensible and too poor in logical content to enable us to rise often to this third stage of thought. The symbolic scheme appears only with an effort of comprehension, that is on the occasion of abstract thought. These three ways in which the concept appears to non-reflective thought correspond therefore to the three clearly-defined attitudes of consciousness. In the first I orient myself, I look about me. In the second, I remain among the objects but I call forth the very class, the collection of these objects as such in my consciousness. In the third, I completely turn away from things (as a unity or a collection) to their relations. The relationships between the concept and image therefore present no problem. In fact, there are no concepts and no images. But there are two ways in which the concept can appear: as a pure thought on the reflective level and on the non-reflective level, as an image.

But a more serious question arises: in the image, thought itself becomes a thing. Will this not cause thought to undergo profound modifications? Can we admit that a purely reflective thought and a spatialized thought have exactly the same meaning; is not thought as an image, an internal form of thought? We must distinguish between two cases, and this way that thought has of being a prisoner of a spatial representation carries different consequences for the ultimate course of consciousness, depending on whether the latter (consciousness) supports reluctantly this imprisonment and seeks to free itself from it, or whether it permits itself to be absorbed by the image like water by sand. In the first case the subject is conscious of the insufficiency of this way of thinking at the very moment he forms the image and seeks to free himself from it. Here is an interesting observation of R. A., a professor of philosophy:

"I had the impression of clearly understanding the main thought of Brunschvicg in reading the pages of *L'Orientation du Rationalisme*, which resumes the thought of Schopenhauer: 'There is no object excepting for the spectator.' When going beyond the order of knowledge. M. Brunschvicg, in the very order of being, brings forth the two correlative realities (subject and object) of a spiritual activity, of an original course, I thought I had grasped the final point of his thought and I recalled an image that illustrated, in some way, my intellectual effort. In the center, a kind of schematic, geometric representation of a movement and then, beyond, from the two sides of this moving line, two symmetrical points or rather two small circles very similar to the circle of a target. This image was not, of course, in the forefront of consciousness. Nevertheless I noticed it but felt it to be insufficient because still tainted with some materiality, but it seemed to me that my impression of understanding sprang mainly from the movement of thought to grasp the image and to go beyond it. I felt that if I could think of the spiritual equivalent of that image without the help of any sensible representation, then I would have truly understood M. Brunschvicg because I would have had to see 'with the eyes of the heart' the nature and the spirit (in the second sense), emerge out of this spiritual and creative primitive urge." [1]

The description of R. A. does not permit us to doubt that we are in the presence of a symbolic scheme. Should anyone wish to check up on the preceding chapters, it will be seen that all the characteristics of the scheme are to be found here. But the consciousness of R. A. contains an additional determination which we have not found up to now in any of the descriptions of Flach: the scheme is itself but provisional, insufficient as a step to be surpassed. But did we not say that the symbolic scheme was the essence it represented? How then is it possible that it should present itself at the same time as being and as not being this essence (the genesis in a spiritual movement of

[1] I have met other instances among a number of scholars and professors of this effort to surpass the image at the very moment when it is formed. I had an especially interesting report from M. L. deR., a student of philosophy.

the subject-object combination)? It seems, however, that this structure of consciousness is very common among philosophers, that is, among men who are very much in the habit of "thinking about thinking" as Goethe said, that is, who have delved deeply into the immaterial nature of thinking, who know by long experience that it escapes every attempt to picture it, to define it, to capture it, and who consequently resort to comparisons and metaphors reluctantly and cautiously when they speak of it. The symbolic scheme therefore appears, for them, as but superficial and very deceptive. No doubt it is completely there, but in a form which can deceive. As a result, the scheme presents itself as something external to thought which itself appears as something which cannot be exhausted by anything "external" which it may adopt, and finally, as radically incongruous with its appearances.

As a result, the investigator can have two attitudes in relation to his own thinking. He can either be contented with seizing the scheme as a possible direction, as the open door to a series of further investigations, the indication of a nature through which to grasp some material aspects. In this case, the scheme possesses a characteristic dynamism which derives from the fact that it permits its own over-extension. But, at the same time, *understanding* is not given in act; it is only outlined as possible, as being at the point of the deliverance (enfranchisement) of all the images. Very often the comprehension is only that: the scheme plus the idea that one could—that one should—go further.

Or else the subject actually carries out the operations which are to liberate his thought from their materialistic obstacles. It disengages itself from the scheme, while entirely retaining the thought. But if it remains in the non-reflective attitude, that is, if it is only conscious *of* the object (particular or universal essence, relationships between essences, etc.), on which it forms thoughts, it can turn away from a symbolic scheme only to construct another, and so on to infinity. It will stop sooner or later in these operations. But this cessation remains without importance if the subject stays aware of the unsatisfactory nature of all imagery, whose importance we have just seen, if he can say to himself at the moment when he stops himself what Gide wants to write at the end of *The Counterfeiters*: "Could be continued." In that case, the essence searched for appears as not being in any of the forms it has assumed, nor in the infinity of those it might have assumed. It is *different*, radically different. And, from the very fact that the subject *does not cease to affirm this heterogeneity*, all these imagined coatings, all these schemes are without danger for thought. But thought, although we could express ourselves upon it without keeping account of the images in which it reveals itself, is never directly accessible to us, if we have once taken the imaginative attitude in forming it. We will always go from image to image. Comprehension is a movement which is never ending, it is the reaction of mind to an image by another image, to this one by another image, and so on, in a straight line, to infinity. To substitute for this infinite regression the simple intuition of a bare thought calls for a radical change in attitude, a veritable revolution, that is, passing from the non-reflective plane to that of the reflective. On this plane thought presents itself as thought at the very time that it appears: and so it is completely transparent to itself. But we can never discover any connecting path which permits us to elevate ourselves progressively from non-reflection to reflective thought, that is, from the idea as an image to the idea as idea. The simple act of intellection on the reflective plane has for its correlative the infinitive idea of approximations through symbols on the non-reflective plane. The result of this equivalence is that the two processes, on the two planes, are equivalents for the progress of knowledge.

It is altogether different when the scheme absorbs thought and presents itself as *being* itself the essence or the relationship to be determined. *Non-reflective thought is a possession*. To think of an essence, a relationship, is on this plane to produce them "in flesh and bone," to constitute them in their living reality (and naturally under the "category of absence" which we defined in the first chapter of Part I) and at the same time to see them, to possess them. But, at the same time, it is to constitute them *under a certain form* and to consider this form as expressing exactly their nature, as *being* their nature. Here thought encloses itself in the image and the image presents itself as adequate to the thought. There follows a warping—possible at any moment—of the further course of consciousness. In fact, the object under consideration (essence, relation, a complex of relations, etc.), does not present itself only as an ideal structure: it is also a material structure. Or rather ideal and material structure are but one. But the material structure implies certain determinations of space, certain symmetries; certain relations of position, and sometimes even the existence of things and persons (see above, for instance, the worker who is pounding his hammer). While the evolution of these determinations remains governed by the *ideal sense* of the image, while the transformations of the scheme remain commanded by those of thought, the development of the idea is not altered. But this subordination of material structures to the ideal structures is possible only if the material structures are grasped as not exhausting the ideal structures, as if a relative independence were posited between the two. This happens only in the attitude we have described in the preceding pages when the subject, although in the non-reflective attitude, retains a sort of vague recollection of pure knowledge touching the nature of the pure idea in general. But in the very great majority of cases the material structure occurs as *being* the ideal structure, and the development of the figure, of the scheme, in its spatial nature is given as exactly identical with the development of the idea. We can see the danger; a slight preference is enough, it is enough to consider for a moment for themselves the spatial relations of the scheme and to permit them to affirm themselves or to modify themselves in accordance with the laws of belonging to spatiality: the thought is hopelessly warped, we no longer follow the idea directly, we think by analogy. It has appeared to us that this imperceptible debasement of thought was one of the most common causes of error, particularly in philosophy and in psychology.

In the imaginative attitude, in fact, we find ourselves in the presence of an object which presents itself as an analogue to those which can appear to us in perception. This object, in as much as it is constituted as a *thing* (pure determinations of geometric space, common object, plant, animal, person) is the correlative of a certain knowledge (empirical—physical or biological, laws—or *a priori*—geometric laws), which has served to constitute it but which has not exhausted itself in that constitution. This knowledge presides at the ultimate developments of the image, it is this knowledge which orients them in this or that direction, which resists when we want to modify the image arbitrarily. In short, soon as I constitute the image of an object, the object has a tendency to behave as an image in the same way that other objects of the same class do in reality. Flach cites some fine examples, but does not seem to grasp their importance. "The subject imagines, for instance, balls thrown in the air. He then feels in his arms the resistance of the air to the rising of the balls. We have made no deeper studies on synaesthesias since it is established that these phenomena really belong to intuition and do not form an important characteristic of the symbolic scheme as such. They apply as well to cases of illlustrations of thought by simple association."

In this excellent example cited by Flach no associations are, in fact, involved, but rather the interpretation of a knowledge which becomes conscious of itself only in the form of an image. All that the subject clearly envisions is the trajectory of the balls tossed in the air. But he cannot think of this trajectory without at the same time thinking of the resistance of the air; although this resistance was not deliberately thought of, the body imitates it as the indispensable complement of the object. Left to itself, the image thus has its own laws of development, and these depend in their turn on the knowledge which has served to constitute it. Here is an observation that will enable us to see this more clearly:

"I wanted to speak of an automobile that climbed hills easily and I was searching for an expression which would describe this abstract idea—unformulated—that would be comical : 'It climbs the hills is if it were pulled up by a weight, as if it were falling towards the top and not the bottom.' I had an image. I saw the automobile climbing a hill; I had the feeling that it was climbing by itself and without a motor. But I just could not imagine this reversing of the weight: the image resisted and offered me but an equivalent: I had the vague feeling of the presence on top of the hill of an ill-defined object, a sort of loadstone, that pulled the automobile. Since this image was not the one I had wanted to produce, there resulted from it a wavering and I could not find the adequate expression. I had therefore to look for a subterfuge and I said: 'One is obliged to check the ascent.' This introduction of a new element modified my image and gave it an entirely different nuance, while its elements nevertheless remained the same; instead of being pulled by a loadstone, the same automobile climbed the hill by itself: it was no longer a machine but a living being which was moving spontaneously and whose ardor I had to control."

In this example the subject wanted to construct, as an intermediary between the abstract thought "reversing of the weight" and his verbal expression, a concrete image the substance of which would have passed into the discourse. But this image would not permit itself to be constructed because it is its nature to contradict the concrete knowledge that had presided at its formation; its searched-for structure had been missing, one slid to the right or left, one struck the living automobile-beast, the magnetized automobile, but this reversed weight, although conceived, was not grasped as an image. From these concrete laws that preside at the individual development of every image, nothing is more typical than the transformation of the automobile into a living being after the phrase "one is obliged to check the ascent." This automobile which must be checked in its ascent ceased being a machine due to this very command. The mere fact of imagining this restraint and these circumstances completed itself spontaneously by the annexation to the machine which was being restrained with a sort of living force. Thus, although the mind is always free to vary no matter which element of the image, we must not believe that the mind could change, at the same time, *all* the elements at its pleasure. All happens as if the transformations of the image were sufficiently rigorous by the laws of *compassibility*. These laws cannot be determined *a priori* and depend upon the knowledges which enter into combination.

Let us now return to our problem: when I produce, in the course of my reflections, an image of the type of those Flach calls "symbolic" (whether of a scheme or any other representation), it seems that there is a conflict in this image between what it is and what it represents, between the possibilities of development which come to it from the idea it embodies, and its own dynamism. On the one hand stones, a hammer, a flower could be symbols of a mass of abstract essences; on the other, this flower, these stones, this hammer, have their own nature and tend to develop into an image in keeping with this nature. When I conserve this dissatisfaction with images of which we have spoken at the very heart of the images, the thought does not suffer from this ambiguity because I leave no time for the image to develop in accordance with its own laws, I leave it as soon as I formed it; I am never satisfied with it. Always ready to be engulfed in the materiality of the image, thought runs away by gliding into another image, this one into another, and so on. But in the majority of cases, this defiance of the image, which is like a recollection of reflection, does not appear. In that case, the laws of development that belong to the image are often confused with the laws of the essence that is under consideration. If that essence appears as a stone that is rolling down an incline, this descent of the stone, which draws all its necessity from my physical knowledge, develops and reinforces the symbol, confers upon it its rigor. The following instance will show the dangers of this substitution. "I would have liked to convince myself of the idea that every oppressed person or every oppressed group draws from the very oppression from which it suffers the strength to destroy it. But I had the clear impression that such a theory was arbitrary and I felt a sort of annoyance. I made a new effort to think: at this very moment there arose the image of a compressed force. At the same time I felt the latent force in my muscles. It was going to break out the more violently the more compressed it was. In a moment I felt to the point of certainty the necessity of the idea of which I could not persuade myself the moment before." [1]

We see what is involved here: the oppressed *is* the force. But on the other hand, *on* the compressed force we can already read with confidence the strength with which it will be discharged: a compressed force represents clearly potential energy. This potential energy is evidently that of the oppressed, since the oppressed *is* the force. Here we see clearly the contamination between the laws of the image and those of the essence represented. This idea of potential energy which increases in proportion to the force exercised on the object, is the force which *presents* it, it is upon it that it can be apprehended. Change the term of comparison, and substitute an organism for the force, and you will have the absolutely inverse intuition, something which could be expressed in the phrase: "the oppression demeans and debases those who suffer from it." But the image of the force left to itself and envisaged purely and simply as an image of force, would

[1] Observation of R. S., a student.

not be enough to convince us. No doubt that the force gathers strength. But never enough to get rid of the load which weighs upon it, because the force it gathers is *always inferior* to that which compresses it. The conclusion we then draw from the image will be this: "The oppressed gains in strength and in value from the very fact of the oppression, but it will never get rid of its yoke." In fact, as I could explain it to myself, in reproducing in myself the scheme of the force, there is more. The image is falsified by the meaning: the energy that gathers in the compressed force is not felt as a pure passive storing, but as a living force, one which increases *with time*. Here the image of the force is no longer a simple image of force. It is more of something indefinable: an image of a living force. Here there is no doubt a contradiction, but we believe that we have shown in Part III that there is no image without an inherent contradiction. It is in and by this very contradiction that the impression of evidence arises. The image thus carries within itself a persuasive power which is spurious and which comes from the ambiguity of its nature.

4. Image and Perception

At the beginning of this book we showed the difficulties raised by every attempt to interpret perception as an amalgam of sensations and images. We now understand why these theories are inadmissible: for the image and the perception, far from being two elementary psychical factors of similar quality and which simply enter into different combinations, represent the two main irreducible attitudes of consciousness. It follows that they exclude each other. We have already stated that when Peter is envisioned as an image by means of a picture it means that the painting is no longer *perceived*. But the structure of images called "mental" is the same as that of images whose analogue is external: the formation of an imaginative consciousness is accompanied, in this as in the former case, by an annihilation of a perceptual consciousness, and vice versa. As long as I am *looking* at this table I cannot form an image of Peter; but if the unreal Peter arises before me all of a sudden, the table which is before my eyes disappears, leaves the scene. These two objects, the real table and the unreal Peter can alternate only as correlatives of radically distinct consciousnesses; how then, under these conditions, could the image cooperate to form the perception?

It is then evident that I always *perceive more and otherwise* than I *see*. It is this incontestable fact—and which seems to us to constitute the very structure of perception—that the psychologists of the past tried to explain by introducing images into perception, that is, by supposing that we complete the strictly sensory material by projecting unreal qualities on the objects. This explanation naturally demanded the possibility of a strict assimulation between image and sensations—at least theoretically so. If it is true as we have tried to show, that there is here an enormous contradiction, we must look for some new hypothesis. We will limit ourselves to indicating the possible directions of research.

In the first place, the works of Koehler, Wertheimer and Koffka permit us henceforth to explain certain anomolous constants of perception by the persistence of formal structures during our change of position. A thorough study of these forms would permit us, no doubt, to understand why we perceive *in a different way* than we see.

We must now explain why perception includes *more*. The problem would be more simple if we would once and for all give up that creature of reason which we know as pure sensation. We could then say, with Husserl, that perception is the act by which consciousness puts itself in the presence of a temporal-spatial object. Now, into the very constitution of that object there enters a mass of pure intentions which do not posit new objects but which determine the present object in relation to aspects not now perceived. For instance, it is well-understood that this ash-tray before me has a "bottom," that it rests *by means of this bottom* on the table, that this bottom is of white porcelain, etc. These various facts are derived from either a mnemic knowledge, or from ante-predicative inferences. But what we should note well is that this knowledge, whatever its source may be, remains unformed: not that it is unconscious but it sticks to the object, it is grounded in the act of perception. What is envisioned is never the invisible aspect itself of the object, but that visible aspect of the thing to which the invisible one corresponds, namely, the upper surface of the ash-tray in that its very structure as the upper surface implies the existence of a "bottom." It is evidently these intentions which supply perception with its fullness and its richness. Without them, Husserl rightly observes, mental contents would remain "anonymous." But they are not less radically heterogeneous in imaginative consciousness: they do not become formulated, posit nothing apart and limit themselves to projecting into the object as a constituting structure qualities which are hardly determined, all but simple possibilities of development (like that fact that a chair should have two other legs than those seen, that the arabesques of the mural tapestry should extend all the way behind the closet, that the man I see from behind should also be seen from in front, etc.). We see that what is involved here is neither an image that has dropped into the unconscious nor that of an image that has been subdued.

These intentions can no doubt give rise to images and this is the very source of the error which we have exposed. They are the very condition of every image concerning objects of perception, in the sense in which all knowlege is the condition of corresponding images. Only, if I wish to represent for myself the mural tapestry *behind* the cupboard, the pure intentions implied in the perception of the visible arabesques will have to detach themselves, to posit themselves for themselves, to *express* themselves, to *debase* themselves. At the same time they will stop to ground themselves on the perceptual act and become a sui generis act of consciousness. So also, the hidden arabesques will no longer be a quality of the visible arabesques—namely, as *having a sequel*, of *continuing without interruption*. But they will rather appear as isolated to consciousness, as an autonomous object.

There is therefore in perception the charm of an infinity of images; but these can arise only at the cost of the annihilation of perceptual consciousness.

In summary, we can say that the imaginative attitude represents a special function of mental life. If such an image appears, in place of simple words, of verbal thoughts or pure thoughts, it is never the result of a chance association: it is always an inclusive and sui-generis attitude which has a meaning and a use. It is absurd to say that an image can harm or check thought, or then this must be understood to mean that thought hurts itself, loses itself in windings and byways; implying that as a matter of fact there is no opposition between image and thought but only the relation of a species to a genus which it subsumes. Thought takes the timage form when it wishes to be intuitive, when it wants to ground its affirmations on the *vision* of an object. In that case, it tries to make the object appear before it, in order to *see* it, or better still, to *possess* it. But this attempt, in which all thought risks being bogged down is always a defeat: the objects become affected with the character of unreality. This means that our attitude in the face of the image is radically different from our attitude in the face of objects. Love, hate, desire, will, are quasi-love, quasi-hate, etc., since the observation of the unreal object is a quasi-observation. It is this behavior towards the unreal which will now be the subject of our study, under the name of the imaginary life.

Part IV

THE IMAGINARY LIFE

1. The Unreal Object

We have seen that the act of imagination is a magical one. It is an incantation destined to produce the object of one's thought, the thing one desires, in a manner that one can take possession of it. In that act there is always something of the imperious and the infantile, a refusal to take distance or difficulties into account. Thus, the very young child acts upon the world from his bed by orders and entreaties. The objects obey these orders of consciousness: they appear. But they have a very unique existence which we shall attempt to describe.

At the outset my incantation tends to obtain these objects in their entirety, to reproduce their integral existence. Next, these objects do not appear, as they do in perception, from a particular angle; they do not occur *from a point of view;* I attempt to bring them to birth as they are in themselves. I need but produce Peter as "seen at seven in the evening, in profile, last Friday," or Peter as "seen yesterday from my window." [1] What I want and what I get is just Peter. This does not mean that Peter will not appear before me in a certain position, and perhaps even in a certain place. But the objects of our imaginative consciousness are like the silhouettes drawn by children; the face is seen in profile, but both eyes are nevertheless drawn in. In a word, imagined objects are seen from several sides at the same time: or better—for this multiplication of points of view, of sides, does not give an exact account of the imaginative intention—they are "presentable" under an all-inclusive aspect. It is something like a rough draft of a point of view on them which vanishes, becomes diluted. These are not sensible but rather quasi-sensible things.

For the rest, the object as an image is an unreality. It is no

[1] It may happen, however, that I seek to bring before me precisely this or that aspect of Peter. But this demands a particular specification.

doubt present, but, at the same time, it is out of reach. I cannot touch it, change its place: or rather I can well do so, but on condition that I do it in an unreal way, by not using my own hands but those of some phantoms which give this face unreal blows: to act upon these unreal objects I must divide myself, make myself *unreal*. But then none of these objects call upon me to act, to do anything. They are neither weighty, insistent, nor compelling: they are pure passivity, they wait. The faint breath of life we breathe into them comes from us, from our spontaneity. If we turn away from them they are destroyed; in the following chapter we shall see that they are completely *inactive*: they are ultimate terms but never original terms. Even among themselves they have neither cause nor effect.

An objection may be offered that this development of images "by association" entails a sort of passivity of mind. If I bring before me a mental picture of a murder I "see" the sunken knife; I "see" the blood flowing and the sinking of the body of the victim. No doubt: but I do not see them in spite of myself: I produce them spontaneously, *because I think of them*. These details do not appear because of a tendency of the object to complete itself automatically, in the sense of Wolff's "*reditur integra-perceptio*," but because of a new consciousness formed on the imagined object. This is what the works of Janet on psychaesthenics show: the tragic nature of the obsession is derived from the fact that the mind forces itself to reproduce the object of which it stands in fear. There is no mechanical reappearance of the haunting image nor a monoideism in the classical sense of the term: but the obsession is *willed*, reproduced by a sort of dizziness, by a spasm of spontaneity.

This passive object, kept alive artificially, but which is about to vanish at any moment, cannot satisfy desires. But it is not entirely useless: to construct an unreal object is a way of deceiving the desires momentarily in order to aggravate them, somewhat like the effect of sea water on thirst. If I desire to see a friend I make him appear as an unreality. This is a way of *playing* at satisfying my desire. But I play at it only because my friend is in fact not there in reality. I give nothing to the desire; what is more: it is the desire that constructs the object in the main: in the degree to which the desire projects the unreal object before it to that degree does it specify itself as desire. At first it is only Peter I desire to see. But my desire turns into a desire for that smile, of that physiognomy. It then limits and aggravates itself at the same time, and the unreal object is precisely—at least as far as its actual aspect is concerned—the limitation and the aggravation of that desire. It is but a mirage, and in the imaginative act desire is nourished from itself. More exactly, the object as an image is a *definite want;* it takes shape as a cavity. A white wall *as an image* is a white wall *which is absent from perception.*

We do not mean to say that Peter himself is unreal. He is a creature of flesh and bones who is in his room at the moment. The imaginative intentions that grasp him are equally real, as is also the affective-propelling analogue which they animate. Nor is it to be assumed that there are two Peters, the real one of Ulm Street and the unreal one who is the correlative of my actual consciousness. The only Peter I know and envision is the real one, who really lives in that real room in Paris. It is therefore that Peter that I call forth and who appears to me. But he does not appear to me *here.* He is not in the room where I am writing. He appears to me in his real room, in the room in which he really is. But in that case, it may be said, he is no longer unreal. We must make ourselves clear: Peter and his room, real in so far as they are situated in Paris, three hundred kilometers away from where I really am, are not so anymore as far as they appear to me now. Even if I thought, on producing an image of Peter: "He is unfortunately not there," it does not mean that I make a distinction between Peter as an image and the Peter of flesh and bone. There is but one Peter and he is precisely the one who is not there; *not to be there* is his essential quality: in a moment Peter occurs to me as being in D . . . Street, that is as being absent. And this absence of Peter, that which I see directly, which constitutes the essential structure of my image, is precisely a nuance that colors the image completely, and it is this we call his unreality.

In general it is not only the material itself of the object that is unreal but all the spatial and temporal determinations to which it is subjected participate in this unreality.

For space, that is obvious. The space of the image is obviously not that of perception. Nevertheless, since certain special cases present some difficulties we must outline a general discussion of the problem. If I recall my friend Peter all of a sudden, I shall "see" him in his grey suit in this or that position. But most of the time he will not appear to me in a certain particular place. This does not happen because every special determination is faulty, since Peter does have certain qualities of position. But the topographical specifications are incomplete or entirely lacking. We may perhaps be inclined to say that Peter appeared to me on the left, a few yards from me, level with my eyes, with my hands. Many descriptions made by well-educated subjects (in the investigations of the Würtzburg psychologists or those of M. Spaier) mention these alleged localizations. But it is easy to discover the error of these subjects: by admitting in effect that Peter appears at my left he does not also appear at the same time to the right of the armchair which is actually before me. This localization must then be illusory. The explanation of it is that in order to have Peter appear as an image we must *animate* certain kinaesthetic impressions which make us aware of the movements of our hands, eyeballs, etc. We have tried to describe the process of these "animations" in the third part of this book. Now, by the side of these "informed" impressions there are others which belong to the same organs and which keep all of their kinaesthetic meaning, and which arrive in our consciousness as so many instructions concerning our hands, our eyes. And these latter are so close to the former that they establish themselves there imperceptibly. For instance, I can very well interpret the movements of my eyeballs as the static form M; by which we must understand that I animate with a new intention the impressions that come to me from the contraction of orbicular muscles and from the rolling of the eyes against the orbits. But other regions of the orbits, the superciliary muscles, etc., supply me with immutable kinaesthetic impressions, so that the motor analogue cannot completely detach itself from its kinaesthetic environment. There thus results by contamination a sort of lateral and spontaneous localization of the object as an image, which is the reason why I place it "to the left," "to the right," above," or "below." But these spatial specifications, although they can mask the unreal character of imagined space, can in no way qualify the unreal object.

If we discard these false localizations it will be easier for us to understand an important characteristic of the object, which we might call its coefficient of depth. Peter as an image appears to me at a certain distance. Here the contamination of the motor analogue by its environment could not serve as a valid explanation. But, is Peter, moreover, at a given distance from me? This is not possible; he bears no relationship to me since he is unreal; he is no more five yards from me than a hundred. Shall we say that he appears to me as if "seen by me at a distance of five yards?" But just at the time that I produce Peter as an image I have no idea at all that I see him, that I attempt to put myself in immediate communication with an absolute. Peter is five yards from no one; if he were five yards from me he would have his perceptual size and aspect, that's all. This is a sort of absolute quality. We have tried to show just now that in the image the object appears as a complex of absolute qualities. But on the other hand, each of these absolute qualities draws its origin from a sensible appearance of the object, therefore from a relative quality; the image does not create conditions of absolute existence for the object: it carries the sensible qualities to the absolute, without stripping them however of their essential relativity. From this there naturally arises a contradiction, but one which is not glaring, due to the confused character of the unreal object. Already in the perception I attribute to Peter an absolute height and a natural distance in relation to me. Consequently when I reproduce Peter as an image I give him his absolute height and his natural distance. But these qualities will no longer appear as relationships between Peter and other objects: they have been interiorized: the absolute distance and the absolute height have become intrinsic characteristics of the object. This is so true that I can reproduce as an image my friend R. who is very short with *the shortness of his stature* and his absolute distance, and do so without evoking any object in relationship to which that shortness is recognizable. In perception I can never know whether an object is large or small unless I have the means of comparing it with other objects or myself. But the object as an image carries its smallness within itself. No doubt that in the image I can vary the stature and the distance of objects. But what varies, when, for instance, I imagine seeing a man in the distance who is coming towards me, are internal qualities of that unreal man: his color, visibility, and his absolute distance. It cannot be his distance in relationship to me which does not exist.

This analysis has led us to recognize that space as an image has a character much more qualitative than does perceptual extension:[1] all spatial determination of an object as an image presents itself as an absolute property. This is in keeping with what we have said in the previous chapter that it is impossible to count the columns of the Pantheon as an image. The space of the unreal object has no parts. But, it will be said, does not Berkeley's "esse est percipi" hold without exception for all unreal objects, and, if so, does it not follow that consciousness does not expressly confer this space without parts to unreal

[1] Which itself is far from being a pure quantity.

objects? The fact of the matter is that consciousness affirms expressly nothing about unreal space: it is the object it grasps and the object presents itself as a concrete whole which includes extention along with other qualities. The space of the object is, therefore, as unreal as is its color or its form.

Let us now suppose that I produce an image of Peter in his room in D . . . Street. Here the question is more complicated since a specification of topographical space is added to the absolute extension of the unreal object. Our observation on this case is that this localization is produced by a special intention which is added to the central imaginative intentions. It is a matter of an additional specification. It can happen that without this specification the object might appear to me with a vague spatial atmosphere: Peter is vaguely "surrounded by his room." But the latter, vaguely included in the affective analogue, is not explicitly affirmed. For the room to be given in fact as the container of Peter it would have to be the correlative of an act of a specific affirmation, synthetically united to the act of consciousness which constitutes Peter as an image. But once this affirmation is made, the room that appears does not occur in its relationships to the real space where I live. A vague feeling of direction, which, moreover, does not strongly accompany the object, could hardly be noticed. Otherwise, the room naturally appears with its "normal" proportions, or, more specifically, "natural size" is never *placed* in relation to my real space: if it were, the distance of my body would be at least outlined in perspective, since the room did not appear to me *here* where I am, but *yonder* where it is. In reality, it is placed in reference to Peter, as *his* surrounding, *his* milieu. Of course it cannot be made an intrinsic quality of Peter and yet it has no purely contiguous external relations with him. Produced by a secondary intention, which has meaning only in relationship to the central intention, it might be called an "*appurtenance*" of the main object. Naturally, it is certainly the real room I see, just as I see the real Peter. But it occurs as absent; and at the same time his character is greatly modified since the external relationship of contiguity which unites it to Peter is transformed into an internal relationship of appurtenance.

It is more difficult to admit that the temporal aspect of the object as an image is unreal. Is not the object in fact contemporaneous with the consciousness that forms it and is not the time of the consciousness very real? Nevertheless, in order to think adequately on this question, we must review once more the principal that has guided us thus far: the object of consciousness differs in nature from the consciousness of which it is the correlative. Therefore nothing is proven by the fact that the flow of time in the consciousness of the image is the same as the time of the object of the image. We shall see, on the contrary, by means of several examples, that these two durations are radically separated.

There are unreal objects which appear in consciousness without any temporal determinations. If, for instance, I imagine a centaur, the unreal object belongs neither to the present, the past, nor the future. Moreover, it does not last in front of the consciousness that elapses, it remains invariable. I, who imagine the centaur, change, I submit to external entreaties, I hold the unreal object before me with more or less effort; but from one moment to another of my time the centaur has not changed, has not aged, not "taken" a second more: it is without time. There is a temptation to give it *my* present, just as *my* space is given to Peter as an image. But we shall find out soon that that would be committing the same error. Certainly the consciousness to which this centaur appears is present. But the centaur is not: it does not allow of temporal determination.

Other objects, without being any better localized, do possess a sort of contracted compressed duration, a non-temporal synthesis of particular durations. For instance, *the* smile of Peter that I now represent to myself is neither his smile of last evening nor of this morning. Nor are we dealing here with a concept but with an unreal object which gathers into one invariable synthesis the many smiles that occurred and disappeared. So that even in this immutability he retains a "density" of duration that distinguishes him from the centaur of which we just spoke.

These objects remain motionless in every way before the flux of consciousness. At the extreme opposite we find objects that run off more rapidly than does consciousness. It is well known that most of our dreams are very short. Nevertheless the oniric drama can last several hours, several days. It is impossible to make this drama which unfolds during a whole day coincide with the rapid course of the consciousness that dreams it. We may attempt to reduce the duration of the dream to the oniric consciousness by turning the *dreamed story* into a rapid march of images. But the explanation is very ambiguous. What is to be understood here by image? Does it mean the imaginative consciousness or the object imagined? If it means the imaginative consciousness it is evident that it cannot flow any faster or slower than it does flow: all that can be said is that it absolutely fulfills its duration and that it is this very fullness that measures this duration. In what concerns the imaginative object, can we really speak of a more rapid succession? But we are not here at a cinema where a more rapid unwinding of the film produces the impression of a "slowing down." Objects, on the contrary, run off *more slowly* than does real consciousness, for consciousness really lives several seconds while the world of the unreal lasts for several hours. Never does a very rapid flow of images produce the impression of a very long duration, *if that flow is referred to the time of the consciousness*. The error here comes from the identification of image and consciousness, which gives rise to the supposition that a very rapid succession of images is also a very rapid succession of a conscious process and since hypothetically (since the sleeper is cut off from the world) every attempt at comparison fails, it is believed that the relationships are reserved for the different contents. This view, which harks back to the principle of immanence and all its contradictory consequences, must be abandoned. It is useless to object that the unreal object is made up of several truncated scenes which I *imagine* from a coherent whole. For we mean to say nothing else. Of course, I imagine that these scenes have a very long duration. We must therefore admit a phenomenon *of belief;* a positional act. The duration of unreal objects is the strict correlative of this act of belief: I *believe* that these truncated scenes join each other to form a coherent whole, that is, that I join the present scenes with the past scenes by pure intentions accompanied by positional acts.[1] However, I *believe* thoroughly that together these scenes last for several hours. The duration of the object as an image is thus the transcendant correlative of a special positional act and consequently participates in the unreality of the object.[2]

This conclusion also emerges from an examination of intermediary cases, that is, those in which the unreal duration of the object and the real duration of consciousness run off parallel, with the same rhythm. I can take ten minutes to imagine a scene that lasted ten minutes. But it would be childish to think that because of this the scene would be more exactly detailed. *The time I take* to reconstruct it matters little. What matters is the determination of the unreal duration that I give it.

There is an absence of time as of space. In the end, the time of an unreal scene which duplicates exactly an actual scene which is happening right now remains an unreal time. If, while Peter is pouring himself a drink behind my back, I

[1] These intentions are analogous to those that constitute a static form beginning with the kinaesthetic impressions.
[2] The objection will be made that this duration in the dream is presented as real just as are the objects that occupy it. This objection is based on a misconception of the basic nature of the dream. Later on we shall see what this nature is.

imagine that he is pouring himself a drink at this moment, the two events, the real and the unreal do not coincide. On the one side we have the elements of consciousness and the real gesture of Peter which occur together, on the other the presence of the unreal gesture. Between these two events there is no simultaneity.[1] The apprehension of the one coincides with the annihilation of the other.

These diverse characteristics of unreal duration are fully comprehensible only if that duration is conceived as being like unreal space, that is, without parts. Duration is also a quality of the object, and just as it is not possible to delineate the columns of the Pantheon in imagery, so it is impossible to specify and count the instants of an unreal act. It is rather a matter of a vague consciousness, of the flow and a coefficient of duration projected on an object as an absolute property. But let it not be believed that this undifferentiated duration resembles in any way the Bergsonian duration. It is rather something like the space-time that this philosopher describes in *Les Données immédiates de la Conscience.* This holds that in keeping with the principle of quasi-observation, the duration of the imagined object has actually undergone a radical change of structure, or rather, an inversion: the event, the gesture we want to realize as an image appears as commanding the previous instants. I know where I'm going and what I want to produce. This is why no development of the image can take me by surprise, whether the scene I produce is a fictitious one, or one of the past. In both cases, the previous in-

[1] Naturally this does not hold for the intentions that grasp in perception on the objects perceived certain qualities not perceived but whose existence we affirm. These are given from the beginning as existing in the time and space of the perceived objects. A simple example will show the difference: I see Peter from the back. This very perception on the back of Peter implies that he has a front, a "before" and Peter's face, etc. are already envisioned in my perception of his back. They are given virtually in the same space. But if I want to recall the face of Peter in an explicit manner, I leave at once the domain of perception, the face of Peter becomes "disengaged" in some way from the body that I see from the back; I see it as an unreality in an unreal space. The same is, of course, true of the temporal determinations.

stants and their contents serve as means to reproduce the posterior instants considered as ends.

There are, however, cases when the time of the object is a pure succession without temporal localization. If I imagine the course of a centaur or of a naval battle, these objects do not belong to any moment of duration. They belong neither to the past, future, nor above all, to the present. There is nothing present but the *real me* while I imagine them. They are without any attachments, without temporal relationships to any other object or my own duration. They are characterized only by a subjective duration, by the pure before-after relation, which is limited to marking the relationship of the different states of the action.

Thus the time of unreal objects is itself unreal. It has no characteristics whatever of perceptual time: it does not run off (as does the duration of this piece of sugar which is melting), it can expand or contract at will while remaining the same, it is not irreversible. It is a shadow of time, like the shadow of the object, with its shadow of space. Nothing separates the unreal object from me more surely: the world of imagery is completely isolated, I can enter it only by unrealizing myself in it.

When we speak *of the world* of unreal objects, we use an inexact expression for the sake of greater convenience. A world is a unit in which each object has its fixed place and bears certain relationships to the other objects. The very idea of a world implies the following twofold condition for its objects: they must be rigorously individualized, and they must be in equilibrium with a milieu. It is for this reason that there is no unreal world since no unreal object can meet this twofold condition.

At first objects are not individualized. There is both too much and not enough in them. At the very beginning too much; these phantom-objects are fleeting and ambiguous; at once themselves and something other than themselves, they become the supports of contradictory qualities. Often, to carry the reflective analysis to the end, we discover that there are several in one. This essential ambiguity of the unreal object appears to us to be one of the main factors of the fear of imagination. A clear and distinct perception is, from a certain point of view eminently reassuring. No doubt the sudden appearance of a tiger is frightening: but this is another fear. If we experience fear in the night when alone, it is because the imaginary objects that haunt us are suspicious by nature. And this *suspicious* character is the reason why an imaginary object is never fully itself. Anything of which we are afraid in this way is *impossible* in the degree to which objects escape the principle of individuation. We deliberately declare that this ambiguity constitutes the only depth of the object as an image. It represents in itself a semblance of opacity.

Furthermore, there is not enough in an unreal object for it to constitute a definite individuality. None of its qualities are pushed to the limit. It is this we called in the second part of the book an *essential poverty*. When I perceive Peter I can always approach him close enough to see the grain of his skin, to observe his enlarged pores, and even the theoretical possibility of my examining his microscopic cells and so on to infinity. This infinity is implicitly contained in my actual perception, it overflows it infinitely by everything I can specify about him at each moment. It is this which constitutes the "massiveness" of real objects, but the nature of Peter as an image is to be thinned. This object that I pretend to produce in its totality and as an absolute is reduced basically to a few meager relationships, several spatial and temporal determinations, which, no doubt, have a sensible aspect but which are *stopped*, which contain nothing more than what I posited explicitly—aside from that vague ambiguity of which I just spoke. No doubt I can still assert that if I so desired I could approach this unreal object and see it microscopically enlarged (in an unreal way). But I also know that the new qualities which will appear to me are not *in* the object in its implicit state. They are added to it synthetically and a particular intention of my consciousness would be needed to affirm that the new object before me is also the old view under a new aspect. Thus I can stop the existence of the unreal object at any moment, I am not dragged along despite myself to the specification of its qualities: it exists only while I know it and want it.

It is for this reason that the voluntary modifications I might bring to the object can only produce two kinds of effects: either they bring no other changes than themselves to the objects—or they drag into it radical changes affecting its identity. For instance if I give Peter as an image a flat or turned-up nose it will not give his face a new aspect. Or supposing I attempt to represent my friend with a broken nose. It may happen that I fail to do so and in order to complete the form thus produced I evoke the face of a boxer which is no longer at all that of Peter: as it happens in dreams when the least change in the facial features causes a change of personality. In both cases I missed what I was grasping, that is, the veritable transformation of Peter's face, a transformation in which something remains and something disappears, and when what remains takes on a new value, a new aspect, while also retaining its identity. Unreal changes are inefficient or radical: what may be called the all or nothing law. There is a threshold below which the changes are inefficient for the whole form, above which they drag in the constitution of a new form, having no relationship to the preceding. But the threshold itself, the state of equilibrium cannot be reached.[1]

Nevertheless it is often said: "Yes, I imagine vividly that he wore a high hat on his head, etc." So Goethe pretended to be able to produce a flower as a bud, make it grow, blossom, open, close, flower, etc. But it seems to us that these claims

[1] It is for this reason that the spelling of a word cannot be decided without writing it. It is impossible for me to feel before the unreal object the change of physiognomy that the addition of one or several letters will bring.

that contradict our theory are not absolutely sincere. No doubt, a high crown can be made to appear, as well as the figure of Peter. Perhaps they are seen simultaneously, and perhaps one may even succeed in seeing the face of Peter below a high crown. But what one will never see as an image is *the effect* of a *high crown on* the face of Peter: such contemplation actually calls for passivity and ignorance; it demands that at a given moment we should be able to stop *producing* that synthetic form, to *verify* the result. Thus the painter having put a spot of paint on his picture steps back and forgets himself as a painter in order to examine the result as a spectator. This cannot happen in imaginative consciousness. Only, and we shall come back to this, the mind surpasses this impossibility; it makes a sort of spasmodic effort to realize the contact and this effort misses its mark, but it serves at the same time as the indication of the synthesis that it must operate; this appears as a limit, an ideal; the face and hat must be held together in the same act. One is about to get there, one touches the goal, one almost divines the effect to be obtained. But all of a sudden everything collapses leaving the subject enervated but not vanquished; or rather everything changes and a head appears under a high crown only it is not the head of Peter. One nevertheless says of it "I imagine very well the head he would have," because it seems one was very close to the goal, a bit short of it or a bit beyond it with a slight correction of range one would have hit it.

But, it will be said, I can make these unreal objects move. Here we must distinguish between will and spontaneity. The imaginative consciousness is an act which forms itself at one stroke by will or pre-voluntary spontaneity. But it is only pre-voluntary spontaneity that can draw final developments from this consciousness without the disintegration of the original object. I can certainly produce by voluntary *fiat* an unreal object in motion, on condition that the movement appear at the same time as the object: the movement (created at a single stroke by the imaginative apprehension out of kinaesthetic material) constitutes the very stuff of the object; it may be said that what appears to me is not a fist in motion but a movement which is a fist. But I cannot voluntarily animate afterwards an unreal object which is initially motionless. Nevertheless what the will cannot obtain might be produced by the free spontaneity of consciousness. We know as a fact that the real noetic elements of the imaginative consciousness consist of knowledge, movement and affectivity. An imaginative consciousness can appear suddenly: it can of itself freely vary in conserving for a moment its essential structure: for instance it can have a free development from the affective factor, an evolution from knowledge, etc. From this there result variations for the unreal object which is the correlative of this consciousness which will continue in respecting the identity of the object while the essential structure of consciousness will be conserved. But it must be added that, in the condition of normal vigilance, these structures do not delay their disintegration and that imaginary objects do not have a long life. It appears to us that these free transformations of the imaginative object can be identified by what Kant calls in his *Critique of Judgment* the free play of the imagination. But the will soon reclaims its rights: the image is to be developed under all circumstances (excepting sometimes in hypnagogic hallucinations when consciousness is caught. It happened to me that, irritated by the sight of an illuminated wheel which was turning clockwise, I wanted to make it turn inversely but without success. Naturally this curious phenomenon is not to be understood as the object resisting consciousness but as consciousness resisting itself—as when we are led to produce the obsessing representation just because we do not wish to do so).

Thus I can produce at will—or almost at will—the unreal object I want but I cannot make of it what I want. If I want to transform it I must actually create other objects; and between them there will necessarily be gaps. The object as an image thus acquires a discontinuous, jerky character: it appears, disappears, comes back and thus is no longer the same; it is motionless and it is useless to attempt to give it a movement: I only succeed in producing a movement without motion which I attribute to it in vain. Then all of a sudden it reappears in motion. But all these changes do not come from it: just as the movements of that beautiful violet blot which remains in my eyes while I looked at the electric lamp do not come from the lamp but from the spontaneous as well as the voluntary movements of my eyeballs. So in the unreal object there is but a single power and it is negative. It is a force of passive resistance. The object is not individualized; and here is a primary reason why the unreal does not build itself up in the world. In the second place, every unreal object carrying its own time and space occurs without any solidarity with any other object. There is nothing I must accept at the same time along with it and by means of it: it has no environment, it is independent, isolated—through lack and not through excess; it acts on nothing and nothing acts on it: it is *without consequence* in the full sense of the term. If I want to recall an image, a scene which is somewhat long, I must do so by putting together a number of isolated objects that occurred by fits and starts and by establishing between them some "intramundane" ties with a stroke of empty intentions and decrees.

Consciousness is thus constantly surrounded by a retinue of phantom objects. These objects, although at first sight possessing a sensible aspect, are not the same as those of perception. Of course, they can be plants or animals, but these consist of qualities, of species, of relations. Soon as we try to observe one of them we find ourselves confronted with strange creatures beyond the laws of the world of realities. They always occur as indivisible wholes, as absolutes. At once ambiguous, impoverished and dry, appearing and disappearing in a disjointed manner, they invariably occur as a perpetual "elsewhere," as a perpetual evasion. But the evasion to which they invite is not only of the sort which is an escape from actuality, from our preoccupations, our boredoms, they offer us an escape from all worldly constraints, they seem to present themselves as a negation of the condition of being in the world [1] as an anti-world.

2. The Unreal and Behavior

It has often been said that "images aroused by a central associative mechanism of sensory excitations can have the same effect as does a direct stimulation. It has already been mentioned that the idea of darkness involves a dilation of the pupils of the eye, the image of a close object involves reflexes of accommodation with convergence and contraction of the pupil, the thought of a disgusting object causes vomiting and the hope of a tasty dish produces salivation if one is hungry." [2]

In accordance with the above text—and a host of others of like nature—the image, that is, the unreal object, should serve as a stimulus for action, just as a perception does. This view implies necessarily that the image is a detached bit, a piece of the real world. Only a revived sensation, no doubt a weaker one, than that of a perception but of the same nature, could stimulate such an actual and perceptible movement as that of the dilation of the pupils. We, who have drawn a distinction from the very outset, between the real imaginative consciousness and the unreal object, cannot possibly admit a causal

---

[1] This is how we translate the "in-der-Welt-sein" of Heidegger. We shall see in the conclusion that this is but an appearance and that every image is really built upon "a realistic foundation."

[2] Pieron in the "Nouveau Traité" of Dumas, T. H., p. 38. We should mention that we have conducted numerous experiments without being able to confirm this alleged pupillary dilation in our subjects. We even raise the question whether this may not be one of the psychological legends which are unfortunately to be found in some of the most serious works. But since we may be charged with faulty experimentation we draw no conclusions other than that the fact itself implies no contradiction. Besides, there are undeniable facts of the same sort which call for the same explanation: for instance, the erection of the penis on the occasion of a sensual image.

relation going from the object to consciousness. The unreal cannot be seen, touched, smelled, otherwise than in an unreal way. Conversely, it can act only on an unreal being. It is, however, undeniable that the different reflexes mentioned do occur when images arise. But every image rests on a layer of real existences, and it is this we have called the imaginative consciousness. It is here, then, that the real origin of these real movements must be sought.

We must distinguish between two sorts of layers in a complete imaginative attitude: the primary or constituent layer, and the secondary layer, the one that is commonly called the reaction to the image. On the ground of perception we draw a parallel distinction between the perceptual act as such and the affective or idea-motor reactions that join it in the unity of a single synthesis. Thus far we have spoken only of the primary or component layer, that is, of the real elements which correspond in consciousness exactly to the unreal object. But we must also remember that we can react in the second degree, love, hate, admire, etc., etc., the unreal object we have just built up, and although these feelings naturally occur with the analogue properly so called, in the unity of the same consciousness, they represent, nevertheless, different articulations with the logical and existential priority having to be granted to the constituent elements. There are thus intentions, movements, a knowledge, sentiments that combine to form the image, and intentions, movements, sentiments, knowledges which represent our reaction, more or less spontaneous, to the unreal. The former are not *free*: they obey a directing form, a first intention, and are absorbed into the constitution of the unreal object. They are not aimed at for their own sake, do not at all exist for themselves, but through them consciousness aims at the object as an image. The other factors of the psychic synthesis are more independent, they exist for themselves and develop freely. They are easily recognized, classified and named: they do not confer any new qualities on the object. Consequently, when we speak of feelings and movements that are supposed to be "reactions to the unreal object" we must distinguish between these two layers of consciousness.

Vomiting, nausea, pupillary dilation, reflexes of ocular convergence, erection, appear to us to belong, with their corresponding feelings, to the strictly constituent layer. Nothing is more clear than this once it is admitted, as we hold, that the image is not a simple content of consciousness among others, but that it is a *mental form*. From this it follows that the entire body participates in the make-up of the image. No doubt some movements are more particularly called upon to "configurate the object"; but into the immediate constitution of that object, there enters a part of spontaneous pantomime. It is not because the unreal object appears close to me that my eyes are going to converge, but it is the convergence of my eyes that mimics the proximity of the object. Just as a feeling is quite something else than a simple physiological disorder so there are no feelings without a harmony of bodily phenomena. The very feeling of disgust, which is absorbed in constituting in the object the quality of "disgusting," which is completely objectified and becomes aware of itself only as an unreal property, this very feeling is produced by the intentional animation of certain organic phenomena. No doubt, for most persons the affective element that constitutes the analogue is reduced to a simple emotional abstraction. In such a case the affective factor is completely exhausted in the constituent act. We become aware only of this special nuance of the object, the quality of "repugnant"; and nothing we might add to it later can confer on the object any new quality, it belongs to the secondary layer. It is because of this that certain persons exclaim "this is frightful" or "what horror" on hearing an account of an accident or at a recital of misery, and imitate the horror by means of several schematic gestures. It is evident that they have been somewhat touched and that the characteristic of "frightful" or "horrible" of the scene has been conferred on the images that they formed from the material of a simple affective scheme. But it can also happen that imaginative feelings are violent and develop with force. In that case they are not consumed in constituting the object, they envelop it, dominate it and drag it along. Nausea and vomiting, for instance, are not the effect of the trait "repugnant" of the unreal object, but the consequences of the free development of the imaginative feeling which over-reaches in some way its function and, if I may say so, which "is over-zealous." This happens particularly when the affective ground where the constituent consciousness feeds is already prepared. Pieron recognizes this implicitly when he says, in the text we have cited, that images of a palatable dish cause salivation "when one is hungry." Likewise one must be disturbed or about to be if voluptuous images are to cause an erection. In a general way it is not the unreal object that calls forth these manifestations; but the constituent forces that are prolonged and expanded well beyond their function.

The outcome of these manifestations is variable. They may become incorporated, like the feeling or pantomime out of which they flow, into the very constitution of the object. Such is the case, for instance, of slight nausea. But if they exceed normal intensity these reactions will attract attention and proclaim themselves in their own right. Vomiting, for instance, could not be founded solely in the general imaginative attitude and passes away unperceived. But it is to be noted that at the moment when these reactions become the real object of our consciousness, the unreal object of the preceding consciousness will have become a memory. States of consciousness therefore follow each other in the following order: consciousness of a repugnant unreal object; consciousness of real vomiting occurring jointly with the mnemic consciousness of the repugnant object. This means naturally that the unreal object happens in the consciousness of vomitings as the real cause of the real vomitings. By this very fact it loses its unreality and we fall into the illusion of immanence: memory thus confers upon it a quality which actual consciousness could not have given it, namely, as the *real cause* of the organic phenomena. So, as we have already seen, if immediate consciousness can distinguish by nature the object as image from the object that is present, memory confuses these two types of existence because real and unreal objects appear before it as memories, that is, as the past. It has seemed to me that these differences in the strength of the constituent feelings account for what is called differences in the liveliness of imagination. It is not true that unreal objects have more or less power or vivacity depending on the individual. An unreal object cannot be strong since it does not act. But to produce an image of greater or lesser liveliness is to react with greater or lesser liveliness to the producing act, and by the same token to attribute to the imagined object the power of giving birth to these reactions.

Nevertheless we must not believe that the unreal object, which is a final term, an effect which is never itself a cause, is a pure and simple epiphenomenon, and that the development of consciousness is exactly the same whether that object does or does not exist. Certainly the unreal always receives and never gives. There is no way to give it the urgency, the exigencies, the difficulty of a real object. Nevertheless we must not fail to recognize the following fact: before producing an image of a roasted chicken I must be hungry and yet I do not salivate; before I produce an image of a voluptuous scene, I am perhaps disturbed; after a long period of continence my body may have a diffuse sexual desire, but I have no erection. It cannot be therefore denied that my hunger, my sexual desire, my disgust undergo an important modification in passing through the imaginative state. They have been concentrated, become precise, and their intensity has increased. This calls for a phenomenological description: how does the passage through the imaginative stage modify the desire in this way?

Desire, disgust are at first diffuse, without precise intentionality. In organizing itself with a knowledge into an imaginative form, desire becomes precise and concentrated. Enlightened by the knowledge, it projects its object outside itself. By this we must understand, however, that it becomes conscious of itself. The act by which feeling becomes conscious of its exact nature is limited and defined, the act is one with that by which it presents itself with a transcendental object. And this is readily understandable: desire is actually defined by its effect, and so is repulsion, or scorn, etc. It is impossible to think without contradiction that the image could link itself to desire from the outside; this would involve the supposition that desire is a sort of anonymity by nature, a perfect indifference to the object on which it will fix itself.

Whereas, the affective state, *being consciousness*, could not exist without a transcendent correlative. Nevertheless, when feeling is directed on a real thing, actually perceived, the thing sends back to it, in the manner of a screen, the light it has received from it. And, by a game of going and coming the feeling itself is enriched constantly as the object imbibes affective qualities.[1] The feeling thus obtains a unique depth and richness. The affective state follows the course of attention, it develops with each new discovery of perception, it assimilates all the aspects of the object; as a result its development is unpredictable since it is subordinated to the development of its real correlative even while remaining spontaneous: at each instant perception overflows it and sustains it and its massiveness, its depth comes from its being confused with the perceived object: each affective quality is so deeply incorporated in the object that it is impossible to distinguish between what is felt and what is perceived.

At the time of the constitution of the unreal object, the knowledge plays the role of perception: it is to it that the

[1] Such as "gracious, disturbing, sympathetic, light, heavy, fine, troublesome, horrible, repugnant," etc.

feeling is incorporated. Thus is born the unreal object. It is at this point that we should repeat what we constantly maintained: the unreal object exists, it exists as unreal, as inactive; of this there is no doubt; but its existence is undeniable. Feeling then behaves in the face of the unreal as in that of the real. It seeks to blend with it, to adapt itself to its contours, to feed on it. Only this unreal, so well specified and so well defined, pertains *to the void*; or, if one prefers, it is the simple reflection of the feeling. This feeling therefore feeds on its own reflection. That is why it knows itself at present as disgust with that dish, which it will develop into nausea. It is possible to speak here of a sort of affective dialectic. But naturally the role of the object differs completely from what it was in the world of perception. There my repugnance, guiding my disgust, forced me to discover in the real dish a thousand repugnant details which ended in vomiting. But in the case of imaginative disgust, the object is indispensable but as a witness. It is posited beyond the affective developments as the unity of these developments but, without it, the reaction of disgust could not be produced of itself. If the disgust swells beyond all measure and reaches the point of vomiting this happens because it is confronted by the unreal object; it reacts to itself as disgust *of* that object. As to the *real* scope of this development, it is a sort of dizziness: it is because it knows itself as *such* a disgust that, without receiving the same enrichment, the disgust swells without effect. In this repugnance before the unreal there is therefore something *sui generis*. It is not reducible to a repugnance before a perception. At first there is in it a sort of liberty, or, if one prefers, of autonomy: it is determined by itself. But this is not all: it participates in some way in the emptiness of the object to which it addresses itself. It can swell to the point of nausea, and there is nothing to prevent its swelling by itself. It is lacking that part of passivity which makes for the richness of the feelings that constitute the real. It sustains itself by a sort of continued autocreation, by a sort of tension without repose: it cannot let itself go without disappearing with its object, it exhausts itself in affirming itself and at the same time in swelling up, in reaching itself. Hence, a considerable nervous expenditure. Every person can confirm by his own experience that it is exhausting to maintain before him the repugnant or graceful features of an unreal object. But, it will be said, we do vomit. Yes, no doubt, but in the degree to which we undergo our irritations, our obsessing ideas, or the obsessing tunes that we hum. This is a spontaneity we cannot control. But from the beginning to the end of the development nothing positive on the part of the object can compensate for that quality of nothingness that characterizes the whole process; we were stirred, carried away, we vomited *because of nothing*.

Let us take a real object, as, for instance, this book. It is completely imbued with our affectivity and as such it appears to us with this or that affective quality. These qualities enter into the constitution of the perceived object, and, as such, cannot detach themselves and appear separately to the reflective eye. We have just examined the corresponding layer in the imaginative consciousness. But, before this book I do not remain inactive, I act in this or that manner: I pick it up or put it down, I do not like its binding, I pronounce judgments of fact or of value. These various reactions do not aim to constitute the object but rather to indicate our orientation in relation to it. No doubt these reactions appear to the nonreflective consciousness as qualities of that object. But these qualities occur directly as relations to us: it is the book *I like*, that I placed on the table, that I should read tonight. They are but posited on the object and are easily detached to occur by themselves and for themselves, as judgments, feelings, volitions, to the reflective eye. It is only here that we can speak of behavior in the strict sense of the term, since the behavior is separable and can appear as such to reflective consciousness.

Similar behavior naturally occurs before the unreal. It is

expedient to distinguish this behavior carefully from the simple development of the imaginative feeling. The difference is readily understood if we envisage the following two cases: in one, for instance, some thought arouses my love for Annie or my indignation against Peter. This love or indignation attaches itself synthetically to a knowledge, passes through the imaginative stage, and causes the birth of the unreal face of Annie or the gesture that made Peter hateful. In that case the image occurs as the meaning, the theme, the pole of unification of the spontaneous affective development. No doubt these are infected with an essential "emptiness," no doubt they are quickly exhausted or change in nature because they cannot feed on a real object. But all the processes are free, non-reflective, automatic in the sense we have given that term above. In a word, it is my love for Annie that causes her unreal face to appear to me, and not the unreal face of Annie that excites a glow of love for her. Likewise, if Peter displayed an offensive gesture yesterday that bewildered me, what is reborn first is the indignation or hatred. These feelings grope blindly for a moment in order to understand themselves and then, illuminated by meeting with a knowledge cause the offending gesture to emerge.

But a second case may arise: once the image is constituted I can react to it deliberately with a new feeling, a new judgment which is not carried away with the unreal object in the unity of the same constitutive movement, but which posits itself clearly as a *reaction*, that is, a beginning, the appearance of a new synthetic form. For instance I can produce an image which is in itself not strongly charged with feeling and yet be indignant or rejoice before that unreal object. Yesterday, for instance, a graceful gesture of Annie's aroused in me a gust of tenderness. No doubt this tenderness could, on revival, cause the unreal rebirth of the affective gesture. In this way I could no doubt revive *both* the gesture and the tenderness in an unreal manner both of which would retain their date and their "absenteeism." [1] But it may also happen that I reproduce the gesture in order to *revive* the tenderness. In that case what I aim at is not yesterday's tenderness, nor Annie's gesture as such; what I want is to re-experience a real present tenderness, but analogous to that of yesterday. What I want is to be able to "recover," as we commonly say, my feelings of yesterday. It is that new situation that we want to envisage.

When we reproduce the charming gesture that moved us yesterday it appears to us that the revived situation is exactly the old one: that gesture that made such a strong impression on us when it occurred, why does it not do it again now that it is here as an image? However, the process is radically different. In the first case, that is yesterday, it was the real gesture that aroused my tenderness. It appeared to me as an entirely unexpected although a natural phenomenon. At the same time this upsurge occurred, now under the form of a quality of the object, now under its subjective aspect, and probably it appeared first under its objective aspect. But today that tenderness appears at first as an end, although in a more or less clear manner; the reflective knowledge thus precedes the feeling itself and the feeling is aimed at under its reflective form. Besides the object is reproduced for no other purpose than to arouse the feeling. That is, we already know in con-

---

[1] We have long opposed the existence of an affective memory. But our reflections on imagination caused us to change our opinion. It is not true that on recalling yesterday's shame there is nothing in my consciousness but a present cognition of an abstract emotional present (or a complete feeling) but the abstract emotional serves as material for a special intentionality that aims through it at the feeling I had yesterday. In other words, the real feeling does not necessarily occur for itself: it can serve as "hylé"—on condition that it is not very strong. In this case we are confronted with an imaginative consciousness whose correlative will be yesterday's feeling present as an unreality. We therefore admit the existence of an affective memory and an affective imaginaton. For it is by a similar process that we attempt to realize the feelings of a stranger, or of a madman, or a criminal, etc. It is not exact that we limit ourselves to producing in ourselves a real emotional abstraction. Our desire is to evoke the feelings of the madman, the criminal, etc., in an unreal state in so far as these belong to him.

nection with that affective state and we evoke the object because it possesses as one of its qualities the power of giving
birth to this upsurge of tenderness. We are here naturally confronted with a determination which is still abstract, it is a
potentiality in the object. But it follows that the object reproduced is already not entirely the same as the one we want
to reproduce. In fact, the gesture of yesterday aroused my
tenderness while it was occurring, that is after a certain duration and precisely when that tenderness appeared. But the
power of the unreal object appears with it, as one of its absolute qualities. In brief, the ultimate developments of my affective state are foreseen, and the entire evolution of that state
depends upon my prevision. This does not mean that it always
obeys it, but when it does not obey it, it is aware of its dis-
obedience.

But we also know that the unreal object cannot perform
the function of a cause; in other words, that tenderness I want
to revive cannot be produced by the unreal object. When the
unreal object is reconstructed it is I who must determine to
be tender before it. In brief, I shall affirm that the unreal
object is acting upon me, while being immediately conscious
that there is no real action, nor could there be, and that I
shrivel up to mimic that action. A feeling I shall call tenderness in which I shall be able to recognize yesterday's glow
might appear. But this is no longer an "affection" in the sense
that the object no longer affects me. My feeling, still here, is
wholly activity, wholly tension; it is feigned rather than felt.
I proclaim that I feel tender, I know I should be, I realize
tenderness in me. But this tenderness does not rebound on the
unreal object; it has not fed on the inexhaustible depths of the
real: it remains cut off from the object, suspended; it occurs
to reflection as an effort to rejoin that unreal gesture which
remains beyond its reach and which it does not attain. What
we seek in vain to enact here is the receptivity, the *passion* in
the sense given that term in the seventeenth century. One could

speak of a dance before the unreal, in the manner that a corps de ballet dances around a statue. The dancers open their arms, offer their hands, smile, offer themselves completely, approach and take flight; but the statue is not affected by it: there is no real relationship between it and the corps de ballet. Likewise, our conduct before the object cannot really touch it, qualify it any more than it can touch us in return; because it is in the heaven of the unreal, beyond all reach.

Our tenderness is thus lacking in sincerity, and above all in spontaneity, docility, richness. The object does not sustain it, nourish it, does not communicate to it that power, that flexibility, that unexpectedness which makes for the depth of a feeling-passion. Between the feeling-passion and the feeling-action there is always the difference which can be found between the real anguish of one suffering from cancer and the pain of a psychaesthenic who believes himself to be suffering from cancer. We could, of course, find, in the case of algia (imagined pain) an individual who is completely disorganized, who has lost all control, maddened by fear, enervated and despondent. Not one of these symptoms—nor his starts, his outcries when he is touched on the limb he believes to be ailing—is feigned in the absolute sense of the word; that is, there is no question here of either a "ludisme" or of mythomania. It is true enough that the victim cannot keep himself from screaming, and that perhaps even less so than if his suffering were real. But nothing—whether his starts or his rattlings in the throat—can constitute real pain. The anguish is there, no doubt, but it confronts him as an image, inactive, passive, unreal: he struggles *before it* against his will, but none of his cries, of his gestures is aroused by it. And he *knows it* at the same time; he knows he is not suffering; and all his energy—in contrast with that of the cancerous person, who tries to reduce the effects of his suffering—is used to suffer more. He cries out in order to bring on anguish, he gesticulates in order to bring it into his body. But in vain: nothing will fill in that annoying impression of emptiness which constitutes the very reason and basic nature of his outburst.

From all the preceding we could conclude that there is a natural difference between the feelings before the real and the feelings before the imaginary. For instance, love varies completely in accordance with whether its object is present or absent.

When Annie is gone my feelings for her change in nature. No doubt I continue to call them love, and I no doubt deny the change, pretending that I love her when absent just as much and in the same way as when she is present. But that is not so. Naturally, the knowledge and general behavior remain intact. I know that Annie possesses this and that quality, I continue to show her signs of my confidence, for instance by writing her everything that happens to me; if need be, I would defend her interests as if she were present. Besides, we must recognize the existence of authentic feeling-passions: sadness, melancholy, even despair caused us by such absence. The reason is that it is more the real and present emptiness of our life which evokes them than the unreal and absent Annie; it is the fact, for example, that such gestures, such attitudes, which we have hardly delineated recur without a goal, and leave us with the impression of unbearable uselessness. But all this represents, in some way, the negative of love. It is certain that the positive element remains (the glow towards Annie) deeply modified. My love-passion was subordinated to its object, it is as such that I am constantly informed of it, constantly does it surprise me, I must remake it at each instant, readjust myself to it: it lived by the very life of Annie. As long as it could be believed that the image of Annie was none other than Annie reborn, it could appear evident that this Annie would arouse almost the same reactions in me as the true Annie. But now we know that Annie as an image cannot be compared with the Annie of perception. She has undergone the change of unreality and our feeling has undergone a corresponding change. At first it *stopped*: it no longer "happens," it can barely remain in the forms it has already assumed: it has become somewhat scholastic, it can be given a name, its manifestations can be classified: they no longer overflow their definitions, they are exactly limited by the knowledge we have of them. At the same time the feeling is *debased* since its richness, its inexhaustible depth comes from the object: there is always more to love in the object than I actually love, and I know it, so that love as it occurred before the real was under the thematic unity of an idea, in the Kantian sense: the idea that Annie as a real individual is inexhaustible and that, correlatively, my love for her is inexhaustible. Thus the feeling that surpasses itself at each instant was surrounded by a vast halo of possibilities. But these possibilities have disappeared just as did the real object. By an essential reversal, it is now the feeling that produces its object and the unreal Annie is no more than the strict correlative of my feelings for her. It follows that the feeling *is never more than what it is*. It now has a basic poverty. Finally, it has passed from the passive to the active stage: it plays with itself, it mimics itself: it is wanted, it is believed. It occurs at each moment as a great effort to reproduce the real Annie because it knows well that when it can also restore her body to her it will reincarnate itself. Little by little the feeling will schematize itself and congeal into rigid forms while the images we have of Annie will correspondingly become banal.[1] The normal evolution of knowledge and feeling demands that at the end of a certain time this love lose its own *nuance*: it becomes *of love* in general and becomes somewhat rationalized: it is now that by-word sentiment which psychologists and novelists describe: it has become typical; Annie is no longer there to confer upon it that individuality which made it into an irreducible consciousness. And even if I were to continue to behave myself right now as if I loved Annie, remaining faithful to her, writing

[1] Cf. the book by Philippe: "L'image," very remarkable for the period.

to her daily, thinking of her constantly, longing for her, something is nevertheless lacking, my love is radically impoverished. Barren, scholastic, abstract, directed towards an unreal object which itself has lost its individuality, it evolves slowly towards the empty absolute. It is about such a moment that one writes: "I no longer feel close to you, I have lost your image, I am more than ever separated from you." This is the reason, we believe, why letters are awaited with such impatience: not so much for the news they contain (provided of course we have nothing special to fear or hope) as for their real and concrete nature. The stationary, the black letters, the perfume, etc., all these replace the faltering affective analogue; by means of all these I grasp a more real Annie. We have already seen the imaginative role that signs can play. As the love becomes impoverished and schematized (formulized) it also becomes very weak. In every person we love, and for the very reason of its inexhaustible wealth, there is something that surpasses us, an independence, an imperviousness which exacts ever renewed efforts of approximation: The unreal object has nothing of this imperviousness. It is never more than what we know of it. The first several times we no doubt affirm, as by scruple, this imperviousness, this *strange* nature of the loved person. But we feel nothing of the sort. It is a matter of pure knowledge which is soon attenuated and remains in suspense, because it has no affective material to which to attach itself. So that the unreal object, as it becomes commonplace, will conform more to our desires than would Annie herself. The return of Annie will shatter this entire formal structure. After a period of readjustment which may take a longer or shorter time the impoverished feeling will be replaced by the real feeling. For a moment we may miss the complaisance and simplicity of Annie as an image. But this is because we will have lost the memory of the affective impoverishment which was its indispensable correlative.

Thus we can distinguish two irreducible classes of feelings from the very fact of the extraordinary difference that separates the object as an image from the real object: real feelings and *imaginary* feelings. By this latter adjective we do not mean that the feelings themselves are unreal, but that they appear only before unreal objects and that the appearance of the real object is enough to put them to flight at once, just as the sun dispels the darkness of the night. These feelings whose essence it is to be *debased*, poor, irregular, spasmodic, schematic, need non-being in order to exist. They attack the enemy continuously in thought, make it suffer morally and physically, but are actually helpless in its real presence. What has happened? Nothing, except that the enemy now really exists. A while ago, the feeling alone gave the meaning of the image. The unreal was there only to permit the hatred to objectify itself. Now the present overflows the feelings completely and the hatred remains in suspense, foiled. This is not what it hated; it is not adapted to that man of flesh and bone, very alive, new, unpredictable. What it hates is but a phantom tailored exactly to its measure and what was exactly its replica, its sense. It does not recognize this new creature that opposes it. Proust has well shown this abyss that separates the imaginary from the real, he has clearly indicated that there is no passage from the one to the other, and that the real is always accompanied by the ruin of the imaginary, even if there be no contradiction between them, for the incompatibility comes from their nature and not their content. It must be added that the imaginary actions I project have no consequences other than those I wish to give them, which is due to the essential poverty of images. If I strike my enemy in image the blood will not flow or it will flow only as much as I wish. But before the real enemy, before that real flesh I anticipate that real blood will flow which is enough to deter me. There is therefore a continuous hiatus between the preparation of an action and the action itself. Even if the real situation is almost the one I had imagined, there is something in which it differs in nature from my imaginings. I am not surprised by the event but by the change of the universe. At the same time, the springs of the projected action disappear or change signs because they are only imaginary. If I nevertheless perform the projected action, I do so most of the time because I am caught short and have no other at my disposal. Or it may be through some sort of obstinacy which shuts its eyes and will not notice the change that occurred. This is the source of the stiff and abrupt actions of people who "say what they have to say" without paying attention to their interlocutor, in order not to abandon completely the realm of the imaginary before they have become too involved to be able to retreat. Thus we can recognize two distinct selves in us: the imaginary self with its tendencies and desires—and the real self. There are imaginary sadists and masochists, persons of violent imagination. At each moment our imaginary self breaks in pieces and disappears at contact with reality, yielding its place to the real self. For the real and the imaginary cannot Co-exist by their very nature. It is a matter of two types of objects, of feelings and actions that are completely irreducible.

Hence, we may think that individuals will have to be classified in two large categories, according to whether they prefer to lead an imaginary life or a real life. But we must understand what a preference for the imaginary signifies. It is not at all a matter of preferring one sort of object to another. For instance, we should not believe that the schizophrenic and morbid dreamers in general try to substitute an unreal and more seductive and brighter content for the real content of their life, and that they seek to forget the unreal character of their images by reacting to them as if they were actual objects actually present. To prefer the imaginary is not only to prefer a richness, a beauty, an imaginary luxury to the existing mediocrity *in spite of* their unreal nature. It is also to adopt "imaginary" feelings and actions for the sake of their imaginary nature. It is not only this or that image that is chosen, but the imaginary state with everything it implies; it is not only an escape from the content of the real (poverty, frustrated love, failure of one's enterprise, etc.), but from the form of the real itself, its character *of presence*, the sort of response it demands of us, the adaptation of our actions to the object, the inexhaustibility of perception, their independence, the very way our feelings have of developing themselves. This unnatural, congealed, abated, formalized life, which is for most of us but a make-shift, is exactly what a schizophrenic desires. The morbid dreamer who imagines he is a king will not put up with a real throne, not even with a tyranny, or all his wishes would be granted. A desire is in fact never satisfied to the letter precisely because of the abyss that separates the real from the imaginary. The object I desire might be given me, but it is on another level of existence to which I must adapt myself. Here it is now confronting me: if I am not pressed by the action I must hesitate for a long time, surprised, not able to recognize this reality so full and rich in consequences: I must ask myself: "It is really *this* I wanted?" The morbid dreamer will not hesitate: it is not this he wants. At first the present calls for an adaptation which he can no longer supply; it calls for a sort of indetermination of our feelings, a real plasticity: because the real is always new, always unforeseeable.[1] I would want Annie to arrive: but Annie whom I desired is only the correlative of my desire. Here she is, but she overflows my desire in every respect, an entirely new apprenticeship is needed. But the feelings of the morbid dreamer are solemn and congealed; they always return with the same form and the same label; the sick person has had all the time

---

[1] It is not so much because one predicts the future by means of the past, as we usually say: this argument is valid only when presented against the old conception of images. But rather because the real is foreseen by means of the unreal, that is, the one whose riches are infinite by means of schemes of an essential poverty.

to construct them; nothing in them is left to chance, they will not stand for the least deviation. Correlatively the traits of unreal objects that correspond to them are stopped forever. Thus the dreamer is able to choose from the storeroom of accessories the feelings he wishes to put on and the objects that fit them, just as the actor chooses his costume. Today it is ambition, tomorrow sexual love. It is only the "essential poverty" of objects as images that can satisfy the feeling submissively, without ever surprising it, deceiving it or guiding it. It is only unreal objects that can come to nothing when the caprice of the dreamer stops, since they are but his reflection; it is only they whose consequences are no other than what is desired of them. It is therefore a mistake to look upon the world of the schizophrenic as a torrent of images possessing a richness and a glitter which compensates for the monotony of the real: it is a poor and meticulous world, in which the same scenes keep on recurring to the last detail, accompanied by the same ceremonial where everything is regulated in advance, foreseen; where, above all, nothing can escape, resist or surprise.[1] In brief, if the schizophrenic imagines so many amorous scenes it is not only because his real love has been disappointed, but, above all, because he is no longer capable of loving.

[1] For this essential poverty of reveries see: *Moments d'une Psychanalyse*, by Dr. Blanche Reverchon-Jouve and Pierre-Jean Jouve, in the N.R.F., March, 1933.

"It was at the beginning of the war (1915) and at the age of eleven that Mlle. H . . . became more and more attached to a unique dream which became gradually systematized, had grouped a certain variety of elements while becoming more set and fixed; a dream whose interest she upheld by all sorts of researches in dictionaries and magazines as soon as her fantasy failed her.

". . . Her life was so fatally motivated by the dream that the hour she did not spend in bed dreaming she went to the library looking for new elements with which to enrich, to enlarge the web of the dream." (p. 356.)

The case of Mlle. H . . . is otherwise very interesting, and it is only to be regretted that the psychoanalysis overwhelmed it with massive, pretentious and absurd interpretations.

3. Pathology of the Imagination

The schizophrenic is well aware that the objects with which he surrounds himself are unreal: and it is for this very reason that he calls them forth. The observations of Marie B.[1] are significant in this connection:

"I recall the crisis I went through once: I said that I was the queen of Spain. At heart I knew well that this was untrue. I was like a child that plays with its doll and who is well aware that its doll is not alive but who wants to believe it. . . . Everything seemed to me to be enchanted. . . . I was like a comedian who played a role and who identified himself with his character. I was conquered . . . but not entirely. I lived in an imaginary world." [2]

Here we meet no difficulty. But it is an entirely different matter when we consider nocturnal dreams, hallucinations and pariedolies: it can even be said that in substituting a new theory for the old one concerning the image, we fall into the inverse difficulty. Having assimilated the image to the sensation Taine found no difficulty in explaining hallucination: in fact, perception is already "a true hallucination." He encounters no difficulty until he is called upon to explain how, among all these hallucinations, some true and others false, we distinguish immediately between images and perceptions. Conversely, we, who started out with the fact that these subjects recognize immediately that their images are images, do we not take the risk of finding our stumbling block in the problem of hallucination? Are we not dealing here in fact with an image which is no longer recognized as an image? But let us first define the problem.

[1] Borel and Robin. *Les Rêveries morbides.* Annales médico-psychol., March, 1924.

[2] Nor was Mlle. H., whom we cited above, deceived about the reality of her images; "Mlle. H. always knew that the story was fictitious, but also thought that it contained the truth in what concerned her." *Ibid.,* pp. 362–368.

If it is true that the hallucinated person "mistakes an image for a perception" what do the words "mistake for a perception" mean? Do they mean, as some psychologists hold, that the hallucinated person confers externality to his image, "projects" his image into the world of perception? This would be simply absurd. As we have already seen, the image is in fact a vague term which means at once a consciousness and its transcendent correlative. What then could the hallucinated person externalize? Certainly not consciousness: it is not in fact possible that what is consciousness should occur as something else than consciousness. The Cartesian Cogito retains its rights even with psychopaths. But neither could the object of the imaginative consciousness be externalized, for the reason that it is already such by nature. If I form the imaginative consciousness *of* Peter, Peter brings along with him his unreal space and places himself before consciousness, he is external to consciousness (Cf. above). The problem is therefore entirely different: the object of the image differs from the object of perception: (1) in that it has its own space, whereas there exists an infinite space which is common to all perceived objects; (2) in that it occurs immediately as unreal, whereas the object of perception originally set up, as Husserl says, a claim to reality (Seinsanspruch). That unreality of the imagined object is the correlative of an immediate intuition of spontaneity. Consciousness has a nonthetic consciousness of itself as a creative activity.[1] This consciousness of spontaneity appeared to us as a transversal consciousness, which is one with the consciousness of the object; this is the very structure of the mental state; and the way we place it renders it independent of the state of health or sickness of the mind of the subject. The following question therefore arises: how do we abandon our consciousness of spontaneity, how do we feel ourselves passive before images which we ourselves form; is it true that we confer *reality*, that is, actual presence upon these objects

[1] Cf. above Part I, Chapter I, Section V.

which occur to a sane consciousness as absent. Finally, since, as we have seen,[1] perception and imaginative consciousness are two alternating attitudes is it possible that we fuse the space of the image with that of the perception in the case of hallucination, as does an hallucinated person who says, for instance: "on this (real) chair I saw the (unreal) devil"?

To the last question we can answer at once: nothing proves in fact that the patient realizes the fusion of the two spaces. In short, we have no other guarantee than her reports which should be taken with caution. As Janet observed, it practically never happens that the patient has hallucinations *in the presence* of the physician (at least visual hallucinations)—which we can interpret as follows: a systematized activity in the realm of the real seems to exclude hallucinations. This is what gives seemingly a certain efficacy to the "tricks" used by the patients to put a stop to hallucinations. The patient who mutters and concentrates his attention on what he is saying can delay the appearance of the voices that threaten or insult him for a few minutes if it is absolutely necessary to do so. Dumas' observation concerning the confused deliriums caused by war shock is perhaps more striking. For instance, the soldier Grivelli seemed at first to have taken into account the large size of the room in which he was to set the stage for his delirium. But when the physician changed the appearance of the room it had no effect on the course of the delirium. On the contrary, if Professor Dumas called out loudly and close to him, "Wipe your nose," the delirium of the patient stopped for an instant and he wiped his nose gently. Everything here seems to point to an alternation of perception and delirium. It will no doubt be objected that oniric confusion is closer to the dream than to hallucination. This we will not deny. But what concerns us here is to disengage certain traits which may well be common to these two pathological forms. Briefly, it

[1] Part 4, Chapter 5.

seems to us that hallucination coincides with a sudden anni-hilation of perceived reality. It does not occur in the real world: it excludes it. It is this point that M. Lagache explains so well in his recent book in connection with this comment on Janet.[1]

"Auditory hallucination does not have the congruence of auditory perception with environmental conditions and espe-cially with the present features of perception; the persecuted person rarely believes that he is hurt by a person who is with him and who is speaking to him in a normal way; it is later that the distinction between the person who "hurts" and the person who is "hurt" becomes delicate; it is also unusual to meet with auditory hallucinations. . . ."

However, it does not seem to us to be necessary to reduce the hallucination, as Janet seemingly tries to do (at least so with auditory hallucination, verbal motor hallucination being something entirely different) to a recital accompanied by the belief which the patient makes of it. There is certainly an hallucinatory act, in our opininion; but this act is a pure event that appears suddenly to the patient while his perception dis-appears. It follows that when the patient narrates his sensory hallucinations he localizes them in perceptual space. At first, however, and as Lagache has shown in connection with verbal hallucinations:

". . . spatialization is not a primary quality of auditory hal-lucination, but depends, on the one hand, on intellectual en-dowments, and on the other, on the motor attitudes. So that distance is infinitely variable and the patient localizes his voices in a far-off town or behind a wall, on the ceiling, under the floor, under the pillow." [2]

These few observations are enough to show the unreal nature of the localization. In short, the spatialization of the

[1] Lagache, *Les hallucinations verbales et la parole*, Alcan, 1934. Cf. also Janet, *L'Hallucination dans le délire de persécution*, Revue de Philo., 1932. *Op. cit.*, 164.

hallucination is very much like the localization of the image. The uttered word could have been spoken in a distant town. Nevertheless it is heard. But is it even heard? No more than Peter as an image is seen. Lagache makes some pertinent observations on this point:

"All verbal hallucinations entertain a receptive attitude towards an ideo-verbal or verbal content felt by the hallucinated to be of strange origin. Now, to have a receptive attitude towards words is to listen. Every verbal hallucination is therefore in a sense heard, and we might even go as far as to say that every verbal hallucination is auditory, if this means only a receptive attitude without assuming sensory, acoustic characters of the heard words." [1]

In other words, the injuring word "appears" to the subject. It is there and the subject submits to it, is in a receptive state towards it. But this receptivity does not imply necessarily a sensory event.

Besides, even in those cases in which the localization is made in relation to real space (in the room of the patient, for instance) it must be said that localization is made after the fact. According to us, the visual or auditory hallucination is accompanied by a provisional state of crumbling of perception. But when the hallucinatory attack is over the world reappears.[2] It therefore seems natural that the patient, in speaking of the scene he has just witnessed, feels it to be a part of the world that surrounds him: "I am *here;* I who just saw the devil" easily becomes "I just saw the devil here."

But what does *being here* mean to the hallucinated person? Is it because he enumerates correctly the furniture of the house that he feels that he saw them as we do? Let us not forget the curious sort of hallucinations which give the impression of

[1] *Op. cit.,* 89.
[2] Dr. T., specialist in diseases of the nervous system, told us of a patient who, following an attack of encephalitis, was able to adjust himself correctly to a social situation (as for instance to a conversation with his physician) but who, when alone, fell into a somnolence accompanied by hallucinations.

being absolute realities but without spatio-temporal traits, namely, mental hallucinations.

Thus, from whatever angle we look at it, the localization of hallucinations appears to us to be a secondary problem, presenting no great difficulties of principle and which is subordinate to the much more general question: *how can the patient believe in the reality of an image which occurs in essence as unreal.*

Merely raising the question shows us that what is involved here is an alteration of belief or, if one prefers, of thesis. But let us not be deceived about it: the constitutive thesis of the image cannot be changed; and it matters little whether the consciousness is or is not "morbid"; it is an essential necessity that the unreal object be constituted as unreal; we have often said that the spontaneity of consciousness is identical with the consciousness of that spontaneity—and consequently the one cannot be destroyed without the other. This is the reason why the excellent accounts given by Lagache of verbal motor hallucination fall short of explaining auditory hallucination (provided there is one of them which is really independent of verbal hallucinations), or visual or mental hallucinations. Here we must fall back on the distinction made by Descartes: it is possible to speak or to breathe without being aware of doing so. But I cannot *think* that I am speaking without *knowing that I think that I am speaking.* Consequently, the recourse of what Lagache calls the introspection (that is, the "orientation" of the subject towards the psychological problem and the part he takes in the solution) to feelings (of influence, of imposition, of hallucination) and to the diminution of vigilance cannot attain the result that the production of the unreal object coincides with the consciousness of its unreality. In the case of the verbal motor hallucination, on the contrary, no other explanation is needed to show speech as movement detaching itself from the subject and as opposing itself to him.

We therefore reach the following first conclusion: in the

hallucination, in the dream, nothing can destroy the unreality of the object as an image as an immediate correlative of the imaginative consciousness. After this first examination it therefore appears that we end up in an impasse and that we must change something in our theory or abandon some one of our claims.

But perhaps hallucination is not characterized by the alteration of the primary structure of the image; perhaps it occurs rather as a radical destruction of the attitude of consciousness in respect to the unreal. Briefly, it may be that what is involved here is a radical alteration of all of consciousness and the change of attitude towards the unreal can only appear as the counterpart of the weakening of the sense of the real. A simple observation will make it clear to us. Lagache observes that "in some cases, no phenomenological event seems to distinguish between the language of the deranged and that of the normal person; the patient knows straight off that it is not he who is speaking, as if he had decided it, without our being able to grasp the concrete means that determine and motivate his decision."

And he cites a patient, Paul L., whose voice "remains the same when others speak to him but (who) *knows* when it is they who speak and when it is he." Naturally we are here dealing with those motor hallucinations which interest us less for more reasons than one. But we can raise the following question concerning these hallucinations: "If Paul L. *knows* at once, without a change of voice and 'as if he had decided it' that it is someone else who is speaking, if he can practice so easily 'the intentional social objectification' of which Janet speaks, is this not so because at the very moment that he seems to us to have normal perception he in fact does not perceive as we do?" [1] What strikes us is what he enacts at the beginning

[1] This follows from the fact that at the time he pretends to be speaking he also pretends to be speaking to X who is absent. This is enough to turn the actual into something strictly abnormal.

of his dialogue, namely, that it is I who am speaking. And since it is true that he is speaking at that moment we are inclined to conclude from it that these mental operations are correctly executed. Then, when he continues to keep on talking and pretends that the spoken words have been uttered by another person we suppose that he is presenting a pathological process. But how can we fail to notice that the voice which he takes for his own is *on the same level* with the one he pretends to hear, which is an essential condition of the *dialogue* he pretends to be conducting. Consequently, if the one is a hallucination to us we must accept the other as being likewise, no matter how paradoxical this may appear to be at first; the patient is as much hallucinated when he assumes that the words he is emitting are his own as when he attributes them to another. In fact, in order that such a phrase should appear to the patient simultaneously as *connected* with the preceding phrase, and as uttered by another than himself, it is necessary that the entire conversation have an hallucinatory character, that in some way he is dreaming that the phrase he is attributing to himself belongs to him, although he does not know it; unless the transition from one speaker to the other occurs so suddenly that the conversation is no longer possible.[1] But what does this mean if not that it is like the famous madman who, according to Stoics "said that it is daytime in broad daylight" and that in fact he perceived nothing in that conversation. All these observations are applicable to visual and auditory hallucinations. No doubt there are moments when the patient, in speaking to the physician, seems to perceive correctly; but at that time he has no hallucinations. When he hallucinates he is alone, he lets himself go: the hallucinatory event as such detaches itself as a positive disturbance on a foundation of

[1] Likewise we must not believe that in the conversation imagined by a schizophrenic his interlocutor is unreal while he himself retains a coefficient of reality: both are unreal and the phrases they utter to each other (so long as these can be effectively muttered) are unreal. Note also further on the role of the Self in the dream.

perceptual apathy in which objects appear as unreal. So that, in our opinion, if the hallucination rejoins the world of perception it does so insofar as the latter is no longer perceived but dreamed by the patient insofar as he himself has become unreal.

We shall perhaps grasp the consequences of the idea more clearly if we compare with the hallucination a phenomenon that seems to us to have a like structure, namely, the obsession.

The contrast between the stereotyped nature of the obsession as compared with the inexhaustible imagery of the hallucination, has no doubt been noticed for a long time. But this is to take the accounts given by patients at their face value. The fact of the matter is that modern psychiatrists are agreed concerning the poverty of the hallucinatory material. Aside from verbal motor hallucinations we find that auditory hallucinations are in the main a play of very banal affronts ("stinker, thief, drunkard"), while visual hallucinations always have the same forms and personages. The hallucination thus presents itself as the intermittent reappearance of certain objects (auditory or visual). It is therefore very much like the obsession which can also be an intermittent apparition of more or less stereotyped scenes. The difference does not lie in that the object of hallucination is externalized. It is very evident, for instance, that the scene of the consecrated wafer, so common among Janet's hallucinated patients,[1] is immediately externalized (that is, projected into an unreal space). This comes out of the very notion of the image. Besides, if one follows the view of many psychologists, hallucination and obsession *impose themselves* on the mind. But it is precisely here that we must make some reservations and seek to determine exactly what is meant by "to impose."

Since the work of Janet, it has been recognized that the obsession is not a strange body that occupies consciousness in spite of itself like a stone in the liver. In fact, the obsession *is a consciousness*; and consequently it has the same traits of spon-

[1] See *La Psychasthénie*, Vol. I.

taneity and autonomy as do all other consciousnesses. In the majority of cases it is an imaginative consciousness which has become a taboo, that is, the psychaesthenic has prohibited its formation. It is precisely because of this that he does form it. Basically the content of the obsession is of little importance (so little that at times there is no content at all, as in the case of the patient who has the obsession of having committed a horrible crime but who cannot even imagine what the crime was); what matters is the sort of vertigo that causes the very prohibition in the patient. His consciousness is captivated, as it is in the dream, but in a different way: it is the very fear of the obsession which causes it to be reborn; every effort "not to think of it" is transformed spontaneously into obsessing thoughts; if it is at times forgotten for a moment, the patient suddenly asks himself, "But how calm I am! Why am I so calm? It is because I have forgotten . . . , etc., etc." And the obsessing object is reproduced by means of vertigo. Consciousness is here a sort of victim of itself, clinched in a sort of vicious circle and every effort made to get rid of the obsessing idea is precisely the most effective means to bring it about. The patient is perfectly aware of this vicious circle and several reports of Janet's patients show that they understand fully that they are at once the victims as well as executioners. It is in this sense, and in this sense only, that the obsession "imposes itself" on consciousness. The psychaesthenic does not lose for a moment the consciousness of spontaneity nor, in the least, the formal impression of personality; not for a moment does he mistake imaginary objects for real ones. If some of them maintain that their obsessions have an hallucinatory trait it is a lie which Janet has completely hunted down. Likewise the sense of the real is in no way blunted: even the depersonalized perceive very correctly. Nevertheless something has disappeared: the feeling of belonging to oneself, or what Cloparede calls the "myselfness." The reconnecting of the phenomena to the self and to the non-self is correctly effected, but, so to speak, on a neutral foundation. The violent opposition between the self and non-self, so obvious to the normal person, is attenuated. Now the self is no longer an harmonious integration of enterprises in the external world. There are some spasms of the self, a spontaneity that liberates itself; it occurs as a resistance of the self to itself.[1]

When we turn to the hallucinated we find first these spasms of consciousness which cause the sudden appearance of an imaginative consciousness, whether "auditory" or "visual." No doubt these consciousnesses are thoroughly spontaneous: no other consciousnesses can exist. And no doubt it is also a stereotype caused by an obsessive vertigo. The hallucination obeys, in fact, the principle of quasi-observation. The patient who presents verbal motor hallucinations *knows* who is speaking with his mouth, without the voice changing.[2] It is therefore usurped by this knowledge; it does not apprehend the content of these hallucinations, but suddenly its total attitude is transformed: it is no longer he who is speaking, but X or Y. Naturally this holds for auditory and visual hallucinations, and especially for mental hallucinations, in which the patient insists upon this trait, since he is not baffled by the quasi-sensory nature of the apparitions. The patient therefore has an *intention* towards the image which can be anterior to the constitution of the imaginative object, a transition from the intentional knowledge to the imaginative consciousness. The patient is not surprised by his hallucination, he does not contemplate it: he realizes it. And he no doubt realizes it as does the obsessed, precisely because he wants to escape it. We can even ask ourselves whether the patient does not very often know in advance at which moment of the journey the hallucination will occur: he must be expecting it and it

---

[1] Under the influence of certain conditions, however, psychaesthenics can present for a moment a delirium of influence.
[2] It can change from high to low, for instance, but this is not indispensable.

comes because he is expecting it. The hallucination does therefore bear a resemblance up to a certain point to the obsession: in the latter as in the former, consciousness is attracted by the idea that it can produce a certain object. Only in the case of the hallucinated, a very important modification has arisen, namely, disintegration.

No doubt the unity of consciousness is retained, that is, the synthetic conjunction of the successive mental moments. This unity of consciousness is the condition of mental disturbances as it is in the normal functioning of thought. But it forms the indifferent ground on which the revolt of the spontaneities disengages itself in the case of a psychosis of hallucination. The higher forms of mental integration have disappeared. That indicates that there is no longer an harmonious and continuous development of thought, realized by a personal synthesis and in the course of which other thoughts could be posited as possible, that is, envisaged for a moment without being *realized*. But the course of thought, although it still pretends to be a coherent development, is broken at each instant by adventitious lateral thoughts, which can no longer be suspended in the state of possibilities, but which realize themselves as a counter-current. Dizziness is always involved, but it is no longer a whole personality which enters into a contest with itself: but partial systems which can no longer remain in the state of simple possibilities but which, hardly conceived, carry off consciousness to realize them. Here, even more so than anywhere else, we must guard against a mechanical interpretation: the morbid consciousness remains a consciousness, that is, an unconditional spontaneity. All these phenomena have been well described by Clerambault under the name of "little mental automatism." [1]

"The auditory hallucination, properly so-called, and the psycho-motor hallucination are later phenomena in the dis-

[1] Clerambault, *Psychose à base l'automatisme et syndromes d'automatismes.* Annales médico-psychologiques, 1927, p. 193.

course of the mental automatism. . . . Intuitions, thought that is overtaken, the echo of thoughts and nonsense are the initial phenomena of mental automatism. Certain facts of mental automatism are well known (see Séglas). Other phenomena of mental automatism have been left in the shade: on the one hand verbal phenomena: explosive words, plays on syllables, long strings of words, absurdities and nonsense; on the other hand, purely mental phenomena, abstract intuitions, the curbing of abstract thought, the secret reeling off of memories. Such are ordinarily the initial forms of mental automatism. The ideo-verbal processes: commentaries on acts and memories, questions, self-answering ideas, come, in general, later." [1]

These mental disturbances bring forth or develop in the hallucinated a feeling and a behavior that distinguish it absolutely from the psychaesthenic: what is known as the syndrome of influence. The patient believes himself to be under the influence of one or more persons. But what has been rarely carefully examined is that this belief in an "influence" is the way the patient has of still affirming the spontaneity of his ideas and of all his mental events. When a patient declares "evil thoughts are given me, I am forced to have obscene ideas," we must not believe that he feels these evil thoughts to be lying about him or floating like bits of wood on the water. He feels their spontaneity and he does not think of denying it. Only he sees that this spontaneity occurs in isolation, as a cross-current, breaking the unity if not of the consciousness then at least of the personal life. There lies the basic meaning of the idea of influence: the patient feels at the same time that it is he who is producing these thoughts as a living, animated spontaneity, and at the same time that he did not will them. Hence the expression "I am forced to think. . . ." So the syndrome of influence is nothing else than the recognition by the patient of the existence of a counter-spontaneity.

[1] Cited by Lagache, op. cit., p. 119.

The pure and ineffable experience (what corresponds to the cogito) of the patient always gives him this absurd or inopportune idea as something a propos of which the cogito can be effected; but the idea eludes him at the same time, he is not responsible for it, he does not recognize it.

It is on this basis of influence that the first hallucinations appear. Can they be called "hallucinations" even at this stage? "I am forced to see" he says in speaking of visual hallucinations. Even there the intuition of spontaneity is not abandoned. An image is formed which occurs as an image, which has preserved its unreal character. It presents itself simply for itself, it arrests the flow of ideas. But the patient has not lost sight of the fact that his persecutors can give him this or that "vision" or "audition" only through his own creative activity. Besides, it seems that at this level the personality undergoes only some slight and rapid alterations. It is possible that there occurs only a liberation of lateral, marginal, spontaneities on the occasion of a strong concentration of the subject. I myself was able to observe a short hallucination when I had administered to myself an injection of mascalin. It had exactly this lateral trait: someone was singing in the room near by and as I tried to listen—stopping completely to look in front of me—three small parallel clouds appeared before me. The phenomenon naturally disappeared as soon as I tried to get hold of it. It was not in keeping with the full and clear visual consciousness. It could exist only by stealth and as a matter of fact it occurred as such; there was, in the way in which these three small clouds appeared in my memory, right after they had disappeared, something at once inconsistent and mysterious, which, it seemed to me, only translated the existence of these freed spontaneities *on the margins* of consciousness.

When we pass to true hallucinations (heard voices, apparitions, etc.) the disintegration is much more serious. No doubt that the unity of consciousness remains intact as that which makes possible cock-and-bull stories, contradictions, etc.[1] But these new forms of synthetic connection are incompatible with the existence of a personal synthesis and with oriented thought. The first condition of the hallucination appears to us to be a sort of vacillation of personal consciousness. The patient is alone, his thoughts suddenly become entangled, scattered; a diffuse and degraded connection by participation takes the place of the synthetic connection by concentration. This decline of potential brings into consciousness a sort of leveling; and, at the same time and correlatively, perception is dimmed and thrown into confusion: object and subject disappear together. It is conceivable that this crepuscular life, being incompatible with the attention or the conception of possibilities as such, is prolonged for a moment without another modification. We may also admit the appearance of phenomena of fascination or of auto-suggestion. But in the case that concerns us there occurs only the sudden formation of a partial and absurd mental system. This system is necessarily partial because it cannot be the object of any concentration of consciousness. There is no longer a center of consciousness or a thematic unity, and it is precisely for this reason that it appears. It occurs in its very structure as anti-thematic, that is, as something which cannot furnish the theme of a concentration of consciousness. Let us explain: every perception occurs as being subject to observation; every idea occurs as subject to meditation, that is, held at a distance and contemplated. But these systems *cannot be observed* in any manner whatsoever because they are the correlatives of a leveling of consciousness; they appear only in a consciousness that has no structure, since they are precisely the negation of all structure. They therefore occur always as being "furtive" which is constitutive of their being: their essence is to be imperceptible, that is, never to stand *before* a personal consciousness. They are words one hears but to which one cannot listen,

[1] Contradiction being a synthesis supposes a general form of unification.

faces one sees but at which one cannot look. From here are derived these frequent characteristics that the patients themselves report: "it was a whispering voice, someone spoke to me over the telephone, etc."

The second characteristic of these systems, we have said, is their absurdity. They occur as cock-and-bull stories, a play upon words, puns, rough abuses, etc. It is this very absurdity which gives us the key of their formation. For us, in fact, all existence, in consciousness, must express itself in terms of consciousness and we cannot admit a spontaneity which springs from a shadowy zone without being conscious of itself, even when the superstructures are affected. This way of conceiving the spontaneity is but an implicit manner of admitting the existence of an unconscious. It therefore seems to us that these absurd systems are nothing else than the way in which consciousness thinks its present state, that is, this crepuscular leveling. But it is not a matter of a normal thought positing an object before the subject, nor of a thought *on* this crepuscular state. But, somewhere in this consciousness, incapable of concentrating itself, on the margin, isolated and furtive, appears a partial system which *is* the thought of this crepuscular state, or, if one prefers, which is the crepuscular state itself. We are here confronted with an imaginative symbolic system[1] which has an unreal object for its correlative—absurd phrases, puns, inopportune apparitions. It appears and presents itself as spontaneity, but, above all, as impersonal spontaneity. In fact we are very far from a distinction between the subjective and the objective. These two worlds have collapsed: we are dealing here with a third type of existence which no words can describe. Perhaps the simplest thing to do would be to call them unreal lateral apparitions, the correlatives of an impersonal consciousness.

Such is what we may call the *pure event* of the hallucina-

[1] We shall explain this symbolism more clearly in our chapter on the dream.

tion. But this event does not coincide with the pure experience of hallucination: in fact an experience implies the existence of a thematic consciousness with a personal unity, and this type of consciousness is denied by the hallucinatory event which always happens in the absence of the subject. In a word, the *hallucination happens as a phenomenon, the experience of which can be made only by memory*. And this memory is immediate, that is, there would be no hallucination if these partial systems would continue to develop in a neutralized consciousness: we would be closer to the dream in that case. The hallucination implies a sudden reaction of consciousness to the partial system by a sudden concentration with a sudden reappearance of the thematic unity. At the unexpected and absurd appearance of the unreal object a wave of surprise or of horror should spread over consciousness, an awakening occurs, a re-grouping of forces, somewhat like the sudden awakening of a sleeping person by a violent noise. Consciousness is up in arms, orients itself, it is ready to observe, but, naturally, the unreal object has disappeared; confronting it is nothing but a memory. We now must describe how this memory comes about.

First of all, the fact must be insisted upon in particular that if the unreal object is not itself before consciousness, there is at least an immediate memory, which is as strong and concrete as possible, one of those memories which cannot give rise to doubt, which develops the immediate certainty of the existence of its object. But the essential trait with which the unreal object is delivered by memory is the externality in relation to the actual personal consciousness. It occurs as having been unforeseen and not being subject to voluntary reproduction. It cannot enter into the present synthesis; it can never belong to it. This externality and this independence are evidently very close to those of an object of the world of reality. At the same time, however, the object retains the characteristics of a spontaneity: it is capricious, furtive and full of mystery. But, it will be asked, does it not retain its unreal nature? It keeps it in such a way that the coefficient of unreality, joined to the unexpectedness and externality, as we have defined it, only helps to accentuate the contradictory and fantastic nature of the hallucination. No longer does the patient in the least translate his experience into out language by saying "I saw, I heard. . . ." But the object does not truly occur in memory as unreal: in fact it had no position of unreality during the event; the production of the unreal object was simply accompanied by the non-thetic consciousness of unreality. This non-thetic consciousness does not pass into the memory because, as we have explained, the memory of the perceived object yields us an unreal object just as it does a real one and, in order that the one may be distinguished from the other in recollection, it is necessary that at the moment of their appearance they must have been the object of explicit positions whether of reality or of unreality.[1] It rather appears to us that the hallucinatory object will retain in memory a neutral character. It is the general behavior of the patient which will confer a reality upon these apparitions and not the immediate memory. The proof of this is that in a condition of overwork or intoxication anyone can have an hallucination but it so happens that his immediate memory delivers it to him as an hallucination. Only, in the case of the psychosis of influence a crystallization operates and the patient organizes his life in accordance with the hallucinations, that is, he will think them over and explain them. It seems also that these spontaneities, completely unexpected and fragmentary as they are, can become charged gradually with a certain ideo-affective material. This calls for a slow action on the part of the patient upon his hallucinations, as demonstrated by the apparition of protectors in an advanced state of chronic hallucinatory psychosis. This action operates naturally by cementation and participa-

[1] Naturally these explicit positions do not have to be articulated judgments.

tion rather than by direct action. In all cases it is obvious that in a constituted psychosis the hallucination has a functional role: the patient no doubt adapts himself to his visions *above all*, but the apparitions and voices can be penetrated and from this reciprocal accommodation there results no doubt a general behavior of the patient which can be called hallucinatory.

4. The Dream

A like problem arises in connection with the dream. Descartes states it in his first Meditation:

"I must always consider that I am a man and that consequently I am in the habit of sleeping and representing in my dreams the same things, or very similar things, which I experience when awake. How often have I thought during the night of being in that place, that I was dressed, that I was close to the fire, whereas I was lying naked in my bed. It now seems obvious that it is not with sleeping eyes that I am looking at this paper, that this head I am shaking is not drowsy; that it is deliberately and purposefully that I stretch this hand and that I feel it: what happens in sleep is not at all as clear, as distinct as all this. But in thinking of it carefully, I recall being often deceived during sleep by similar illusions, and, in pausing at that thought, I see very clearly that there are no certain indications by which it is possible to distinguish clearly the wakeful from the sleeping state, that I am completely astonished by it; and my astonishment is such as to almost persuade me that I am asleep." [1]

This problem could be stated as follows: If it is true that the world of the dream occurs as a real and perceived world, whereas it is constituted by a mental imagery, is there not at least one case when the image occurs as a perception, that is, a case where the production of an image is accompanied by the non-thetic consciousness of imaginative spontaneity? And if

[1] Descartes, *Meditations*: First Meditation.

this is so, is not our theory of the image likely to fall completely apart? The dream certainly raises many other questions: for instance, that concerning the symbolic function of images and also that concerning revery, etc. etc. But these questions do not directly concern this book: here we shall limit ourselves to a discussion of the problem of the thesis of the dream, that is to say, of the type of intentional affirmation constituted by the dreaming consciousness.

An initial observation can guide us: there is a sophism in the passage of Descartes we have cited. As yet we know nothing about the dream which is difficult to grasp since we can describe it only by using recollections of it when we are awake. But I can easily grasp a term of comparison established by Descartes, namely, the consciousness which is awake and which perceives. At each moment I can turn it into an object of a reflective consciousness which will show me its structure with certainty. That reflective consciousness gives me precise knowledge at once: it is possible that in the dream I am imagining that I perceive; but what is certain is that when I am awake I cannot doubt that I perceive. Anyone can try to feign for a moment that he is dreaming, that the book he is reading is a dreamed book, but he will see soon enough and without being able to doubt it, that this fiction is absurd. And, in truth, its absurdity is not less than is that of the proposition: perhaps I do not exist, a proposition which is downright unthinkable in the case of Descartes. That is, that in effect the proposition *cogito ergo sum* results—provided it is well understood—from the intuition that consciousness and existence are one and the same. But this concrete consciousness which is certain of existing, exists and has the consciousness of existing while it has a certain individual and temporal structure. This cogito can surely be the intuition of the intimate connection of certain essences and it is thus that phenomenology, which is eidetic science, conceives it. But in order that it be such, it must first be an individual and concrete reflective operation which can always be operated. Now, to think that I exist thinking is to make an eidetic proposition, of which the proposition that I exist perceiving, for instance, is a specification. Thus, when I perceive, I am not certain that the objects of my perception exist but I am certain that I perceive them. It should also be noted that Descartes did not establish the doubtful nature of perception on a direct inspection of the perception, as he would do if he said: When I perceive, I never know for certain whether I am perceiving or dreaming. On the contrary, he takes it for granted that the man who perceives is conscious of perceiving. He does no more than state that the person who is dreaming has a similar certainty on his part. No doubt that we have the familiar formula: "I pinch myself to see whether I'm dreaming," but what we have here is essentially a metaphor which corresponds to nothing concrete in the mind of those who use it.

Now, this evidence of perception we can confront at first with the frequent cases in which the dreamer, passing suddenly to the reflective level, discovers for himself, in the course of his dream, that he is dreaming. We shall even see presently that all appearances of the reflective consciousness in the dream correspond to a momentary awaking,[1] just as often the weight of the consciousness which is dreaming is such that it soon annihilates the reflective consciousness, like a nightmare in which the dreamer thinks desperately, "I am dreaming" without being able to wake up, because his reflective consciousness immediately disappears and he is "recaptured" by his dream. These few examples will suffice to show us that the position of existence of the dreamer cannot be likened to that of the person who is awake, because the reflective consciousness, in the one case, destroys the dream, by the very fact that it presents it for what it is, whereas

[1] It will be objected that in the course of a dream everyone has had the experience of saying to himself: "This one time I am not dreaming" and that in consequence reflection itself seems to be subject to error in the dream. Later on we shall see what this objection amounts to.

in the case of perception reflective consciousness confirms and reinforces the perception itself. But if we think more carefully about the matter we shall notice in addition that the non-thetic consciousnesses of the dream and of the wakeful state must differ in some respects in the way each presents the objects. In fact, the reflective consciousness draws its assurance from the sole fact that it develops and presents as object what is an implicit and a non-thetic structure of the reflective consciousness. My reflective certitude of dreaming comes therefore from the fact that my primitive and non-reflective consciousness had to contain in itself a sort of latent and non-positional knowledge which reflection then made explicit. Besides, were this not the case, then the dreamer would have to draw his judgment, "I am dreaming," from reasonings and comparison which would show him the incoherence or the absurdity of his images. But such an hypothesis is most obviously improbable: for if the dreamer is to reason and compare he must be in full possession of his discursive faculties, and therefore awake. It is therefore absurd to say that at the very moment when he is sufficiently awake to formulate judgments of resemblance, he says to himself that he is dreaming. All he can say is that he has been dreaming. This often happens, but it is something entirely different from what concerns us. The dream therefore appears to us right away as something fragile which the perception cannot po. sess: it is at the mercy of a reflective consciousness. Only, what produces it and what saves it is that most often this reflective consciousness does not appear. Why this is so we must explain. At this point, however, we should note that the primary and non-reflective consciousness, if it is—at the same time as the position of the object—non-thetic consciousness of itself, cannot be so under the form: "I am dreaming." First of all, because this judgment would suppose a thesis and next because this total definition of a consciousness could be given only by reflection. In order to make ourselves clearer let us use an example that will serve us presently. If I say: I believe that Peter is friendly to me, the judgment is one of reflection. It at once involves a doubt of the object of the belief. I can at once say to myself: it is true, I believe it, but I do not know it, I even conclude that Peter has no friendship for me. And surely, if Peter's friendship for me appears to me as the object of my belief it is that my non-reflective consciousness of this friendship was a non-thetic consciousness of itself as simple belief; but from this we must not conclude that the scepticism of the reflection was also a non-positional structure of the non-reflective consciousness. When I am conscious of the friendship of Peter I am conscious of it as an object that is *believed*, and if I believe in it it is just because I do not doubt it. So, it is precisely because I believe in the friendship of Peter than my non-thetic consciousness of believing does not carry the least doubt of that friendship. It is completely belief. It is therefore blind confidence since to believe is to have confidence. Only, in so far as it is consciousness of believing, it is not consciousness of knowing. But this restriction can appear only as a result of reflection. So we see that the non-thetic consciousness of dreaming permits of none of the restrictive and negative characteristics that we find in the judgment: "I am dreaming." ("I am dreaming," therefore I am not perceiving.) A non-thetic consciousness can be negative of nothing because it is completely full of itself and only of itself.

We have now arrived at the certain conclusion that the theme of the dream cannot be that of perception, even if it appears to resemble it on first sight. This we can also see from a simple inspection of a reflective consciousness directed on a perceptive consciousness: To affirm that I perceive is to deny that I am dreaming, or, in other words, it is a sufficient and necessary motivation for my affirming that I am not dreaming. But if the dream affirmed that it is a perception of the same sort and of the same certainty as that of the perception then the judgment "I perceive" would be but a probability and we would have to support it anew by comparing objects of perception with each other, by the cohesion of perceived scenes, by their resemblance, etc. We have shown elsewhere[1] that these comparisons never occur in consciousness as operations that are really accomplished and that also no distinction between perception and imagery can be drawn from them. It can likewise be shown that neither can they serve as a basis for a distinction between the wakeful and the dream state. In reality, perception, like the truth of Spinoza, is *index sui* and it cannot be otherwise. And the dream also resembles the conception of error in Spinoza: error may appear as the truth but it suffices that the truth be possessed in order that error disappear of its own accord.

All this is, however, not enough. If we study the dream and perception somewhat more deeply we shall see that the difference that separates them is, from one point of view, like that between belief and knowledge. When I perceive a table I do not *believe* in the existence of that table. I have no need to believe in it since it is there by itself. There is no supplementary act by which, in addition to perceiving that table, I can confer upon it a *believed* or *believable* existence. The table is discovered, unveiled, given to me, in the very act of perception: and the thesis of the perceiving consciousness does not need to be confounded with an affirmation. Affirmation arises from voluntary spontaneity while the thesis represents the very nuance of intentionality. It is that which corresponds, from the side of the noese, to the noematic-presence of the object itself. The very evidence of perception is therefore in no way a subjective impression which could be likened to a specification of belief: the evidence is the presence for consciousness of the object itself, it is the "fulfillment" (erfüllung) of the intention. Likewise, for a reflecting consciousness directed upon a perceiving consciousness, the perceptual nature of the reflective consciousness is no longer an object of

[1] Cf. my little book, *L'Imagination*, Alcan.

belief, it is an immediate and evident presentation. This is inescapable. An evidence is a presence. Where evidence is presented belief is neither useful nor even possible. But, the dream is a belief. Everything that happens in a dream is something I believe. I do no more than believe in it: that is, the objects are not themselves present to my intuition.

However, we have only shifted the problem. We will certainly be asked: how does it happen that you can believe in the reality of dream images since it is you yourself who construct the dream as images? Their intentional nature as images should exclude every possibility to believe them to be realities.

The reason is that I also said that the dream was a phenomenon of belief, but not a belief in the images as realities. To know exactly what is involved here we must return to hypnagogic imagery. This imagery which is founded on imaginative apprehension of phosphenes, on muscular contractions, on internal speech, is of a richness which is sufficient to furnish the material of the dream. And Leroy has noted, as have many other writers, that the transition from hypnagogism to the dream can often be seized. They are the same images, he says, only our attitude towards them has been changed. This is confirmed by numerous observations: all persons who experience hypnagogic images can report that they are often surprised in the course of the dream without a change occurring in the very content of the hypnagogic imagery. Only, on suddenly waking up, they become aware of having dreamed. The representative analogue is naturally enriched, in the course of the night, with coenesthetic sensations, and, finally, with all sensations that are strong enough to clear the threshold of consciousness and too weak to cause a dream. They are all grasped, in fact, not for what they are but as analogues of other realities. It was in this manner that Proust, on waking suddenly, noticed that in his dream he pronounced the words "stag, stag, Francis Jammes, fork," but that these words made up a coherent phrase and suited the situation of the dream.

In other words, they *stand for* other words which were not actually uttered. The red coloration of the solar light passing across a screen is also experienced, in a famous dream, as standing for blood. A very common error used to hold that the dream is composed of *mental* images. That is not at all so: for how could it be said that the red light *arouses* the mental image of blood? This would imply that the light remained unconscious, which is absurd—or that it was experienced as a red light, which assumes the dream. In reality, it is the red light that is experienced *as* blood. It is the way we have of apprehending it. Certain dreams cited by Janet show clearly how a successively repeated noise is experienced as *standing for* a number of different objects but never *for itself*: in the dream consciousness *cannot perceive*, because it cannot emerge from the imaginative attitude in which it has enclosed itself. Everything is an image to it, and it is precisely because of this that it cannot dispose of mental images which, although exclusive of perception, can arise only as if a constant transition from perception to imagination were possible and, so to speak, only upon the constantly present foundation of perception. The dream is a consciousness that is incapable of leaving the imaginative attitude. Nevertheless a change has evidently occurred at the outset of the hypnagogic imagery since reflection enables us to grasp a transition from hypnagogism to the dream. Must we admit that this modification is a change of the theme? In other words, does the dream appear when we mistake the hypnagogic *images* for perceptions? This we pronounce as impossible *de facto*. If consciousness would affirm the images as realities it would constitute itself in relation to them as a perceiving consciousness and the immediate result would be to make them disappear. It is just this modification which often brings about the dream: the noise of an alarm clock is at first experienced as an analogue of the noise of a fountain, the ringing of bells, the rolling of a drum, etc. But if we wake up we pass precisely to the perception of the noise of daytime. This does not mean that we make judgments like: "this is the striking of an alarm clock," it only means that we suddenly apprehend the striking *for what it is* (that is a succession of shrill and vibrant sounds) and for nothing else than itself. It matters little whether we do or do not realize later the origin and cause of the noise: I can be aroused by a noise whose true cause I always ignore. I may not even experience it as a noise when I wake up: this name may perhaps imply a complicated play of identifying and recognitory operations. For me to pass from the attitude of the dream to the wakeful state it is quite enough that I apprehend it as something that exists. It matters little even if I deceive myself: the creaking of furniture can be experienced in my night dream for the sound of steps; thereupon I can wake up and interpret the creaking as the sound of steps above my head. There is however an abyss between these two assimilations. In the dream the creaking is a noise of steps as an image; in perception it is experienced as a reality and as itself (although mistaken), as noise of steps. Alain says that to perceive is to dream and wake up immediately. But this is a serious mistake: a false perception is not a dream, to correct a perception is not to wake up. We hold, on the contrary, that the world of the dream is explainable only if we admit that the dream consciousness is completely deprived of the faculty of perceiving. It does not perceive, nor does it seek to perceive, nor can it even conceive what a perception is. But we must not believe that this consciousness which is isolated from the real world, imprisoned in the imaginary, will allow itself to take the imaginary for the real, because it lacks the power to compare it with a reality which performs the function of reducer. This is not at all our idea, first because an image presents itself for what it is, without being in need of inviting a comparison with perception, next because what characterizes the consciousness that is dreaming is that it has lost the very idea of reality. It therefore cannot confer this quality on any one of its noemes. But what we want to show is that the dream is the perfect realization of a shut imaginary consciousness, that is, a consciousness for which there is absolutely no exit and towards which no external point of view of any sort is possible.

If we consult our consciousness at the moment when a noise has just awakened us, after the sudden descent from the hypnagogism into the dream, we shall see that what brings about the judgment of "I was dreaming," is the seizure of the character "interesting" of the hypnagogic images. This character did not exist at all in the pure hypnagogism. By "interesting" is not to be understood bound to *me*, as Leroy seems to believe. The presence of the *me* in the dream is frequent and almost necessary in the case of "deep" dreams, but numerous dreams occurring immediately after one has fallen asleep can be cited in which the me of the sleeper plays no part whatsoever. Here is one, for instance, communicated to me by Mlle. B.: At first there appeared a book engraving of a slave kneeling before his mistress, then the slave set out to look for the pus with which to cure himself of the leprosy he had contracted from his mistress; the pus had to be that of a woman who loved him. During the entire dream the sleeping woman had the impression that she was *reading* the story of the slave. At no time did she play a part in the events. It also happens often that dreams—in my case, for instance—occur at first as a story that I am reading or to which I am listening. And then, suddenly, I identify myself with one of the characters of the story: which becomes my story. We cannot fail to notice the neutralized theme that marks the dream of Mlle B. or the beginning of my dream. Can we really believe that the theme modifies itself and assumes a position of existence because I suddenly became one of the characters of the dream? But let us forget for the moment the role of the Me in the dream and, since there are dreams without the Me, let us see what distinguishes them from hypnagogic images. We already know that it is neither by their relation to

the person of the sleeper nor by a sudden position of the
images as reality. It is sufficient to consider the dream of Mlle.
B. and to compare it to preoniric images to see the difference
clearly: a hypnagogic image is isolated, shut off from other
images; if, by chance, two or three images stand in the relationship of interdependence, the group remains isolated in
every case: there is no hypnagogic world, preoniric visions
have no past, no future, there is nothing behind them nor
alongside of them. At the same time I posit every one of them
as an image. This character of the image marks the dream of
Mlle. B.: she *reads* the story, which is a way of neutralizing
the theme. But each image appears as a moment of a temporal
unrolling which possesses a past and a future. The slave is not
seen for himself, as in preoniric imagery. In the latter it appears simply as a "slave." But in the dream, when it comes to
the sleeping person, it does so as sick-slave-searching-pus-to-
cure-himself. At the same time that his image refers to a before
and an after it appears on a foundation of a very rich spatial
world: while the slave is looking for his remedy I do not
lose sight of the fact that he has a mistress who gave him leprosy nor that this mistress continues to exist somewhere, etc.
But the hypnagogic image never occurs as being somewhere.
We "see" a star as an image and it is a few inches from us but
we do not know at all where this image is an image, it is not
surrounded by an imaginary universe. But the person of the
dream is always somewhere, even if the place where he is is
figured schematically as in the Elizabethan theatre. And this
"somewhere" is himself situated in relation to a whole world
which is not seen but which is all about him. Thus the hypnagogic image is an isolated appearance "in the air," while the
dream, we might say, is a world. To tell the truth, there are as
many worlds as there are dreams, and often even as there are
phases of a dream. It would be more just to say that every
dream image appears with its own world. This is at times
enough to differentiate a single oniric image from a preoniric

image. If the face of the Agha-Khan appears to me and if I simply think that it is the face of the Agha-Khan as an image, it is a hypnagogic vision. But if I already sense behind this face a world heavy with threats and promises, I would wake up at once, it's a dream. But this does not yet give a full account of this "interesting" characteristic of the dream. Because of the fact that a dream carries us suddenly into a temporal world, every dream appears to us as *a story*. (In the case of the appearance of the face of the Agha-Khan, it was a story gathered up into a single vision and which had no time to unroll.) Naturally the spatio-temporal world in which the story unrolls is purely imaginary, it is the object of no position of existence. In fact, it is not even imagined, in the sense in which consciousness imagines when it presents something by means of an analogue. As the imaginary world it is the correlative of a *belief*, the sleeper *believes* that the scene unrolls in a world; that is, that this world is the object of empty intentions which are directed upon him beginning with the central image.

Nevertheless these few remarks do not contradict that great law of the imagination: *there is no imaginary world*. In fact, it is but a matter of belief. This world of the image we do not analyze, we do not concern ourselves with details, we do not even consider doing it. In this sense the images remain isolated from each other, separated by their essential poverty, subservient to the phenomenon of quasi-observation "in the void"; there is no other relationship between them than the ones consciousness can conceive at each moment in constituting them. Nonetheless each image presents itself as surrounded by an undifferentiated mass which poses as an imaginary world. Perhaps it would be better to say that each imaginary act in the dream brings with it a special and constitutive quality of its nature which is "the atmosphere of the world." We have seen above that the space and time of the imaginary occur as internal qualities of the thing imagined. Here we must make a similar observation: the "worldliness" of the dreamed image does not consist of an infinity of relations with other images. It is but a matter of the immanent property of the oniric image; there are as many "worlds" as images, even if the sleeper in passing from image to image "dreams" that he remains in the same world. It is therefore proper to say that in the dream each image surrounds itself with a worldly atmosphere. But for greater convenience we shall use the expression "world of the dream," since it is in current use, with the warning not to take it without reservation. We now see the noetic modification of consciousness when it falls from preonirism in the dream: the hypnagogic image was the sudden conviction into which consciousness suddenly dropped; I was suddenly persuaded that such and such an entoptic blot *was* a fish as an image. Now I am dreaming and this sudden belief grows heavy and becomes enriched: I am suddenly persuaded that this fish has a story, that he was caught in that river, that he will appear on the table of the archbishop, etc. River, fish, archbishop, are all imaginary but they constitute a world. My consciousness is therefore that of a world, I have projected all my knowledge, all my interest, all my memories, and even the necessity of being-in-the-world which imposes itself upon the human being, I have projected all that, but I did so in the imaginary mode in the image which I now construct. What has happened if not that consciousness was completely taken in? It entered completely into the game and it itself was determined to produce syntheses in all their richness, but only in an imaginary way. This is possible only in the dream. Even the schizophrenic, whose condition is very much like that of the sleeper, retains the possibility of perceiving himself as being in the process of playing a game. But here attention no longer exists, nor its power to present its object as transcendent, consciousness is fascinated by a swarm of impressions, it grasps them *as* being this or that object as an image, as *standing for* this or that, and then, suddenly, it is completely in the game, it apprehends these shining impressions as *standing for* an object which is at the farthest remove from a world the contours of which are lost in the fog. So long as the dream lasts consciousness is unable to engage in reflection, it is carried along by its own decline and it continues to lay hold of images indefinitely. This is the real explanation of oniric symbolism: if consciousness can never take hold of its own anxieties, its own desires, excepting as symbols, it is not, as Freud believed, because of a suppression which compels it to disguise them: but because it is incapable of laying hold of what there is of the real under its form of reality. It has completely lost the function of the real and everything it feels, everything it thinks, it cannot feel or think otherwise than under the imagined form. This is also the reason why, as Halbwachs has shown, there is no *memory* in the dream (recollection does not occur in the dream). There is no question here of social frameworks. The least *real* memory will cause the sudden crystallization before consciousness of all of reality, because it will situate itself in the end in relation to this real room, to this real bed in which I am lying. The image of the crystallization can serve us doubly: a single preoniric image can evoke the crystallization of the noemes of consciousness into noemes of imaginary worlds, a single reality grasped or perceived as a reality causes the crystallization of the real world before consciousness, it is all the one or all the other. It is at this point that we must depict the degree of belief of consciousness in these imaginary worlds, or if one prefers, the dullness of these worlds. Let us return to the dream of Mlle. B. The mere fact that the dream happens as a *story* should permit us to understand the kind of belief we attribute to it. But the sleeping woman instructs us still better, she tells us that she *believed herself to be reading* this story. What does she mean if not that the story presents itself to her with the same kind of interest and credibility as that of a read story. The reading is a sort of fascination and when I am reading a detective story I believe in what I am reading. But this does not mean in the least that I fail to look

upon the adventures of the detective as imaginary. What happens simply is that a complete world appears to me as an image
by means of the lines of the book. (I have already shown
that words serve as analogue.[1]) And this world closes again
on my consciousness, I cannot free myself from it, I am fascinated by it. It is this sort of fascination without existential
position which I call belief. Not only is consciousness conscious
of itself as being enslaved but it is also conscious of being
without help against itself. This world is sufficient unto itself,
it can neither be dissipated nor corrected by a perception,
since it does not belong to the domain of the real. It is its very
unreality which puts it beyond reach and which gives it a com-
pact opacity and a strength. While consciousness perseveres
in this attitude it can neither find nor even conceive of any
motive for changing itself so that the transition to perception
can only occur by a revolution. The power of the dreamed
world is of this nature, but with even greater force: as a
noematic seizure of the object, this power is the correlative of
the non-thetic consciousness of fascination. This is the reason
why the world of the dream like that of the reader occurs as
completely magical; we are haunted by the adventures of the
persons of our dream as we are by the heroes of a novel. It
is not that the non-thetic consciousness of imagining ceases
to grasp itself as spontaneity but it grasps itself by itself as a
spellbound spontaneity. This is what gives the dream its
unique nuance of fatality. The events occur as if not being
able not to happen, in correlation with a consciousness which
cannot help imagining them. However, the dream image continues to possess strictly only the characteristics conferred
upon it by consciousness: the phenomenon of quasi-observation holds here as elsewhere. Only, at the same time, it possesses an obsessing trait which is due to the fact that consciousness has determined itself by its own fascination to form it, an
"equivocal" trait which derives from its magical nature and

[1] Book II, Chapter I: Knowledge.

a fatal trait whose origin it will be well for us to explain more clearly.

In an imaginary world there is no dream of *possibilities* since possibilities call for a real world on the basis of which they are thought of as possibilities. Consciousness cannot get perspective on its own imaginations in order to imagine a possible sequence to the story which it is representing to itself: that would be to be awake. This is what we do, for instance, when on waking up we imagine a happy ending to the nightmare we just had. In a word, consciousness cannot anticipate because that would mean to imagine the second power, and therefore to possess the reflective consciousness of the imagination of the first degree. All anticipation at a given moment of a story derives from the very fact that the anticipation appears as an episode of the story. I cannot entertain, conceive another ending, I have no choice, no recourse, I am compelled to narrate the story to myself: there is no "blow for nothing." So each moment of the story occurs as having an imaginary future, but a future I cannot foresee, which will come of its own accord, in its own time, to haunt consciousness, against which consciousness will be crushed. So, contrary to what could be believed, the imaginary world occurs as world without freedom: nor is it determined, it is the opposite of freedom, it is fatal. Thus, it is not by conceiving other possibilities that the sleeper is reassured, saves himself from embarrassment. It is by the immediate production of reassuring events in the story itself. He does not say to himself: I could have had a revolver, but suddenly he does have a revolver in his hand. But too bad for him if at that very moment a thought should occur to him which in the waking state would assume the form of "what if the revolver had been locked!" This "if" cannot exist in the dream: this rescuing revolver is suddenly locked at the very moment when it is needed.

But the world of the dream is not so closed that the dreamer himself does not get to play his role in it. Hence many dreams occur as the adventures of the dreamer himself. "I dreamed that I was . . ., etc." is generally the way we begin to narrate our dreams. How is this appearance of the dreamer himself in this imaginary world to be understood? Are we to believe that it is truly *he*, in person, as a real consciousness who is introduced into the midst of oniric imagery. This hypothesis seems to me to be senseless. For in order that the sleeper introduce himself as a real consciousness into the imaginary drama enacted in the dream, he must be conscious of himself, as a real being, that is, as existing in a real world,.in a real time, and marked by real memories. But these are exactly the conditions that mark the wakeful state. Introduce suddenly a real person into the dream and the dream explodes completely, and reality reappears. Besides, what does this mean exactly? Surely, my consciousness when I am awake is characterized by its "being in the world," but just because this "being in the world" characterizes the relationship of consciousness with reality, it cannot be applied to the consciousness which is dreaming. A consciousness cannot ."be in" an imaginary world, unless to be itself an imaginary consciousness. But what is an imaginary consciousness if not a certain object for a real consciousness? In fact, a consciousness which is dreaming is always a consciousness that is non-thetic of itself while it is held in the grip of the dream, but it has lost its being-in-the-world and recovers it only on waking up.[1]

All we need do in order to solve the problem is recall certain dreams which are at first made up of impersonal scenes and into which the person of the sleeper is suddenly introduced. Every one has dreamed of witnessing the adventures of an imaginary person (for instance, of the slave of whom Mlle. B. dreamed), and then suddenly the sleeper perceives *that it is he* who is the slave. The term "perceive" is in fact

---

[1] The question is, in fact, much more complicated, and even in the dream consciousness does retain its "being-in-the-world" at least in some way. But we may hold on to this idea of a lost "being-in-the-world," at least in a metaphoric sense.

not the right one, since the entire course of the dream is naturally one of quasi-observed phenomena: but rather, after various motivations, the sleeper is suddenly overwhelmed by the belief that the slave who is fleeing before the tiger *is* he himself, just as in hypnagogism, he is all at once overwhelmed by the belief that this bright spot was a man's face. Let us examine this transformation more closely: the slave, in becoming myself, does not lose his constitutive nature of unreality. On the contrary, it is I who, projected into the slave, become an imaginary me. In many cases, I continue to see the slave fleeing Selfness, like Claparède. The constitutive nature of this slave has its own nuance which penetrates it completely, a way of being constitutive which is one that may be called, to use a neologism of Claparède in a sense not originally intended by him, Selfness. The constitutive nature of that slave is that he is me. But he is me in an unreal way, he is me in virtue of imagination. In order to see more clearly what happens here we might resort again to the comparison with the reader. We all know that when reading we identify ourselves more or less with the characters of the story. This happens in particular when the novel is written in the first person, and writers take advantage of this identification to make their story more pressing, more urgent, for their readers. Nevertheless, the identification is never complete, first of all because authors most often make use of "esthetic distance," they write their books "in the past," for instance, etc., which enables the reader to survey their characters. Besides, the possibility of a reflective consciousness is present. A condition results which is worthy of being described for its own sake, and in which I *am* the unreal hero, while remaining different from him; I am myself and another. But let us suppose for a moment that these barriers are broken: I am invaded by the belief that what is menaced by all these romantic dangers is unreally but *absolutely* myself. At this moment my interest in the novel becomes a different sort: it is

I who am menaced, who am pursued, etc. I am involved in an adventure that is happening to me in an unreal way. Up to then the dangers the hero encountered fascinated me and aroused in me great interest, but the basis of which was still—in spite of my partial identification with him—sympathy. Now, the feeling that is aroused is a feeling of belonging; in this imaginary world, in which one must be unreal if he is to enter it, an unreal me represents me, suffers, is in danger, even risks an unreal death which will put an end at once to him and to the world that surrounds him. An unreal game is going on with my unreal self as its stake. Now this condition of trance which cannot be completely realized in the reader (and which interferes with the aesthetic appreciation of the book) is just what realizes itself in the dream. Once an unreal self occurs in the fascinating world of the dream the imaginary world is at once closed; it is no longer an *imaginary spectacle* which is *before* me because of the fact that I am viewing it: now I am represented in it, I am "in danger" in it, I have my place in it and it closes in on me. It is not only represented unreally, but it is also unreally born, it acts and suffers unreally. At the same time its relation to my consciousness is modified since up to then it was a relationship uniquely representative (perhaps like that possessed by the affective impressions created by this world). From the moment that an imaginary self is "inside" everything changes: that self holds on to my consciousness by a relationship of *emanation*. I not only see the fleeing slave, but I *feel* myself to be that slave. And I do not feel myself to be *him* in the intimacy of my consciousness, as I can feel myself in the wakeful state, the same as yesterday, etc. No, I *feel* myself to be him, outside, in him, which is an unreal affective quality (like the despair of René, the wickedness of Menardier, the kindness of Jean Valjean) that I grasp on him. In one sense it is, therefore, transcendent and external since I still see him running and, in another sense, transcendent without distance since I am present in him unreally. But this change the slave undergoes is also undergone by the imaginary world since it is for him (who is me) a hated and feared world, etc. There remains therefore, in one sense, a purely represented world, and, in another sense, a world immediately lived. It gains there a sort of dull presence, and without distance in relation to my consciousness. I am taken. Naturally I do not change the theme because of this, I am taken as I am in the game. But there are games in which one is strongly taken, and, on the other hand, I cannot break the enchantment, I can put a stop to the imaginary adventure only by producing another imaginary adventure, I am compelled to live the fascination of the unreal to the dregs. Here we have the perfect and complete instance of a consciousness for which the category of the real does not exist at all.

We must not believe that in his personal dreams the sleeper always begins by identifying himself with a person who has existed before in an impersonal dream. A dream can be personal from the beginning. Only it is necessary that the imagery of the dreamer produce some object which he can believe, whether immediately or at the end of a certain time, to be himself, whatever else that object may be. In fact, this is the only way that the sleeper has of entering into that world which does not exist: he must identify himself with one of the objects of that world; in other words, a material substratum is needed for his impression of being-in-the-unreal-world. He himself, in fact, we have noted, cannot be there but he can be invaded by the belief that such an imaginary object, which already possesses his being-in-the-unreal-world, is *himself*; and at the same time he can produce this object and the belief that it is he. From this there results that curious trait of the dream when everything is seen and known from both a superior point of view, which is that of the sleeper representing to himself a world, and from a point of view relative and limited which is that of the imaginary me plunged into the world. As a matter of fact, the imaginary me does not see this world and the sleeper does not put himself *in the place* of that particular being in order to see the things from his point of view: it is always from his own point of view, from his point of view of creator that he sees things. Only, at the very moment he sees them, he sees them oriented in relation to that object-me that suffers them and lives them. The enraged dog who is about to bite does not approach the sleeper but the object-me and the sleeper grasps his distance from the object-me as an irreversible absolute, exactly as in the wakeful state I grasp the distance of the dog-who-is-about-to-bite-me from myself as absolutely oriented from the dog to me. This space is full of vectors of tensions, of lines of force called by Lewis a hodologic space. Only, instead of surrounding me, it surrounds and crowds a certain object which I imagine in the midst of others and which is the object-me. The result is that a dream could in no way be represented in the world of perception. Here, for instance, is a dream of mine of last year. I was pursued by a forger. I took refuge in an armor-plated room but he began to melt the armor plate from the other side of the wall with a welding torch. So I saw *myself*, on the one hand, chilled in the room while waiting—while believing myself to be safe—and on the other hand, I saw him on the other side of the wall in the process of drilling. I therefore knew what was going to happen to the object-me, which was still unaware, and yet the thickness of the wall that separated the forger from the object-me was an absolute distance, oriented from him to the object-me. And then, all of a sudden, at the moment when the forger was about to finish his work, the object-me *knew* that he was going to pierce the wall, that is, that I suddenly imagined him as knowing it, without in any way trying to justify this new knowledge, and the object-me escaped just in time through the window.

These few observations enable us to understand better the

distinction everyone is obliged to make between imaginary feelings and real feelings which we experience in the dream. There are some dreams in which the object-me is terrified and yet we do not call them nightmares, because the sleeper himself is very peaceful. He has therefore limited himself to endowing the object-me with feelings which he must have felt for the very verisimilitude of the situation. There are imaginary feelings which do not "take hold of" the dreamer any more than do those usually called "emotional abstraction." It is that the dream does not always motivate real emotions in the sleeper; no more than does a novel, even if it narrates horrible events does it always succeed in moving us. I can witness impassively the adventures of the object-me. And yet it is always this unreal self to whom they happen. Inversely the content of a nightmare is not always terrifying. It is that the real affectivity of the sleeper, for reasons which we do not have to survey here, sometimes precedes the dream and the dream "enacts" it in some way on the imaginary terrain. Sometimes there follow terrible adventures, but sometimes also nothing serious happens; only what does happen is intentionally grasped as being sinister because the sleeper who produces these imaginings is really sinister. It is then the atmosphere of the dreamed world that is nightmarish.

We can likewise explain that apparent anomaly we just indicated in a note in the same way. I have often dreamed that I was walking in New York and found it to be most pleasant. To me this dream always was not only what we are in the habit of calling a "disappointment" but rather that sort of disillusionment we experience after we leave the theatre. I also seemed to tell myself while dreaming that this time I am not dreaming. Here I seem to have performed a reflective act which was deceitful, which would question the very value of the reflection. But this reflective act, has in reality not been carried out: it is an imaginary reflective act, operated by the me-object and not by my own consciousness. This me which is walking between the high walls of New York is the one which says to itself suddenly: I am not dreaming, it is in him that the certitude of being awake arises, just as a hero of a novel can rub his eyes and suddenly declare: "Am I dreaming? No, I am not dreaming." The consciousness which is dreaming is determined once and for all to produce only the imaginary and its cares, its preoccupations, as we have seen, are projected before it in a symbolic and unreal form. The anxious hope that one is not dreaming, not running to the disillusionment which in the end follows from the representation, could not express itself really without awakening the sleeper, just as the spectator could not think "I wish that life was like this play," without detaching himself from the stage and placing himself on the soil of reality (*real* wishes, *real* personality, etc.). Here this desire not to dream, which is only a desire, becomes conscious of itself *outside*, in the transcendence of the imaginary and it is also in this imaginary transcendence in which it finds satisfaction. Thus *I imagine* that the me-object desires to be in New York *for good* and I imagine it with my own desire to be there, and because of this the me-object finds itself—in keeping with the very terms of fiction—in actuality and not in a dream on the streets of New York. In here there is therefore nothing of *real* reflection and we are very far from the wakeful state. The same is true, naturally, of all the reflections which can produce the object-me, such as "I am afraid," "I am humiliated," etc.—reflections which are, moreover, very rare.

On the contrary, the only means that disposes the sleeper to come out of the dream is the reflective declaration: I am dreaming. And to make this declaration nothing is needed but to produce a reflective consciousness. But this reflective consciousness is almost impossible to produce because the types of motivations that ordinarily call it forth are precisely of the sort which the "enchanted" consciousness of the sleeper no longer permits itself to conceive. In this connection nothing is more strange than the desperate efforts made by the sleeper in certain nightmares to *remind himself* that a reflexive consciousness is possible. Such efforts are made in vain, most of the time, because he is forbidden by the very "enchantment" of his consciousness to produce these memories in the form of fiction. He struggles but everything glides into fiction, everything is transformed in spite of him into the imaginary. Finally the dream can be broken only by two motives. The first is the eruption of a reality which forces itself, as, for instance, real fear aroused by the nightmare, which "gets hold" of the nightmare itself and ends up by becoming so strong that it breaks the enchantment of the consciousness and motivates a reflection. I become aware of what I am afraid of and by the same stroke of what I am dreaming. Or some external stimulus is injected, whether because it comes as a surprise and cannot be at once grasped as an analogue, or because of its violence which determines a real emotional shock, which calls forth suddenly the object of a reflection, or because of the resistance of certain orders through sleep.[1] The second motive which can put a stop to the dream is often found in the dream itself: it is possible in fact that the story being dreamed ends with an event which itself occurs as something final, that is, as something for which a sequence is inconceivable. For instance, I often dream that I am about to be guillotined and the dream stops at the very moment when my neck is placed on the block. In this case it is not fear that motivates the dream—for, paradoxical as this may appear, this dream does not always occur as a nightmare—but rather the impossibility of improving an *afterwards*. Consciousness hesitates, and this hesitation motivates a reflection, which is waking up.

We can conclude that the dream—contrary to Descartes—does not at all occur as an apprehension of reality. On the

---

[1] The persistence of these orders could themselves be made the subject of a long investigation, but we cannot attempt this investigation in this book.

contrary, it would lose all its sense, its own nature if it could posit itself as real even for a moment. It is primarily a *story* and our strong interest in it is of the same sort as that of the naive reader in a novel. It is lived as a fiction and it is only in considering it as a fiction which happens as such that we can understand the sort of reaction it arouses in the sleeper. Only it is a "spell-binding" fiction: consciousness—as we have shown in the chapter on the hypnagogic image—has become knotted. And what it lives, at the same time as the fiction apprehended as a fiction is the impossibility of emerging out of the fiction. Just as King Midas transformed everything he touched into gold, so consciousness is itself determined to transform into the imaginary everything it gets hold of: hence the fatal nature of the dream. It is the seizure of this fatality as such which has often been confused with an apprehension of the dreamed world as reality. In fact, what constitutes the nature of the dream is that reality eludes altogether the consciousness which desires to recapture it; all the effort of consciousness turns in spite of itself to produce the imaginary. The dream is not fiction taken for reality, it is the odyssey of a consciousness dedicated by itself, and in spite of itself, to build only an unreal world. The dream is a privileged experience which can help us to conceive what a consciousness would be which would have lost its "being-in-the-world" and which would be by the same token, deprived of the category of the real.

CONCLUSION

1. Consciousness and Imagination

WE ARE now in a position to raise the metaphysical question which has been gradually shaping itself by these studies of phenomenological psychology. We may formulate it as follows: What are the characteristics that can be attributed to consciousness from the fact that it is a consciousness capable of *imagining*. This question can be taken in the sense of a critical analysis under the form: what must be the nature of consciousness in general in order that the construction of an image should always be possible? And, no doubt, it is under this form that our minds, accustomed to raising philosophical questions in the Kantian perspective, will best understand it. But, as a matter of fact, the problem in its deepest meaning can only be grasped from a phenomenological point of view.

After the phenomenological reduction we find ourselves in the presence of the transcendental consciousness which unveils itself to our reflective descriptions. We can thus fix by concepts the result of our eidetic intuition of the essence "consciousness." Now, phenomenological descriptions can discover, for instance, that the very structure of the transcendental consciousness implies that this consciousness is constitutive *of a world*. But it is evident that they will not teach us that consciousness must be constitutive *of* such a world, that is exactly the one where we are, with its earth, its animals, its men and the story of these men. We are here in the presence of a primary and irreducible fact which presents itself as a contingent and irrational specification of the noematic essence of the *world*. And many phenomenologists will call "metaphysics" the investigation whose aim it is to uncover this contingent existant in its entirety. This is not exactly what we would call metaphysics, but this is of little importance here. What will concern us here is this: is the imaginary function a contingent and metaphysical specification of the essence "consciousness" or should it rather be described as a constitutive structure of that essence? In other words: can we conceive of a consciousness which would never imagine and which would be completely absorbed in its intuitions of the real—in that case the possibility of imagining, which appears as one quality among others of *our* consciousnesses, would be a contingent enrichment—or rather, soon as we posit a consciousness, must it be posited as always being able to imagine? This question should be able to settle itself by the simple reflective inspection of the essence "consciousness" and it is thus in fact that we would attempt to settle it, were we not addressing ourselves to a public as yet but little accustomed to phenomenological methods. But since the idea of eidetic intuition is still repugnant to many French readers, we shall resort to a subterfuge, that is, to a method somewhat more complex. We shall begin with the question: what must a consciousness be in order for it to possess the power to imagine, which we shall try to develop by the usual procedures of critical analysis, that is, by a regressive method. Next we shall compare the results we obtain with those the Cartesian intuition gives us of the consciousness realized by the cogito and we shall see whether the necessary conditions for realizing an imaginative consciousness are *the same* or *different* from the conditions of possibility of a consciousness in general.

In truth, the problem stated thus may appear to be completely new and even trifling to French psychologists. And, in fact, as long as we are the victims of the illusion of immanence, there is no general problem of imagination. Images are in fact supplied in these theories by a type of existence strictly like that of things. They are reborn sensations which may differ in degree, in cohesion, in meaning from primary sensations but which belong, as do sensations, to *intra-mundane* existence. The image is as real as any other existence. The only question concerning the image is the problem of its relationship to other existences but whatever this relationship may be the existence of the image remains intact. This is like saying that whether the portrait of King Charles VI is or is not a true likeness, whether the king is dead or alive or even whether he ever existed, the portrait is nevertheless something that exists in the world. There is therefore no existential problem of the image.

But if the image is looked upon as we have viewed it in this work, the existential problem of the image can no longer be sidetracked. In fact, to the existence of an object for consciousness there corresponds noetically a hypothesis or position of existence. Now, the hypothesis of the imaginative consciousness is radically different from the hypothesis of a consciousness of the real. This means that the type of existence of the object of the image *as long as it is imagined*, differs in nature from the type of existence of the object grasped as real. And, surely, if I now form an image of Peter, my imaginative consciousness includes a certain position of the existence of Peter, insofar as he is now at this very moment in Berlin or London. But while he *appears to me as an image*, this Peter who is in London *appears to me absent*. This absence in actuality, this essential nothingness of the imagined object is enough to distinguish it from the object of perception. What then must be the nature of a consciousness in order that it be able to successively posit *real* objects and *imagined* objects?

We must at once make an important observation, which the reader could have made himself if he had studied with us the problem of the relationships between perception and imagery.[1] For an object or any element of an object there is very much of a difference between *being envisioned as nothing* and *being given-as-absent*. In a perception of whatever sort

[1] See Part II.

many empty intentions are directed, from the elements of the object now given, towards other aspects and other elements of the object which no longer reveal themselves to our intuition. For instance, the arabesques of the rug I am viewing are both in part given to my intuition. The legs of the armchair which stands before the window conceal certain curves, certain designs. But I nevertheless seize these hidden arabesques as *existing now*, as hidden but not at all as absent. And I grasp them not for themselves in trying to present them by means of an analogue but in the very way in which I grasp what has been given me of their continuation. I *perceive* the beginnings and the endings of the hidden arabesques (which appear to me in front and in back of the leg of the chair) as *continuing* under the legs of the chair. It is therefore *in the way in which I grasp the data* that I posit that which is not given as being real. Real by the same right as the data, as that which gives it its meaning and its very nature. Likewise the successive tones of a melody are grasped by appropriate retentions as that which makes of the tone now heard exactly what it is. In this sense, to perceive this or that real datum is to perceive it on the foundation of total reality *as a whole*. This reality does not make the object of any special act of my attention but it is co-present as an essential condition of the existence of the reality actually perceived. Here we see that the imaginative act is the reverse of the act of reality. If I want to imagine the hidden arabesques, I direct my attention upon them and I isolate them, just as I isolate on a foundation of an undifferentiated universe the thing I now see. I cease to grasp them in a vacuum as constituting the sense of the perceived reality, *I present them to myself*, in themselves, but precisely as I cease to envision them from the beginning of a present, in order to grasp them by themselves, I grasp them as *absent*, they appear to me as empty data. Of course they really exist yonder under the chair and it is yonder that I envision them but precisely as I envision them where they are not given to me I grasp them as a nothing for me. Thus the imaginative act is at once *constituting, isolating* and *annihilating*.

It is this which turns the problem of memory and that of anticipation into two problems which are radically different from the problem of imagination. No doubt but that recollection is in many respects very close to the image and at times we were able to draw our examples from memory to clarify the nature of the image. There is nevertheless an essential difference between the theme of recollection and that of the image. If I recall an incident of my past life I do not imagine it, I *recall* it. That is, I do not posit it as *given-in-its-absence*, but as *given-now-as-in-the-past*. The handshake of Peter of last evening in leaving me did not turn into an unreality as it became a thing of the past: it simply *went into retirement*; it is always real but *past*. It exists *past*, which is one mode of real existence among others. And when I want to apprehend it anew I envision it *where it is*, I direct my consciousness towards that past object which is *yesterday* and at the heart of that object, I recover the event I am looking for, the handshake of Peter. In a word, just as when I want to *see* actually the hidden arabesques under the chair I have to look for them where they are, that is, remove the chair; so when I recall this or that memory I do not *call it forth* but I betake myself where it is, I direct my consciousness to the past where it awaits me as a real event in retirement. But if I imagine Peter as he might be at that moment in Berlin—or simply Peter as he exists at that moment (and not as he was yesterday on leaving me), I grasp an object which is not at all given to me or which is given to me simply as being beyond reach. There I grasp *nothing*, that is, I posit *nothingness*. In this sense the imaginative consciousness of Peter in Berlin (what is he doing at this moment? I imagine he is walking in the Kurfürstendamm, etc.), is very much closer to that of the centaur (whose complete inexistence I proclaim), than the recollection of Peter as he was the day he left. What is common between

Peter as an image and the Centaur as an image is that they are two aspects of Nothingness. And this it is that also distinguishes the living future from the imagined future. There are in fact two sorts of Futures: the one is but the temporal ground on which my present perception develops, the other is posited for itself but as *that which is not yet*. When I play tennis I see my opponent hit the ball with his racket and I run to the net. Here there is real anticipation since I foresee the course of the ball. But this anticipation does not posit for itself the passage of the ball to this or that point. In reality the future is here but the *real* development of a form induced by the gesture of my opponent and the real gesture of this opponent communicates its reality to the whole form. In other words, the real form with its zones of real-past and real-future is effected entirely as a result of his gesture. *As for my prevision also being reality*, I continue to carry out the form by foreseeing it, because my prevision is a real gesture within the form. Thus, step by step, there is always a real future which occurs simply as the real past, the sense of an actual form in development, or, in other words, as the meaning of the universe. And, in this sense, it is like presenting the unperceived real aspects of objects as a present which is real and envisioned in a vacuum, or as a real future. The arabesques hidden by the chair are also the real complement of the gesture by which I remove the chair as the present and latent existence hidden by the chair. All real existence occurs with present, past and future structures, therefore past and future as essential structures of the real, are also real, that is, correlatives of a realizing theme. But if, on the contrary, while lying on my bed I anticipate what might happen when my friend Peter returns from Berlin, I detach the future from the present whose meaning it constitutes. I posit it for itself and I present it to myself. But I give it to myself exactly while it is not yet, that is as absent, or if one prefer, as nothing. Thus, I can live the same future in reality as a ground of the present (as, for instance, I look for Peter at the station and all my acts have for their real meaning the arrival of Peter at 7:35 P.M), or on the contrary isolate it and posit it for itself but by cutting it off from all reality and by annihilating it, by *presenting it as nothingness*.

We now can see what the essential requisite is in order that a consciousness may be able to imagine; it must have the possibility of positing an hypothesis of unreality. But we must clarify this requisite. It does not mean·that consciousness must cease being consciousness *of* something. It is of the very nature of consciousness to be intentional and a consciousness that would cease to be consciousness of something would for that very reason cease to exist. But consciousness should be able to form and posit objects possessing a certain trait of nothingness in relation to the whole of reality. In fact, we recall that the imaginary object can be posited as non-existent or as absent or as existing elsewhere or not posited as existing. We note that the common property of these four theses is that they include the entire category of negation, though at different degrees. Thus the negative act is constitutive of the image. We have already mentioned, in fact, that the theme is not added to the image but that it is its most intimate structure. But in relation to what is the negation carried out? To answer this question we need but consider for a moment what happens when I grasp the portrait of Charles VIII as *an* image of Charles VIII. At one stroke I stop to consider the picture as forming a part of a real world. It is no longer possible that the perceived object *on* the picture can be changed by the changes of the milieu surrounding it. The picture itself, as a *real thing*, can be more or less brightened, its colors can peel off, it can burn. This is because it possesses—due to lack of a "being-in-the-world" which is restricted to consciousness—a "being-in-the-midst-of-the-world." Its objective nature depends upon reality grasped as a spatio-temporal whole. But if, on the contrary, I grasp Charles VIII as an image on the picture, the object apprehended can no longer be subjected for instance to changes in brightness. It is not true that I can more or less brighten the *cheek* of Charles VIII.

The brightening of that cheek has been, in fact, once and for all, established in the unreal by the painter. It is the unreal sun—or the unreal candle placed by the painter at this or that distance from the face being painted—which determines the degree of the brightness of the cheek. All that a real projector can do is to brighten the part of the real picture that corresponds to the cheek of Charles VIII. Likewise, if the picture burns—it is not Charles VIII as an image who is burning but only the material object which serves as analogue for the manifestation of the imagined object. Thus the unreal object appears at one stroke to be beyond the reach of reality. We therefore see that in order to produce the object "Charles VIII" as an image consciousness must be able to deny the reality of the picture and that it could deny that reality only by retreating from reality grasped in its totality. To posit an image is to construct an object on the fringe of the whole of reality, which means therefore to hold the real at a distance, to free oneself from it, in a word, to deny it. Or, in other words, to deny that an object belongs to the real is to deny the real in positing the object; the two negations are complementary, the former being the condition for the latter. We know, besides, that the totality of the real, so long as it is grasped by consciousness as a synthetic *situation* for that consciousness, is the world. There is then a two-fold requisite if consciousness is to imagine: it must be able to posit the world in its synthetic totality, and, it must be able to posit the imagined object as being out of reach of this synthetic totality, that is, posit the world as a nothingness in relation to the image. From this it follows clearly that all creation of the imaginary would be completely impossible to a consciousness whose nature it would be precisely to be "in-the-midst-of-the-world." If we assume a consciousness placed in the very bosom of the world as one existence among others, we must conceive it hypothetically as completely subjected to the action of a variety of realities—without its being able to avoid the detail of these realities by an intuition which would embrace their totality. This consciousness could therefore contain only real modifications aroused by real actions and all imagination would be prohibited to it, exactly in the degree to which it would be engulfed in the real. This conception of an imagination en-mired in the world is not unknown to us since it is precisely that of psychological determinism. We can affirm fearlessly that if consciousness is a succession of determined psychical facts it is entirely impossible for it ever to produce anything but the real. For a consciousness to be able to imagine it must be able to escape from the world by its very nature, it must be able by its own efforts to withdraw from the world. In a word it must be free. Thus the thesis of unreality has yielded us the possibility of negation as its condition. Now, the latter is possible only by the "negation" of the world as a whole, and this negation has revealed itself to us as being the reverse of the very freedom of consciousness. But at this point several comments force themselves to the fore: first of all we must bear in mind that the act of positing the world as a synthetic totality and the act of "taking perspective" from the world are both one and the same. If we may use a comparison, it is pre-cisely by placing oneself at a convenient distance from the pic-ture that the impressionist painter disengages the whole "forest" or the "white water lilies" from the multitude of small strokes he has placed on the canvas. But, reciprocally, the possibility of constructing a whole is given as the primary structure of the act of taking perspective. It is therefore enough to be able to posit reality as a synthetic whole in order to posit onself as free from it and this going-beyond is freedom itself since it could not happen if consciousness were not free. Thus to posit the world as a world or to "negate" it is one and the same thing. In this sense Heidegger can say that nothingness is the constitutive structure of the existant. To be able to imagine, it is enough that consciousness be able to surpass the real in constituting it as a world, since the negating of the real is always implied by its constitution in the world. But this surpassing cannot be brought about by any means whatever, and the freedom of consciousness must not be confused with the arbitrary. For an image is not purely and simply the *world-negated*, it is always *the world negated from a certain point of view*, namely, the one that permits the positing of the absence or the non-existence of the object presented "as an image." The arbitrary position of the real as a world will not of itself cause the appearance of the centaur as an unreal object. For the centaur to emerge as unreal the world must be grasped as a world-where-the-centaur-is-not, and this can only happen if consciousness is led by different motivations to grasp the world as being exactly the sort in which the centaur has no place. Likewise, if my friend Peter is to be given me as absent I must be led to grasp the world as that sort of a whole in which Peter cannot *actually exist* and *be present to me*. (He can actually be present for others—in Berlin, for instance.) What motivates the appearance of the unreal is not necessarily nor most often the *representative* intuition of the world from some point of view. Consciousness as a fact has many other ways of *surpassing the real in order to make a world of it*: the surpassing can and should happen at first by affectivity or by action. The appearance of a dead friend as unreal, for instance, is built on the foundation of affective expectation of the real as an *empty world* from this point of view.

We shall give the name of "situations" to the different immediate ways of apprehending the real as a world. We can therefore say that the essential prerequisite that enables consciousness to imagine is that it be "situated in the world" or more briefly, that it "be-in-the-world." It is the situation-in-the-world, grasped as a concrete and individual reality of consciousness, which is the motivation for the construction of any unreal object whatever and the nature of that unreal object is circumscribed by this motivation. Thus the *situation* of consciousness does not need to appear as a pure and abstract condition of possibility for all imagination but as the concrete and exact motivation for the appearance of a certain particular imagination.

From this point of view we finally grasp the relation between the unreal and the real. At first, even if an image is not produced at this moment, every apprehension of the real as a world tends of its own accord to end up with the production of unreal objects because it is always, in one sense, a free negation of the world and that always *from a particular point of view*. Thus, if consciousness is free, the noematic correlative of its freedom should be the *world* which carries in itself its possibility of negation, at each moment and from each point of view, by means of an image, even while the image must as yet be constructed by a particular intention of consciousness. But, reciprocally, an image, being a negation of the world from a particular point of view, can never appear excepting *on the foundation of the world* and in connection with the foundation. Naturally the appearance of the image demands that the particular perceptions should be diluted in the syncretic wholeness *world* and that this wholeness should withdraw. But it is exactly the withdrawal of the wholeness which turns it into a foundation, the foundation on which the unreal form must detach itself. Thus, although as a result of producing the unreal, consciousness can appear momentarily delivered from "being-in-the-world," it is just this "being-in-the-world" which is the necessary condition for the imagination.

Thus the critical analysis of the conditions that made all imagination possible has led us to the following discoveries: in order to imagine, consciousness must be free from all specific reality and this freedom must be able to define itself by a "being-in-the-world" which is at once the constitution and the negation of the world; the concrete situation of the consciousness in the world must at each moment serve as the singular motivation for the constitution of the unreal. Thus the unreal—which is always a two-fold nothingness: nothingness of itself in relation to the world, nothingness of the world in relation to itself—must always be constituted on the foundation of the world which it denies, it being well understood, moreover, that the world does not present itself only to a representative intuition and that this synthetic foundation simply demands to be lived as a situation. If these are the conditions that make imagination possible, do they correspond to a specification, to an enrichment contingent upon the essence "consciousness" or are they nothing else than the very essence of that consciousness considered from a particular point of view? It seems that the answer lies in the question. Indeed, what is this free consciousness whose nature is to be the consciousness *of* something, but which, for this very reason, constructs itself before the real and which surpasses it at each moment because it can exist only by "being-in-the-world," that is, by living its relation to the real as *situation*, what is it, indeed, if not simply consciousness such as it reveals itself to itself in the cogito?

Is not doubt the very primary condition of the cogito, that is, at once the constitution of the real as a world and its negation from this same point of view and does not reflective grasp of the doubt as doubt coincide with the apodictic intuition of freedom?

We may therefore conclude that imagination is not an empirical and superadded power of consciousness, it is the whole of consciousness as it realizes its freedom; every concrete and real situation of consciousness in the world is big with imagination in as much as it always presents itself as a withdrawing from the real. It does not follow that all perception of the real must reverse itself in imagination, but as consciousness is always "in a situation" because it is always free, it always and at each moment has the concrete possibility of producing the unreal. These are the various motivations which decide at each moment whether consciousness will only be realized or whether it will imagine. The unreal is produced outside of the world by a consciousness which *stays in the world* and it is because he is transcendentally free that man can imagine.

But, in its turn, the imagination, which has become a psychological and empirical function, is the necessary condition for the freedom of empirical man in the midst of the world. For, if the negating function belonging to consciousness—which Heidegger calls surpassing—is what makes the act of imagination possible, it must be added on the other hand that this function can manifest itself only in an imaginative act. There can be no intuition of nothingness just because nothingness is nothing and because all consciousness intuitive or not is consciousness of something. Nothingness can present itself only as an infra-structure of something. The experience of nothingness is not, strictly speaking, an indirect one, it is an experience which is in principle given "with" and "in." The analyses of Bergson are pertinent in this connection: any attempt to directly conceive death or the nothingness of existence is by nature bound to fail.

The gliding of the world into the bosom of nothingness and the emergence of human reality in this very nothingness can happen only through the position of *something* which is nothingness in relation to the world and in relation to which the world is nothing. By this we evidently define the structure of the imagination. It is the appearance of the imaginary before consciousness which permits the grasping of the process of turning the world into nothingness as its essential condition and as its primary structure. If it were possible to conceive for a moment a consciousness which does not imagine it would have to be conceived as completely engulfed in the existant and without the possibility of grasping anything but the existant. But it is exactly that which cannot be nor could be: all existence soon as it is posited is surpassed by itself. But it must retreat *towards something*. The imaginary is in every case the "something" concrete toward which the existant is surpassed. When the imaginary is not posited as a fact, the surpassing and the nullifying of the existant are swallowed up in the existant; the surpassing and the freedom *are there* but are not revealed; the person is crushed in the world, run through by the real, he is closest to the thing. However, soon as he apprehends in one way or another (most of the time without representation) the whole as a *situation*, he retreats from it towards that in relation to which he is *a lack*, an *empty space*, etc. In a word, the concrete motivation of the imaginative consciousness itself presupposes the imaginative structure of consciousness; the realizing consciousness always includes a retreat towards a particular imaginative consciousness which is like the reverse of the situation and in relation to which the situation is defined. For instance, if I desire to see my friend Peter who is not here now the situation defines itself as a "being in the world" such as Peter is not now given, and Peter is this because the whole of the real is surpassed in order to make a world. But it is not at all the real Peter who, on the contrary, if he were given as present or as envisioned on the basis of the real by empty and presentifying intentions (for instance, if I heard his steps outside the door), would be a part of the situation: this Peter in relation to whom the situation becomes defined is exactly the *absent* Peter.

The imaginary thus represents at each moment the implicit meaning of the real. The imaginative act itself consists in positing the imaginary for itself, that is, in making that meaning explicit—as when Peter as an image rises suddenly before me—but this specific position of the imaginary will be accompanied by a collapsing of the world which is then no more than the negated foundation of the unreal. And if the negation is the unconditioned principle of all imagination, it itself can never be realized excepting in and by an act of imagination. That which is denied must be imagined. In fact, the object of a negation cannot be *real* because that would be affirming what is being denied—but neither can it be a complete nothing, since it is *something* that is being denied. So the object of a negation must be posited as imaginary. And this is true for the logical forms of negation (doubt, restriction, etc.) as it is for its active and affective forms (defense, consciousness of impotence, of deprivation, etc.).

Now we are at the point of understanding the meaning and the value of the imaginary. The imaginary appears "on the foundation of the world," but reciprocally all apprehension of the real as world implies a hidden surpassing towards the imaginary. All imaginative consciousness uses the world as the negated foundation of the imaginary and reciprocally all consciousness of the world calls and motivates an imaginative consciousness as grasped from the particular *meaning* of the situation. The apprehension of nothingness could not occur by an immediate unveiling, it develops in and by the free succession of acts of consciousness, the nothingness is the material of the surpassing of the world towards the imaginary. It is as such that it is *lived*, without ever being posited for itself. There could be no developing consciousness without an imaginative consciousness, and vice versa. So imagination, far from appearing as an *actual* characteristic of consciousness turns out to be an essential and transcendental condition of consciousness. It is as absurd to conceive of a consciousness which would not imagine as it would be to conceive of a consciousness which could not realize the cogito.

2. The Work of Art

It is not our intention to deal here with the problem of the work of art in its entirety. Closely related as this problem is to the question of the Imaginary, its treatment calls for a special work in itself. But it is time we drew some conclusions from the long investigations in which we used as an example a statue or the portrait of Charles VIII or a novel. The following comments will be concerned essentially with the existential type of the work of art. And we can at once formulate the law that the work of art is an unreality.

This appeared to us clearly from the moment we took for our example, in an entirely different connection, the portrait of Charles VIII. We understood at the very outset that this Charles VIII was an object. But this, obviously, is not the same object as is the painting, the canvas, which are the real objects of the painting. As long as we observe the canvas and the frame for themselves the esthetic object "Charles VIII" will not appear. It is not that it is hidden by the picture, but because it cannot present itself to a realizing consciousness. It will appear at the moment when consciousness, undergoing a radical change in which the world is negated, will itself become imaginative. The situation here is like that of the cubes which can be seen at will to be five or six in number. It will not do to say that when they are seen as five it is because at that time the aspect of the drawing in which they are six is *concealed*. The intentional act that apprehends them as five is sufficient unto itself, it is complete and *exclusive* of the act which grasps them as six. And so it is with the apprehension of Charles VIII as an image which is depicted on the picture. This Charles VIII on the canvas is necessarily the correlative of the intentional act of an imaginative consciousness. And since this Charles VIII, who is an unreality so long he is grasped on the canvas, is precisely the object of our esthetic appreciations (it is he who "moves" us, who is "painted with intelligence, power, and grace," etc.), we are led to recognize that, in a picture, the esthetic object is something *unreal*. This is of great enough importance once we remind ourselves of the way in which we ordinarily confuse the real and the imaginary in a work of art. We often hear it said, in fact, that the artist first has an idea in the form of an image which he then *realizes* on canvas. This mistaken notion arises from the fact that the painter can, in fact, begin with a mental image which is, as such, incommunicable, and from the fact that at the end of his labors he presents the public with an object which anyone can observe. This leads us to believe that there occurred a transition from the imaginary to the real. But this is in no way true. That which is real, we must not fail to note, are the results of the brush strokes, the stickiness of the canvas, its grain, the polish spread over the colors. But all this does not constitute the object of esthetic appreciation. What is "beautiful" is something which cannot be experienced as a perception and which, by its very nature, is out of the world. We have just shown that it cannot be *brightened*, for instance, by projecting a light beam on the canvas: it is the canvas that is brightened and not the painting. The fact of the matter is that the painter did not *realize* his mental image at all: he has simply constructed a material analogue of such a kind that everyone can grasp the image provided he looks at the analogue. But the image thus provided with an external analogue remains an image. There is no realization of the imaginary, nor can we speak of its *objectification*. Each stroke of the brush was not made *for itself* nor even for the constructing of a coherent real whole (in the sense in which it can be said that a certain lever in a machine was conceived in the interest of the whole and not for itself). It was given together with an unreal synthetic whole and the aim of the artist was to construct a whole of *real* colors which enable this unreal to manifest itself. The painting should then be conceived as a material thing *visited* from time to time (every time that the spectator assumes the imaginative attitude) by an unreal which is precisely the *painted object*. What deceives us here is the real and sensuous pleasure which certain real colors on the canvas give us. Some reds of Matisse, for instance, produce a sensuous enjoyment in those who see them.

But we must understand that this sensuous enjoyment, if thought of in isolation—for instance, if aroused by a color in nature—has nothing of the esthetic. It is purely and simply a pleasure of sense. But when the red of the painting is grasped, it is grasped, in spite of everything, as a part of an unreal whole and it is in this whole that it is beautiful. For instance it is the red of a rug by a table. There is, in fact, no such thing as pure color. Even if the artist is concerned solely with the sensory relationships between forms and colors, he chooses for that very reason a rug in order to increase the sensory value of the red: tactile elements, for instance, must be intended through the red, it is a *fleecy* red, because the rug is of a fleecy material. Without this "fleeciness" of the color something would be lost. And surely the rug is painted there *for the red* it justifies and not the red for the rug. If Matisse chose a rug rather than a sheet of dry and glossy paper it is because of the voluptuous mixture of the color, the density and the tactile quality of the wool. Consequently the red can be truly enjoyed only in grasping it as the *red of the rug*, and therefore unreal. And he would have lost his strongest contrast with the green of the wall if the green were not rigid and cold, because it is the green of a wall tapestry. It is therefore in the unreal that the relationship of colors and forms takes on its real meaning. And even when drawn objects have their usual meaning reduced to a minimum, as in the painting of the cubists, the painting is at least not flat. The forms we see are certainly not the forms of a rug, a table, nor anything else we see in the world. They nevertheless do have a density, a material, a depth, they bear a relationship of perspective towards each other. They are *things*. And it is precisely in the measure in which they are things that they are unreal. Cubism has introduced the fashion of claiming that a painting should not *represent* or *imitate* reality but should constitute an object in itself. As an aesthetic doctrine such a program is perfectly defensible and we owe many masterpieces to it. But it needs to be understood. To maintain that the painting, although altogether devoid of meaning, nevertheless is a *real* object, would be a grave mistake. It is certainly not an object of nature. The real object no longer functions as an analogue of a bouquet of flowers or a glade. But when I "contemplate" it, I nevertheless am not in a realistic attitude. The painting is still an *analogue*. Only what manifests itself through it is an unreal collection of *new things*, of objects I have never seen or ever will see, but which are not less unreal because of it, objects which do not exist *in the painting*, nor anywhere in the world, but which manifest themselves by means of the canvas, and which have gotten hold of it by some sort of possession. And it is the configuration of these unreal objects that I designate as *beautiful*. The esthetic enjoyment is real but it is not grasped for itself, as if produced by a real color: it is but a manner of apprehending the unreal object and, far from being directed on the real painting, it serves to constitute the imaginary object through the real canvas. This is the source of the celebrated disinterestedness of esthetic experience. This is why Kant was able to say that it does not matter whether the object of beauty, when experienced as beautiful, is or is not objectively real; why Schopenhauer was able to speak of a sort of suspension of the Will. This does not come from some mysterious way of apprehending the real, which we are able to use occasionally. What happens is that the esthetic object is constituted and apprehended by an imaginative consciousness which posits it as unreal.

What we have just shown regarding painting is readily applied to the art of fiction, poetry and drama, as well. It is self-evident that the novelist, the poet and the dramatist construct an unreal object by means of verbal analogues; it is also self-evident that the actor who plays Hamlet makes use of himself, of his whole body, as an analogue of the imaginary person. Even the famous dispute about the paradox of the comedian is enlightened by the view here presented. It is well known that certain amateurs proclaim that the actor *does not believe* in the character he portrays. Others, leaning on many witnesses, claim that the actor becomes identified in some way with the character he is enacting. To us these two views are not exclusive of each other; if by "belief" is meant actually real it is obvious that the actor does not actually consider himself to be Hamlet. But this does not mean that he does not "mobilize" all his powers to make Hamlet real. He uses all his feelings, all his strength, all his gestures as analogues of the feelings and conduct of Hamlet. But by this very fact he takes the reality away from them. *He lives completely in an unreal way.* And it matters little that he is *actually* weeping in enacting the role. These tears, whose origin we explained above (See Part III, Chapter II) he himself experiences—and so does the audience—as the tears of Hamlet, that is as the analogue of unreal tears. The transformation that occurs here is like that we discussed in the dream: the actor is completely caught up, inspired, by the unreal. It is not the character who becomes real in the actor, it is the actor who *becomes unreal* in his character.[1]

But are there not some arts whose objects seem to escape unreality by their very nature? A melody, for instance, refers to nothing but itself. Is a cathedral anything more than a mass of *real* stone which dominates the surrounding house tops? But let us look at this matter more closely. I listen to a symphony orchestra, for instance, playing the Beethoven Seventh Symphony. Let us disregard exceptional cases—which are besides on the margin of aesthetic contemplation—as when I go mainly "to hear Toscanini" interpret Beethoven in his own way. As a general rule what draws me to the concert is the desire "to hear the Seventh Symphony." Of course I have some

[1] It is in this sense that a beginner in the theatre can say that stage-fright served her to represent the timidity of Ophelia. If it did so, it is because she suddenly turned it into an unreality, that is, that she ceased to apprehend it for itself and that she grasped it as *analogue* for the timidity of Ophelia.

objection to hearing an amateur orchestra, and prefer this or that well-known musical organization. But this is due to my desire to hear the symphony "played perfectly," because the symphony will then be *perfectly itself*. The shortcomings of a poor orchestra which plays "too fast" or "too slow," "in the wrong tempo," etc., seem to me to rob, to "betray" the work it is playing. At most the orchestra effaces itself before the work it performs, and, provided I have reasons to trust the performers and their conductor, I am confronted by the symphony itself. This everyone will grant me. But now, what is the Seventh Symphony itself? Obviously it is a *thing*, that is something which is before me, which endures, which lasts. Naturally there is no need to show that that thing is a synthetic whole, which does not consist of tones but of a thematic configuration. But is that "thing" real or unreal? Let us first bear in mind that I am listening to the Seventh Symphony. For me that "Seventh Symphony" does not exist in time, I do not grasp it as a dated event, as an artistic manifestation which is unrolling itself in the Châtelet auditorium on the 17th of November, 1938. If I hear Furtwaengler tomorrow or eight days later conduct another orchestra performing the same symphony, I am in the presence of the same symphony once more. Only it is being played either better or worse. Let us now see *how* I hear the symphony: some persons shut their eyes. In this case they detach themselves from the *visual* and dated event of this particular interpretation: they give themselves up to the pure sounds. Others watch the orchestra or the back of the conductor. But they do not see what they are looking at. This is what Revault d'Allonnes calls reflection with auxiliary fascination. The auditorium, the conductor and even the orchestra have disappeared. I am therefore confronted by the Seventh Symphony, but on the express condition of understanding *nothing about it*, that I do not think of the event as an actuality and dated, and on condition that I listen to the succession of themes as an absolute succession and not as a real succession which is unfolding itself, for instance, on the occasion when Peter paid a visit to this or that friend. In the degree to which I hear the symphony it is *not here*, between these walls, at the tip of the violin bows. Nor is it "in the past" as if I thought: this is the work that matured in the mind of Beethoven on such a date. It is completely beyond the real. It has its own time, that is, it possesses an inner time, which runs from the first tone of the allegro to the last tone of the finale, but this time is not a succession of a preceding time which it continues and which happened "before" the beginning of the allegro; nor is it followed by a time which will come "after" the finale. The Seventh Symphony is in no way *in time*. It is therefore in no way real. It occurs *by itself*, but as absent, as being out of reach. I cannot act upon it, change a single note of it, or slow down its movement. But it depends on the real for its appearance: that the conductor does not faint away, that a fire in the hall does not put an end to the performance. From this we cannot conclude that *the* Seventh Symphony has come to an end. No, we only think that the *performance* of the symphony has ceased. Does this not show clearly that the performance of the symphony is its *analogue*? It can manifest itself only through analogues which are dated and which unroll in our time. But to experience it on these analogues the imaginative reduction must be functioning, that is, the real sounds must be apprehended as analogues. It therefore occurs as a perpetual elsewhere, a perpetual absence. We must not picture it (as does Spandrell in *Point Counterpoint* by Huxley—as so many platonisms) as existing in another world, in an intelligible heaven. It is not only outside of time and space—as are essences, for instance—it is outside of the real, outside of existence. I do not hear it actually, I listen to it in the imaginary. Here we find the explanation for the considerable difficulty we always experience in passing from the world of the theatre or of music into that of our daily affairs. There is in fact no passing from one world into the other, but only a passing from the imaginative attitude to that of reality. Esthetic contemplation is an induced dream and the passing into the real is an actual waking up. We often speak of the "deception" experienced on returning to reality. But this does not explain that this discomfort also exists, for instance, after having witnessed a realistic and cruel play. in which case reality should be experienced as comforting. This discomfort is simply that of the dreamer on awakening; an entranced consciousness, engulfed in the imaginary, is suddenly freed by the sudden ending of the play, of the symphony, and comes suddenly in contact with existence. Nothing more is needed to arouse the nauseating disgust that characterizes the consciousness of reality.

From these few observations we can already conclude that the real is never beautiful. Beauty is a value applicable only to the imaginary and which means the negation of the world in its essential structure. This is why it is stupid to confuse the moral with the esthetic. The values of the Good presume being-in-the-world, they concern action in the real and are subject from the outset to the basic absurdity of existence. To say that we "assume" an esthetic attitude to life is to constantly confuse the real and the imaginary. It does happen, however, that we do assume the attitude of esthetic contemplation towards real events or objects. But in such cases everyone of us can feel in himself a sort of recoil in relation to the object contemplated which slips into nothingness so that, from this moment on, it is no longer *perceived;* it functions as an *analogue* of itself, that is, that an unreal image of what it is appears to us through its actual presence. This image can be purely and simply the object "itself" neutralized, annihilated, as when I contemplate a beautiful woman or death at a bull fight; it can also be the imperfect and confused appearance of *what it could be* through what it is, as when the painter grasps the harmony of two colors as being greater, more vivid, *through* the real blots he finds on a wall. The object at once appears to be *in back of* itself, becomes *untouchable*, it is beyond our reach; and hence arises a sort of sad disinterest in it. It is in this sense that we may say that great beauty in a woman kills the desire for her. In fact we cannot at the same time place ourselves on the plane of the esthetic when this unreal "herself" which we admire appears and on the realistic plane of physical possession. To desire her we must forget she is beautiful, because desire is a plunge into the heart of existence, into what is most contingent and most absurd. Esthetic contemplation of *real* objects is of the same structure as paramnesia, in which the real object functions as analogue of itself in the past. But in one of the cases there is a negating and in the other a placing a thing in the past. Paramnesia differs from the esthetic attitude as memory differs from imagination.

DATE DUE			